Phases of
Burnout

PHASES OF
BURNOUT

Developments in Concepts and Applications

ROBERT T. GOLEMBIEWSKI
and
ROBERT F. MUNZENRIDER

*HF
5548.85
.G63
1988
west*

PRAEGER

New York
Westport, Connecticut
London

Library of Congress Cataloging-in-Publication Data

Golembiewski, Robert T.
   Phases of burnout : developments in concepts and applications /
Robert T. Golembiewski and Robert F. Munzenrider.
      p.   cm.
   Bibliography: p.
   Includes index.
   ISBN 0-275-92980-9 (alk. paper)
   1. Job stress.   2. Burn out (Psychology)   3. Organizational
behavior.   I. Munzenrider, Robert F.   II. Title.
   HF5548.85.G63 1988
   158.7--dc19
                                                    87-38491

Library of Congress Catalog Card Number: 87-38491

ISBN:0-275-92980-9

First published in 1988

Praeger Publishers, One Madison Avenue, New York, NY 10010
A division of Greenwood Press, Inc.

Printed in the United States of America

The paper used in this book complies with the
Permanent Paper Standard issued by the National
Information Standards Organization (Z39.48-1984).

10 9 8 7 6 5 4 3 2 1

To Matthew Alexander

Welcome to the life which, you will come to understand, is pervasively unique for each of us. But certain fundamentals apply, as your mother wrote. Just like most of us, you began as a product of your parents' love, and you will serve as a test of it. Just like most of us . . . , and yet uniquely so.

CONTENTS

ILLUSTRATIONS

TABLES

FIGURES

EXHIBITS

Phases of
Burnout

INTRODUCTION

As this book's title implies, the phase model of burnout has achieved a degree of empirical support that justifies the authors' risking a negative knee-jerk reaction by potential readers. *Phases of Burnout* is not a fetching title; the subtitle, *Developments in Concepts and Applications*, has a daunting quality to it. But so be it. A kind of truth-in-labelling dominates here. The book is about the phases, as well as about developments in their conceptual elaboration and application. Hence we will have to risk losing those readers who make snap judgments after reading only the titles of books.

Some of the work included below was first published in a volume entitled, more felicitously, *Stress in Organizations* (Praeger, 1986), but certain realities urge against merely advertising a "second edition," and would be false to both the *tone* as well as the *approach* to this book.

The forerunner to this volume was hedged with encumbering qualifications, devoting much space to eliminating even low-probability analytic possibilities, and (perhaps above all) going overboard to provide data concerning four or five alternative ways to measure burnout. In tone, the book was often defensive. On occasion, indeed, we inclined to the view that the book's subtitle ought to have been *Obstacles in the Path Toward a Phase Model*, in sharp contrast with the one actually used: *Toward a Phase Model of Burnout*. In part, such reservations were due to a kind of learned skepticism—an attitude of better safe than sorry, often expressed polysyllabically and even passively. In addition, early results with the phase model seemed too good to be true. We were eager for the first disconfir-mation of that model, in effect, so that we could begin the expected fine-tuning. Since early data did not provide it for us, we generated a host of limitations and qualifications for the argument. Some were real enough, but some we developed just to allow for the construction of a possible counter-case.

1

To be sure, the treatment herein is not entirely divorced from that of the first book. Some of the previous findings are reported below, serving as a baseline upon which to build. In addition, chapters five and seven have outlines similar to those used in *Stress in Organizations*. But even here the chapters have been revised, substantially shortened, and updated with new materials and (at times) major extensions of the original theoretic and applied beachheads.

Beyond the basics, the treatment focuses on the major progress—conceptual and, in particular, empirical—that has been made in the three years since the initial materials went to the publisher. The advances may be divided into two classes. One deals with a new and partially tested theoretical context for the phase model; the second involves a substantial inventory of individual extensions of and elaborations on the initial argument.

To sum up, in large part this book is different from its predecessor, both in its tone and in its treatment of the subject matter. We now have a clearer view of the phase model, and—new warts and all—we think it has much to recommend it. We hope *Phases of Burnout* encourages getting on with exploiting the model's usefulness with a minimal waste of either motion or emotion.

A TWO-FACTOR GENERAL THEORY OF AFFECT

No doubt the major advance over *Stress in Organizations* represented by this book consists in the authors' changed relationship to the two-factor theory of affect. This evolution has been for the most part halting and fumbling, but the data we have most recently collected have moved us a long distance from our original moorings. Chapters eight and nine in particular focus upon this development, highlighting the conceptual synthesis we came to adopt from the work of others (e.g., Russell, 1979, 1980).

The irony of this transition deserves a mention. We began our research in a debunking mood, as a solitary initiative that sought to deal with a huge but inchoate body of literature (e.g., Kilpatrick, 1986). But this line of research, via a parallel development, eventually led us to join with other researchers in an attempt to contribute to a parsimonious if general theory of affect that rests on two basic dimensions of human experience: pleasant ←→ unpleasant; and active ←→ inactive (e.g., Russell, 1979, 1980).

The two-factor theory is still very much in development, and thus cannot yet serve as any sort of lodestar. We cannot pretend to have tested that general theory in any complete sense, and offer it as a summary statement of the research reported here rather than as the premise upon which it was initiated. Moreover, for our purposes, we have reframed the pleasant ←→ unpleasant dimension in terms of the phases of burnout. This work—whether ultimately deemed bold or foolish—is nonetheless based on much measurement detail and descriptive analysis, as well as on a successful attempt to ameliorate advanced burnout among a group of corporate officials.

We find the simplicity of the two-factor theory to be attractive and even profound. It is conceptually and practically liberating, even as it encompasses some harsh realities.

Others will have to determine whether, in our shift from debunking to supporting a two-factor theory of affect, we are only dealing with a significant subcase of a wider phenomenon, or whether perhaps we are more likely contributing to the development of the "general theory." For our purposes, at present it does not matter which is the case.

OTHER ELABORATIONS AND EXTENSIONS

In addition to a new theoretic view of the phase model, this volume also advances in numerous particulars well beyond the boundaries of ideas presented in *Stress in Organizations*. To alert the reader to this diverse collection of new initiatives, we introduce eighteen major elaborations and extensions:

- an important test of the congruence in several populations of the three subdimensions of burnout used to assign individuals to phases (chapter one), which reduces the force of basic criticisms of any social or psychological measure as artifactual, ungeneralizable, or culture-bound

- new data on test-retest reliability (chapter one), a significant technical issue

- several replications of the concurrent validity of the phase model as estimated by its regular and robust pattern of mappings on approximately 100 variables (chapters three and eight), reinforcing early findings and extending them substantially

- a test of the causal pathways in burnout, which in the present view derives basically from environmental features, and especially at the work-site (chapter three)

- a pilot test for associations of the phase model with properties of blood chemistry—cholesterol, and so on—which, although the results are tentative, constitutes a significant extension of previous research (chapter four)

- a bit more attention to "hard" or "objective" measures as a complement to self-reports (chapters four, five, and nine), which is an issue of great prominence in measurement

- data on the incidence of the burnout phases in 33 hosts, including over 12,000 members, which more than doubles the original data-set and adds significant weight to the assessment of the magnitude of the "burnout problem" (chapter 6)

- an enhanced test of the association between demographics and burnout, featuring a multivariate analysis of gender (chapter seven)

- the association of self-esteem with the phases and features of blood chemistry, in a preliminary but suggestive way (chapter seven)

- enhanced conceptual and empirical attention given to group properties (chapter seven and, especially, chapter nine), as one way of networking the phase model with more-established areas of inquiry

- data on the persistence over time of the phases at five separate sites (chapter seven), obviously a central element in judging the significance of burnout phenomena

- augmented data on the affinity of particular work groups for the more extreme phases of burnout (chapters seven and nine), which is of great importance in connection with actual intervention to ameliorate burnout, and which serves to reinforce the argument for the relevance of worksite and group features in burnout

- an expanded conceptual concern with two kinds of onset of burnout—chronic and acute—along with some new data (especially in chapter seven), which extend the phase model to a commonplace observation and may help target interventions

- greater emphasis on group and organization culture (chapters eight and nine), which relates burnout to a central feature of life of special interest to today's students of organization

- testing for an association between clinically relevant affective states and the phases (chapter eight), which relates to the basic issue of what burnout is and how it relates to common problems in mental functioning—anxiety, depression, and so on

- conceptual and empirical attention to burnout and kinds of change (chapter eight), which not only ties burnout to a key conceptual issue in the behavioral sciences but also suggests the criticality of burnout in distinguishing kinds of change

- increased attention to active vs. passive modes of response to burnout (especially in chapter nine)

- discussion of a successful intervention in an organization to reduce burnout, which relied on Organization Development values and interventions (chapter nine), and was theoretically guided by the conceptual perspectives underlying the phase model

These eighteen new or augmented conceptual and empirical features variously extend the reach-and-grasp of the phase model and justify this book's title. The planned-change intervention provides the most compelling support for the phase model, following as it does this Lewinian paraphrase: If you really understand some phenomenon, you should be able to influence it in planned ways.

To complement these new or augmented emphases and to reflect them, each of the last eight chapters ends with a section entitled: *Implications for the Phase Model of Burnout*. These often-lengthy discussions reflect the greater confidence the authors now have in the phase model—and in how it can help move us from the analytic *here* to a more comprehensive *there* of rich theoretic and applied performance.

TWO LIMITATIONS

This upbeat image of *Phases of Burnout* does require some qualification. There are two areas in which we sought to do better, but could not.

First, major efforts were made to generate "hard" or "objective" measures so as to complement self-reports in tests of the regularity and robustness of their association with the phases, but these achieved only modest results. Prominent here are data dealing with job turnover and some preliminary features of the chemistry of blood.

Not that we and others always failed in the conventional sense. In a dramatic case, an independent team of researchers succeeded beyond virtually anyone's expectations in identifying associations of the phases with some very important "hard" measures—arguably including the "hardest" measures of human effort— that were uncomfortably regular and robust. The host organization involved has thus far exercised its contractual right to withhold permission to publish the data, one hopes for the purpose of doing something to ameliorate advanced phases of burnout and to change the eminently unsatisfactory levels of performance and productivity associated with them. In addition, other "hard" data studies have been delayed.

Second, it was not possible to include in any direct way all other members of our original team in either the research or the preparation of this volume. Jerry G. Stevenson made meaningful and welcomed contributions to the original research, and we take this opportunity, as apart from distinct references later on in the text, to generally acknowledge those good works.

ACKNOWLEDGEMENTS

Books like this one are less dry, written documents than they are monuments to the risks taken and commitments made by particular human beings. Most prominent in this case were those whose desire to create more humane work sites was greater than their natural concern about "adverse findings." In essence, the search for knowledge is at once a leap into the unknown even as it is a necessary basis for more effective applications. In addition, valuable research assistance was provided by Byong-Seob Kim, and typing was provided with skill and verve by a trio that spanned two countries: Kathy Naylor in Canada, and Sandra Daniel and Bridget Pilcher in America.

1. *MOTIVATORS, CHALLENGES, AND CONVENTIONS CONCERNING MEASUREMENT: INTRODUCING THE PHASE MODEL OF BURNOUT*

One cannot even envision *the* orientation to a phenomenal area as protean as burnout. But if such an orientation is manageable, then we may benefit from it, even if it must be incomplete in its results. The orientation described in this chapter is offered as one way of circumscribing, if only approximately, a complex area of inquiry.

This orientation features *the phase model*, which will be described in this chapter and tested in the eight chapters to follow. The description provides some context for measurement, as well as conventions for measuring. Context here refers to a set of motivators that have inspired the project, as well as to a set of challenges that have both triggered and tempered these motivators.

FOUR MOTIVATORS OF MEASUREMENT

Our original study of burnout reflected a mind-set biased toward debunking the phenomenon. Burnout made a splashy entrance into the public consciousness about a decade ago, and had less substance than star quality. Its spectacular appearance on the social scene has its serious downside, with all the attendant hoopla working to confound research. Indeed, researchers have often had to devote time to establishing that burnout is more than just a darling of pop psychology, more than an equivalent of the fashionable fly of a summer's social commentary. Inasmuch as the term "burnout" was being applied to everything, we reasoned, the probability was strong that nothing much could be explained by it in rigorous terms.

Our opinions changed as our knowledge increased, and thus four other motivators have replaced that of debunking. Let us introduce these motivating themes, to be detailed in due course. First, burnout reflects much that is old. In this aspect, the concept does double-duty, not only permitting us to link the

6

observed phenomena to established pathways of commentary and research, but also raising the challenge of testing for possible theoretical connections. Second, burnout seems phenomenally significant. Although the evidence is not all in, burnout does *not* seem to be an empty category. Conceptually, it seems to be a real something that helps describe our world; operationally, it can be measured with substantial reliability and validity; burnout seems of both practical and theoretical significance, as judged from its associations with a broad range of variables relating to health, well-being, and productivity. Patently, this second aspect demands that we upgrade the quality of burnout research.

Third, our present view stresses that the concept of burnout can lay a strong claim to being something new, at least in the sense that it reflects a novel or highly-augmented contribution to our understanding of an important social phenomenon. Again, this powerfully motivates research.

Fourth, burnout as a metaphor captivates our attention, and there is no way to come to real grips with that metaphor short of understanding burnout.

Burnout as Something Old

Consider only three ways in which one can attribute a longish time-line to the focus of our investigation. First, a growing body of data suggests that, while we may be newly aware of the multiple expressions of burnout, it has been long with us. Thus, we read in the popular press about "teacher burnout," or "NFL-coach burnout," or "rabbi burnout," or "burned-out parents." And the mind's eye starts to envision the antecedents of depletion effects: caring or obsessed people, attempting to cope with complex situations that burgeon more rapidly than do the skills and attitudes that permit successful coping. Litanies of such antecedents only require brief pump-priming before they gush forth (e.g., Schwartz and Will, 1953).

The case of our public schools provides a convenient illustration. In recent decades, the schools have taken on an escalating range of social and familial as well as narrowly educational responsibilities. Why? Not only have more people, with a growing range of abilities and disabilities, become more insistent about having their needs met in schools but the national ethos pays at least lip-service to the rightness of these claims; the legitimacy of formal authority is everywhere questioned even where it is not in total rout; systems of rewards in educational settings have not kept pace and, in many cases, have fallen further behind accumulating demands for technical, interpersonal, and ethical instruction; and so on. No wonder, then, that the "burnout" or "flameout" of teachers and school administrators has come to be a common expression both in the popular press and, more recently, in the research literature.

In this sense, burnout may be seen somewhat in the same light as venereal herpes. Both are now identified and partially understood; no doubt both have been exacerbated by prevailing customs and mores, but have nonetheless probably been with us for a long time, if less obvious in previous times; and, as aggravated by today's cultural mores and practices, both now clearly stand in need of that greater knowledge and caring that alone will permit targeted and efficient amelioration.

Second, we have numerous conceptual jumping-off points congenial to burnout. These may involve "the blahs," the several depressions, free-floating anxiety, stress, or whatever. Given these and their acknowledged demands on people, it requires only a direct if bold extension to link *some* stress with *too much*—accumulating stressors can lead to strain and sufficient strain can induce the coping deficits implied by burnout. Hence a condition like burnout can be seen as an end-product of numerous elements in the vocabulary we have long used to describe our lives and our reactions to life.

Third, some observers have proposed a more radical sense in which burnout is something old. From this perspective, the concept is a vague verbal tent that covers several phenomenal areas, carelessly aggregating what would be better left to stand alone. Alienation, depression, and free-floating anxiety are among those concepts with long and independent traditions of their own, which some charge are being placed under the same conceptual tent.

In this sense, therefore, burnout is not only not something conceptually new; in some versions of this third position the notion exists only by verbal fiat. In being extended to so many phenomenal areas, some propose that its content has been so diluted that burnout is only a categoric and distinction-blurring concept, a vague and perhaps mischievous representation of our troubled age.

Burnout as Something Substantial

The third version of burnout as something old must be challenged, at least in its extreme form. Such a view comes near to denying any substance to burnout at all, and the available data do not support such a conclusion. Subsequent chapters will take up this defense in detail, but here let us note only two points. First, Kahn (1978, p. 61) sees burnout as "a syndrome of inappropriate attitudes toward clients and toward self, often associated with uncomfortable physical and emotional symptoms." Second, the range of these symptoms seems very broad. Maslach and Jackson observe (1981, p. 2) that, along with reductions in the quality of care or service, burnout "appears to be a factor in job turnover, absenteeism, and low morale [and] various self-reported indices of personal distress, including physical exhaustion, insomnia, increased use of alcohol and drugs, and marital and family problems." Others present even longer lists of significant signs and symptoms (Cherniss, 1980b, esp. p. 17).

Burnout as Something New or Newly Heightened

A reasonable case can also be made for burnout as referring to some things that are "new," at least in the sense of a heightened incidence and severity of some "old" things (Cherniss, 1980; Freudenberger, 1980). Five points illustrate the argument that the present interest in burnout derives from some new or at least newly heightened features present in today's world.

First, burnout may reasonably be associated with our escalating pace of life. Not so long ago, to illustrate, youngsters might rely on a long line of elders to provide reasonable guidance about multiple details of their future lives. For example, grandfathers and even great-grandfathers, if still living, could pass on basic job or work skills and values. Today, even fathers often cannot be relied on for this, in the very elemental sense that the majority of job titles in the federal list of occupations did not even exist two or three decades ago. And, even where job titles have remained constant, job content may have changed radically.

Numerous indicators of this escalating pace commonly imply the potential for both greater freedom and greater insecurity. Each of these in turn suggests omnipresent stressors that could reasonably crescendo into the state implied by burnout—a level of strain beyond the individual's normal coping capabilities, a strain whose management absorbs sufficient energies to deplete an individual's reserves as well as to pollute the quality of life.

Second, we are literally living in the first few generations of what have come to be recognized as dramatically extended individual life spans. This implies multiple tensions not only on a personal level, but also in relation to the organization of social, economic, and political institutions built in response to the cadence of less demanding times. Only consider that, 10 to 20 years ago, few people over 80 ever entered hospitals, except to die. Today, the scheduling of major operations for octogenarians has become common and everyone expects almost all of them to leave the hospital alive. This silver lining has its accompanying dark cloud, of course, whose full meaning will become manifest only in the years 2010 and beyond, when the legions of the post-World War II baby boomers approach the age now considered normal for retirement.

Third, our expectations have kept pace, to say the least, with our life spans. These expectations relate to ourselves, our intimates, and to our colleagues at work and our clients (Maslach, 1982). These expectations derive from the escalating demands of work made upon us; and they often involve combined personal and vocational aspirations demanding long-term educational preparation, which in turn generates some form of extended dependence on the part of professionals-to-be extending into people's late twenties or early thirties. Commonly, such heightened expectations have sharply raised the ante we must pay just to live our lives, and substantial psychic costs have come to seem reasonable concomitants.

Fourth, fewer and fewer areas of life will easily tolerate "half-baked" commitment on the part of anyone. Not so long ago, intense commitment was required only of the elite, if them. Various forms of physical and economic coercion sufficed to elicit whatever degree of mass effort was required. Consider war, which only in the last half-century or so has come to directly involve large numbers of noncombatants. Whatever carnage may have occurred at the front lines in earlier wars, ordinarily the involvement of the civilian population, whether immediate or potential, was sharply limited. World War II changed that, decisively, and the thermonuclear age has so accentuated the shift that the most elite warriors are now the safest and noncombatants have become the most vulnerable.

Half-baked commitment suffices far less frequently, nowadays (Freudenberger, 1980). In today's jobs, work often requires higher levels of skill and better self-starting abilities, particularly from "knowledge workers." And new trends like *coproduction* also add to the burdens of what used to be the consumer's role—we now often pump our own gas, and carry ourselves long distances to airport gates so that the airlines can lower their costs while still providing long-distance mass transport. We now provide much "self-help" or "voluntary aid" in myriad public and private contexts, and will probably engage in far more of it in the future.

Fifth, both the sheer number and the shopping lists of share-claimers have been growing exponentially of late, and will probably continue to do so. The social justice obviously due to many of these people only exacerbates the problem of transition and adaptation for society in general (Mason, 1982).

These and similar factors might well contribute to an increasing incidence of burnout in recent years, and such a state of affairs powerfully motivates research, of course.

Patently, it makes a *big* difference how many people have reached what level of burnout, but in obtaining this information we still lack sufficient guidance. Fineman presents one version of the common opinion, and demonstrates that it provides but unsure footing for making any definite generalizations. He notes (1985, p. 153): "The pervasiveness of burnout is unclear. The reader of the mainstream literature could be forgiven for assuming, from its tone, that all social workers and the like are on the path to chronic stress and inevitable burnout. . . . But few studies provide a sense of perspective on the incidence of burnout, and those that do show that it is confined to a modest proportion, 11 percent or less. . . ."

Four Metaphors for Social Life

Burnout appears to be a central topic in the behavioral sciences, perhaps even *the* topic. This may seem overstated, but consider that the current interest in the notion of burnout may stem from the fact that basic problems of modern social life seem to have become so troublesome that the guiding metaphors of past decades cannot effectively deal with them.

To paint with a very broad brush, the past three decades may be seen as reflecting a preoccupation on the part of our society with forms of doing—doing different, good, and well, respectively. Recall that the 1950s were considered the anxious years in which we first learned "to do different"—to live with the bomb and perhaps with permanent and pervasive "free-floating anxiety." The 1960s liberated the "me and mine generation," often characterized by an ardent openness and need to "do good"—to expand human potential by challenging conventional limits on people and their development, especially its mental and emotional aspects. These expansionist tendencies were reflected in various kinds of social awareness, but they also led to narcissistic excesses. "Let people be free" typified the former; drug-induced "mind-blowing" came to represent the latter. Most observers see social consciousness as having lost ground in the late 1970s and beyond, with the emphasis in today's society being on determined professionalism, if not just acquisitiveness. Here the focus shifts to concerns about "doing well."

These characterizations of the three previous decades—generalizations though they are—suggest obvious differences, but they all have some sense of hope about them. They focus on *doing*—whether it be doing different, doing good, or doing well. Divergent and even contradictory as they may be, they share a sense of energy, and they even suggest some directions in which that energy should be applied. In turn, energy and direction both encourage hope.

In contrast, the current emphasis on burnout should cause pause if not alarm. Consider the phenomenon in a general sense. Our world is full of stressors—stimuli that can induce fight or flight responses, and hence can either agitate or energize. Some of these stressors—often called *eu-stressors*—can be powerful motivators. They enhance and enrich; they quicken and enlarge our lives. Thus, simply avoiding stressors will not do. Opening the door to opportunity, so to speak, however, has its costs, because some stressors can create strain, and sufficient strain can challenge and even outstrip our coping capabilities. Great energies may then be directed into maintenance or subsistence activities, leading to physical and emotional deficits and burnout.

If burnout is a suitable metaphor for the life experience of a growing and, perhaps, substantial number of people, it implies more of an end of the road than any sort of ongoing activity—a state of exhaustion rather than one of becoming. And this should cause concern in a world where, patently, so much does need doing, for burnout leaves room for little positive response, except perhaps learning how to avoid it or manage it.

Life cannot be bounded by a simple metaphor, of course, but the metaphor still might capture some of the essence of what is going on, and perhaps help us to explain it. Ideally, an analysis based accurately upon such a metaphor might even help us to modify or even solve the problem.

Notions such as these motivate this research on burnout. Greater clarity about the construct, its character, and its costs may eventually aid us in managing burnout effects, and perhaps even to escape them. That time is not yet at hand in any highly programmatic sense. But visions of the existing seem to be increasingly in-mind if not firmly in-hand. And visions of the possible are beginning to form as, we hope, this book will help to demonstrate.

The early gusher of research has not diminished the boomtown atmosphere associated with the study of burnout (Kilpatrick, 1984). If anything, indeed, accumulating research enlarges the sense of practical and theoretical opportunities associated with this study, even as it heightens the sense of urgency with regard to coping with the problem.

FIVE CHALLENGES TO MEASUREMENT

The flurry of attention notwithstanding, to date the commentary on burnout has been limited in five crucial particulars. First, much of the attention has simply been episodic and anecdotal—if at times compelling and convincing, as in studies made by specialists in organizational development and change (for example, Mitchell, 1977), even when the effects of the phenomenon have been deemed deserving of headlines, as in cases of burnout among teachers, various people-helpers, computer programmers, or NFL football coaches, among others. This "ad hoc-ness" gets reflected in the diversity of the definitions of burnout, which encompasses a very broad and often unclear range of phenomena. With burnout meaning almost anything and everything to various observers, research and experience are, as Cherniss (1980b, p. 16) notes, not likely to generate theoretical formulations of increasing power.

This book nonetheless does not have to be the first explorer of unknown territory. It rests primarily on a program of developmental work on measurement (Maslach and Jackson, 1982), which we seek to extend in several ways. Newton wrote of standing on the shoulders of others as *the* prerequisite for seeing more in nature, and that observation definitely applies here.

Second, the main body of work on burnout has involved people in the helping professions. These include social workers (Barad, 1979), religiously oriented samaritans (Collins, 1977), law-enforcement officials (Maslach and Jackson, 1979), lawyers in legal-services offices (Maslach and Jackson, 1978), day-care workers (Daley, 1979; Pines and Maslach, 1980), and organizational intervenors or change agents (Mitchell, 1977; Weisbord, 1978).

This focus rests on a solid rationale, even though later analysis suggests that too much should not be made of the association between burnout and these professions. The overall evidence shows that burnout is where you find it; that is, everywhere, whether at high levels of organization or low, in various demographic aggregates, and so on. We should not, however, neglect the solid connection between the helping professions and burnout. As Maslach and Jackson explain (1981, p. 1), people in such professions "are often required to spend considerable time in intense involvement with [troubled people, and these exchanges commonly become] charged with feelings of anger, embarrassment, frustration, fear or despair." The resulting chronic tension and stress can be emotionally draining, which leaves the professional "empty" and "burned out."

The association between burnout and helping professions also highlights a critical aspect of the dis-ease—the need for help from others to break out of the inward-spiraling characteristic of burnout. For burnout seems to be accompanied by a curious myopia, perhaps even an incapacity. As Freudenberger (1977, p. 26) notes, those who suffer from it do not see "themselves as the angry, rigid, cynical and depressed human beings others are having difficulty working with." Rather, they find themselves "fatigued, depressed, irritable, bored and overworked," as well as contributing less, while often working longer and having to contend with a growing array and intensity of physical symptoms. And their strong tendency is to externalize their plight. As Freudenberger (1977, p. 26) concludes, they "often fail to see their situation as stemming from inside themselves. Instead they find fault with everything and everyone around them, complaining about the organization and reacting cynically to whatever is suggested or attempted by others."

Thus, those in the advanced stages of burnout require major help from others and yet, as we shall show, one of the symptoms of burnout is a distancing of oneself from others. This not only suggests a profound irony, but also suggests that any successful amelioration of the disease could have major benefits.

Third, the common view of burnout often suggests that it has an off/on character: "I was burned out on this project yesterday, but I'm OK today." Perhaps. However, this view is, at the very least, inelegant and may well be false. Only rare and casual attention has been given to the phases or stages of burnout, or what we call "progressive burnout."

This neglect of degrees of burnout disregards major theoretical and practical possibilities. For example, different phases of burnout might respond to different ameliorative efforts or designs. And if that is even a distant possibility, more of a focus on progressive burnout might well encourage its prevention, or at least its remediation, before "things get too bad."

Fourth, the available literature, as Perlman and Hartman clearly show in their review article (1982), is clear only about the precursors of burnout. Indeed, *anything* can be a precursor of burnout for *somebody* at some time. The argument has numerous variants, and basically, perhaps, burnout does not have a clear epidemiological distribution. Indeed, as Maslach observes (1978a, p. 115), "What is most emotionally painful for one staff person may not pose any special problems for the next." More complicated variants of the same point easily come to mind. For example, one person's strain-inducing stressor at T_1 can be a positive motivator for another person, or even for the initial person at T_2. Concepts of burnout are typically nested in this sort of prototypic model in the literature on stress:

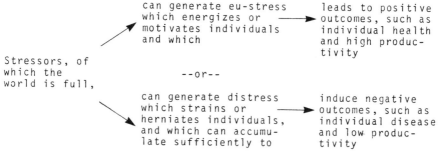

```
                    can generate eu-stress      leads to positive
                    which energizes or     ---> outcomes, such as
                    motivates individuals       individual health
                    and which                   and high produc-
                                                 tivity

Stressors, of
which the                --or--
world is full,

                    can generate distress       induce negative
                    which strains or       ---> outcomes, such as
                    herniates individuals,      individual disease
                    and which can accumu-       and low produc-
                    late sufficiently to        tivity
```

This general view has certain advantages, among which is the convenient explanation it provides for the frequent occurrence, if not the universality, of burnout. In this sense the dis-ease—which some observers see as an expression of *the* contemporary angst—basically refers to an accumulation of stressors great enough to propel individuals beyond their comfortable coping limits and thus powerful enough to create strain, the fight against which uses great amounts of energy. The overall picture suggests a vicious, downward spiral: managing strain absorbs energies that could go into everyday living, and any coping deficits there worsen the strain, which in turn redirects greater energies into bare maintenance, and so on. The vernacular often expresses the short-range fixation usually accompanying this condition in graphic terms—for example, "It's hard to design a drainage system for the swamp when you're up to your hips in alligators."

To focus only on the view above—that any stimulus can be a stressor for someone at some time—has its obvious inadequacies, even though it may be accurate enough. It encourages an emphasis on heightening stress-coping capabilities in individuals, rather than on reducing the stress-inducing potential in (let us say) work environments. The view also leads one to search for types of stressors that may be especially troublesome for many people, even though it remains true that one person's motivator may be another's backbreaker. And, perhaps most significantly, the approach suggests a research dead end, for it provides a ready rationalization for even very different kinds of precursors or outcomes, but without any distinct or helpful explanation of when a specific event will occur. Thus, in a sense this view explains everything, and nothing.

An emphasis on burnout seen in terms of progressive phases potentially provides a way out of this conceptual cul de sac. In a manner of speaking, burnout phases deal with the bottom line of an individual's balance of *eu*-stress over *dis*-stress, whatever the ranges and magnitudes of stressors to which individuals are exposed, and whatever their coping skills. *If* one can develop a valid and reliable bottom-line measure, goes the hope supporting this line of research, then and only then can one test whether certain classes of precursors are dominant in inducing or reinforcing such an effect. And that constitutes the beginning of wisdom on which an arsenal of remedial and, especially, preventive approaches can be built—an arsenal involving behaviors, attitudes, policies, practices, and so on.

Most research has approached the problem more or less the other way around, focusing on the precursors of burnout, or on the "personal psychological factors" (Fischer, 1983, p. 41) that may constitute a "sufficient cause" for a specific event to trigger eustress, distress, or no reaction in a specific person. The focus has not been on the bottom-line measurement of burnout and, in the present view, this bias has encouraged a welter of conflicting findings. Chapter two will provide a conceptual perspective on this critical point, but note here one illustration of the open-ended character of the "deficit model." In the conventional view, burnout derives from the *presence* of strain-inducing stressors that can overwhelm coping capabilities. A second covey of observers shifts the focus to the *absence* of positive motivators—job features like autonomy, variety, and significance (Jayaratne and Chess, 1983), commitment and moral purpose in work (Cherniss and Krantz, 1983), or organizational support (Farber, 1983, pp. 242–43).

There now exists no way to choose between such open-ended orientations, especially given the reliance of various studies on different measures of burnout in different populations, and also given the focus on small and often distinct panels of variables. In short, both "presence" and "absence" orientations suffer from the same basic ambiguities. Some of these ambiguities inhere in the variability of burnout precursors, from person to person; and some of them are exacerbated by idiosyncratic features of specific studies. In general, the main problem is that, using such a model, there is no end of possible precursors or features that can be associated with the phenomenon.

The present approach does not seek to finesse forever the study of precursors—absent or present—but it does assign them a distinctly secondary priority. The first priority goes to the burnout measure that—if reliable and valid—will serve to accurately show the variation in stressors, coping skills of individuals, and so on.

Fifth, the available literature suggests a dreary catalog of *outcomes* associated with specific degrees of burnout, but is neither comprehensive nor specific enough in describing these outcomes. Particularly lacking are statements about organizationally relevant outcomes, and especially about their variation in relation to specific degrees of burnout. For the most part, this shortfall derives from two sources: the clinical or even anecdotal character of most of the available literature, and the tendency to adopt an on/off, all/none view of burnout.

Ample incentive exists for detailing the links between specific degrees of burnout and a varied range of outcomes—especially those which are organizationally relevant—despite the unimpressive record of such attempts up to this time. Burnout has in fact been associated with a broad range of noxious outcomes, for individuals and, by implication, for their employing organizations (Cherniss, 1980b; Freudenberger, 1980; Maslach, 1982a, b).

This volume, then, addresses these five critical shortfalls. They constitute the major analytical targets and, even though the most critical research design lies beyond this volume and the work it reports, it is felt that major progress in relation to these analytical targets has been made.

CONVENTIONS TO GUIDE MEASUREMENT

Most of the targets for measurement will be introduced at appropriate points below, but several basics concerning the *how* and *where* of this research deserve up-front treatment. Four basic aspects of how and where get immediate attention: the features of the general model of burnout underlying this research; the characteristics of the prime research loci; the items for measuring burnout; and the procedure for using the items to generate phases of burnout.

FIGURE 1.1
Environmental or Multiple Outcomes Model Underlying This Research

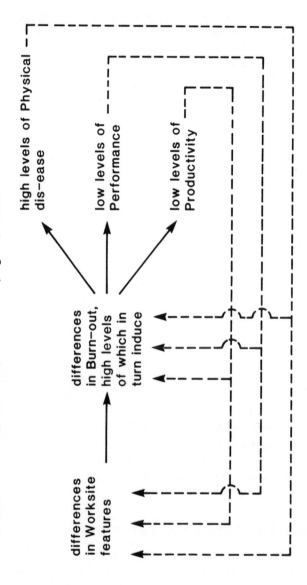

Environmental or Multiple-Outcomes Model of Burnout

To sketch the present approach, the five critical shortfalls of the burnout literature will be approached here in terms of a simple model, sketched in Figure 1.1. For convenience, it may be called an environmental or a "multiple-outcomes" model, because it provides for three broad consequences of progressive burnout, which in turn are seen as triggered by features of the work site. The basic conceptual view is not novel. Its attraction lies in its general acceptance, as by Harrison (1981), Jayaratne and Chess (1983, esp. p. 13), and others. This study adds to this attraction: it tests the basic conceptual view in substantial populations that provide a range of data, both in self-reports concerning work site features and physical health, as well as "objective" archival information about performance appraisals, productivity, and turnover.

This environmental or multiple-outcomes model will not be legitimated in any detailed way. Measurement conventions will be introduced later at several points. Here, note only two inspirations derived from the general model. A long tradition of research on organizational behavior suggests important linkages of features of the work site with individual responses at work, such as those tapped by burnout. So this effort takes guidance from research done by a distinguished collection of students of human behavior—Likert, Argyris, and so on—who have highlighted how work site structures and styles can have profound practical and moral consequences. As Harrison (1981, p. 43) expresses the core agreement of this tradition of research, "role strain and attitudes toward the work itself are near the core of the burn-out problem."

In addition, the general model proposes-for-testing three selected classes of outcomes consistent with the burnout literature. The bulk of available research collectively implies that individuals suffering from advanced burnout will feel worse and perform more poorly than usual, resulting in diminished productivity (Burke, Shearer, and Deszca, 1984). For starters, such results are seen here as direct and multiple outcomes experienced at different degrees of burnout. And we will have to see later what the empirical data imply about that major assumption.

Note also that the general model does not specify any interactions among the three outcomes. Such reinforcing linkages will receive later attention. As a first approximation, however, most observers do expect direct associations among the outcomes, but associations of less strength than the main-line effects tying burnout differences to each of the three multiple outcomes. Main-line effects are indicated by the solid vectors in Figure 1.1 and relate differences in a set of work site descriptors to progressive phases of burnout, whose outcomes will be traced in terms of differences in physical symptoms, performance, and productivity. The model includes feedback effects, which are designated by the broken-line vectors in Figure 1.1. These feedback effects reinforce and help maintain the main-line effects, but they are viewed as conceptually secondary and as occurring later in time.

Profiling the Basic Data Set

Most of the data for addressing the five basic research challenges come from a single data base. Given the ubiquity of this data base throughout this book, eight of its main aspects get early attention. In order, they are:

- a description of Site B, or the work place whose employees provided the bulk of the initial data on which the phase model rests

- the Maslach Behavior Inventory, or MBI, which supplies the items of the basic measurement instrument

- the congruence at five sites of the three subdomains underlying the MBI

- an introduction to the usefulness of a phase model in burnout

- the virulence and prepotency of the three MBI subdomains, which serve as the main conceptual components of the present phase model

- norms for differentiating individuals as high vs. low on the three MBI subdomains, with these assignments being critical in the phase model

- an eight-phase model of burnout, which builds on the three MBI sub-domains, each distinguished as high vs. low

- the reliability of both subdomain scores as well as assignments to the phases

Site B: Division of a Federal Agency

Most data come from a single locus, henceforth called Site B to be consistent with earlier publications (e.g., Golembiewski, Munzenrider, and Stevenson, 1986). Other research loci will be identified later, as appropriate.

The federal employees at Site B perform a range of jobs that can be emotionally arousing, with clients who can be "difficult," and under conditions that are trying. Moreover, the public employees work at numerous sites, nationwide, and they constitute a "horizontal slice" of a federal agency at low- to middle-organization levels involving a narrow range of jobs.

Certain details provide justification for referring to the Site B population as a horizontal slice. The federal respondents come basically from the middle ranges of General Schedule (GS) levels, and encompass four classes of employees, including the following:

- managers and supervisors, largely GS 11-13, who constitute some 12 percent of the total responding population

- a cadre of employees from one of the established professions, at GS 7-12, or 6 percent

- employees who are in contact with clients, at GS levels 5-11, who comprise 70 percent of the respondents

- clerical personnel, generally at GS levels 4-6, who constitute 12 percent of the responding population

Note that the classified federal service distinguishes 18 GS levels, plus the super-grades.

With both management and union support, the national work force of Site B was asked to volunteer responses to a questionnaire dealing with aspects of their work life. The total population numbered 2,869, located at more than 50 sites across the country, with the field units having similar although not identical employee compositions, missions, and roles. Responses vary for different items and for different purposes, but N = 1,535 for the most central usages here. The response rate thus approximates 54 percent, which is considered acceptable for present purposes. Comparisons of several conventional demographics—age, sex, race, and so on—also suggest that the responding population constitutes a near analog of the total population (Stevenson, 1985).

Maslach Burnout Inventory, or MBI

This research relies on the Maslach Burnout Inventory (Maslach and Jackson, 1981) to assess burnout. The MBI consists of 25 items, which tap three subscales:

Depersonalization, high scores on which distinguish individuals who tend to view people as things or objects, and who tend to distance themselves from others;

Personal Accomplishment (reversed), high scores on which indicate respondents who see themselves as not performing well on a task that they perceive as not being particularly worthwhile; and

Emotional Exhaustion, high scores on which come from individuals who see themselves as operating beyond comfortable coping limits, and as approaching "the end of the rope" in psychological and emotional senses.

Extensive factor analyses with a variety of public-sector and non-profit populations (Maslach and Jackson, 1981) assigned MBI items to the three subscales, and later analysis will test the adequacy of these assignments.

Exploratory work with MBI data encourages some modifications of the original instrument, two of which deserve note here. Thus, while the original MBI asks for two ratings on each item—one for frequency and one for intensity—respondents at Sites A and B got simpler instructions:

III. Write a number in the blank to the left of each statement below, based on this scale: To what DEGREE is each of the statements LIKE or UNLIKE you?

Very much UNLIKE me   1   2   3   4   5   6   7   very much LIKE me

Enter one NUMBER in the blank to the LEFT of each statement. Make

TABLE 1.1
Three-factor Structure for 23 MBI Items, Site B (N = 1,535)

MBI Subscales/Items	Rotated Factors*			
	I	II	III	H²
Emotional exhaustion, modified				
148. Emotionally drained	.80			.64
149. Used up	.79			.63
152. Fatigued in morning	.62			.44
159. Feel burned out	.83			.71
164. Feel frustrated	.64			.48
165. Work too hard	.47			.25
171. At end of rope	.57			.44
Depersonalization, modified				
153. Feel uncomfortable about way I treat coworkers			.43	.20
155. See people as impersonal objects			.60	.40
157. Working with people is a strain	.48		.34	.37
161. I've become more callous			.60	.43
162. Hardening me emotionally	.60		.32	.46
166. Don't care what happens to coworkers			.50	.32
167. Working directly with people is stressful	.46		.34	.37
173. Coworkers blame me for their problems			.37	.14
Personal accomplishment (reversed)				
154. Understand how coworkers feel		.40		.21
158. Deal effectively with co-worker problems		.53		.28
160. Positively influencing co-workers		.43		.20
163. Feel very energetic	.42	.46		.39
168. Can create relaxed atmosphere with coworkers		.54		.33
169. Feel exhilarated		.56		.32
170. Accomplished worthwhile things		.55		.45
172. Deal with emotional problems calmly		.42		.18
Eigenvalue	6.1	2.5	1.9	
Percent common variance	26.4	10.9	7.9	
Percent cumulative variance	26.4	37.3	45.2	

*Shows only loadings > .30.

certain you use LOW numbers to describe statements which are *unlike* you and HIGH numbers to describe statements *LIKE* YOU.

_____ 148. I feel emotionally drained from my work.

In addition, two items are dropped, based on a detailed item analysis. The 23 items retained are identified briefly in Table 1.1, along with the item numbers on the survey to reflect how the subscale items are interspersed on the instrument.

Five kinds of evidence suggest the serviceability of the two modifications, which distort neither Maslach's intent nor her findings. First, in a reanalysis of Maslach's data, Ahmavaara's technique (1954) estimates that the intensity and frequency factorial structures share about 96 percent of their variance, in both pattern *and* magnitude (Golembiewski, Munzenrider, and Carter, 1983). Indeed, the authors are not aware of even a single case in the literature that does not lead to the same conclusion. Little is lost by the present convention of neglecting the intensity-versus-frequency distinction.

Second, although the data are omitted here to conserve space (Golembiewski, Munzenrider, and Stevenson, 1986, p. 15), the alpha reliabilities for the three "modified" versus "original" MBI scores increase, on balance, after the two-item deletions. The modified reliabilities are quite acceptable for present purposes. In addition, any further deletions in all cases but Item 165 would lower alpha reliabilities. Finally, the individual items correlate diversely with subscale scores. This implies a synergistic effect of each batch of items, and reinforces their collective contributions to three subscales, as distinct from mere collections of items.

Third, Table 1.1 reflects a relatively clear factorial structure for Site B, when three factors are called for. Factor 1 is loaded by four items from other subscales, but the other two factors get loaded $> .30$ only by items classified *a priori* within their respective subscales by original factor analyses with other populations (Maslach and Jackson, 1981). Note the communalities, or H^2. They reflect at a glance how much of an item's variance is included in the factor analysis. The lowest value is 18 percent, and many are much higher, which indicates the salience of the items to the three-factor construct of burnout.

A separate analysis of data from Site A reveals the same pattern (Golembiewski, Munzenrider, and Carter, 1983). Site A is a commercial product-line division of a multinational firm, N = 292, with the broad range of functions from research through audit and all hierarchical levels from porter to president. Details about this business organization appear elsewhere (e.g., Golembiewski, Munzenrider, and Stevenson, 1986, esp. pp. 9–10).

Fourth, the factorial structures generated by responses to the modified MBI correspond closely to Maslach's original factorial structures, again in relation to data from both Sites A and B. Measures of the correspondence rely on Ahmavaara's (1954) factor comparison technique that estimates the congruence between pairs of structures. For Site A, approximately 80 percent of the variance is shared with Maslach's original structure, considering both the pattern and the magnitude of the sets of factorial structures (Golembiewski, Munzenrider, and Carter, 1983). For Site B, Ahmavaara's technique places that degree of congruence at approximately 70 percent. Specifically, the structure deriving from federal respondents was compared both with Maslach's frequency and intensity factorial structures, with these results:

	Intraclass Correlation	Product-Moment Correlation
Frequency factors	.86	.86
Intensity factors	.83	.84

Fifth, as the factor analysis suggests, the three subscales have correlations that leave most of the variance unaccounted for. This reinforces the usefulness of the three components. In sum:

	Depersonalization	Personal Accomplishment (reversed)	Emotional Exhaustion
Depersonalization	1.00	.28	.55
Personal accomplishment (reversed)		1.00	.27
Emotional exhaustion			1.00

Like other evidence, this pattern of intercorrelation suggests that the three subscales make relatively independent contributions to defining the content of "psychological burnout."

Three-Factor Structure at Five Loci

Convincingly, also, the three-factor structure seems to be very durable between settings. Specifically, Ahmavaara's technique is used to compare the congruency between the factors isolated by the Site B MBI administration with the structures generated by four other MBI administrations involving:

A. a population of middle-level and senior Canadian managers, N = 244 (Cahoon and Rowney, 1984)

B. employees of a Canadian hospital, excluding doctors, N = 299 (Boudreau, 1986)

C. employees of midwestern regional division of retirement communities, N = 942 (Deckard, 1985)

D. employees of a national corporation of nursing homes, N = 284 (Rountree, 1982)

Ahmavaara's technique reveals that the five populations in effect perceive almost the identical structure in their MBI administrations. The product-moment

TABLE 1.2
Congruence of Five Pairs of MBI Factorial Structures

Modified MBI at Site B Paired With	Product-Moment Correlation	Intra-Class Correlation
Case A	.88	.88
Case B	.88	.88
Case C	.97	.97
Case D	.96	.96

correlation estimates the congruency of the *pattern* of a pair of factorial structures; and the intraclass correlation coefficient estimates the similarities in magnitude *as well as* pattern of two correlation matrices. Details are available elsewhere (Munzenrider and Golembiewski, 1986, 1987), but Table 1.2 presents conclusive summary evidence of the congruence of the five factorial structures under consideration here. In sum, the four pairs of factorial structures share an average of nearly 85 percent of the variance, considering both patterning and magnitude.

This constitutes very convincing evidence that the three subdimensions of burnout focused on below are not artifacts of a specific locus. People in a range of settings seem to "see" the same conceptual dimension in the MBI items, in sum, which implies the centrality in nature of the "something" measured by the MBI items and scoring procedure.

Phases of Burnout

The phase model of burnout seeks to extend Maslach's work in three senses, as will become clear. To begin, note that Maslach and Jackson (1981) basically test for the relationships of the three separate subscale scores with a wide range of personal and organizational outcomes. One could also calculate a total MBI score, but this use of the instrument is rare (Golembiewski and Munzenrider, 1981).

This study makes another, triune use of the MBI items. It attributes progressive prepotencies to the three MBI subscales, utilizes norms from the federal population at Site B to distinguish high from low scores on each of the subscales, and then defines phases of burnout in terms of the eight possible high-versus-low combinations of scores on the three subdomains.

Details of these assignments will be presented in the concluding pages of this chapter, but note here that the phases could just as easily have been called "degrees" or "levels." All of these terms can be seen to be imperfect when viewed very critically; no terminology will completely prevent confusion in this area. The only defense against misunderstanding here is, rather, a conceptual one. The phases measure what the following context describes—nothing more, nothing less—despite the various connotations associated with the term, "phases," "degrees," or "levels." Hence, the special significance to this study of the final pages of this chapter.

Virulence and Potencies of MBI Subscales

Essentially, the present phase approach aims to test the relative virulence of the eight phases, which rest on a basic assumption about the relative potencies of the three proposed contributors to burnout. This section seeks to be clear about that assumption, as a prelude to the detailed testing that preoccupies the chapters to follow.

The limited conceptual focus here sketches the rationale underlying the assumed potencies of the three MBI subscales, with restricted attention to MBI subscales, in what may be called an *idealized chronic progression*. Broadly, *Depersonalization* is seen as the usual and least potent entry into burnout. In general, *Emotional Exhaustion* is the most potent contributor, and *Personal Accomplishment* is intermediate. Later analysis will provide much detail about a different progression—*acute onset*.

The relative potencies of the three MBI subscales derive from several sources, with years of organization-watching providing most of the argument for such a view. Let us consider upwardly mobile persons, and especially those in an autocratic organization, by way of gaining some perspective on the present view that increases in depersonalization represent common and least-virulent initiators of progressive burnout. Early "progress" for such persons will be defined largely in rational-technical terms, which encourages depersonalization. Indeed, some degree of "objectivity" or "detached concern" (Lief and Fox, 1963) seems necessary or at least useful for effective performance in many occupations and professions. Beyond some undefined point, however, depersonalization undercuts personal accomplishment. Perhaps the prototypic case involves the depersonalizing salesperson promoted to manager. In episodic contacts with "sales targets," certain attitudes and behaviors may be useful or at least not troublesome—a focus on people that is narrow and instrumental, "snow job" skills that reflect little regard for the broad interests of potential "marks," a characteristic overstatement or elasticity with regard to fact, and so on. In a managerial job, such depersonalizing features may contribute far less to effective performance and may, indeed, undercut it. As depersonalization deepens and personal accomplishment continues to suffer, stressors can result in strain surpassing an individual's normal coping limits, which results in the energy deficit encompassed by the notion of emotional exhaustion.

The hypothetical progression of burnout contributors can also be illustrated by reference to two other critical sorts of situations: when the individual at work experiences too heavy a case load, or is otherwise overstimulated; and when the individual faces an environment containing too little stimulation and challenge (Cherniss, 1980b, p. 45). In both cases, the individual may feel a loss of autonomy and control, which may threaten or diminish his or her self-image. At early stages, he or she may actively seek a constructive way out, but persistence of the condition may eventually encourage one to treat other people as objects—that is to say, one treats others as one is being treated. The resulting depersonalization could then cycle in ways that diminish one's sense of personal accomplishment, and can eventually lead to growing emotional exhaustion.

The basic progression—depersonalization $\longrightarrow$ diminished personal accomplishment $\longrightarrow$ emotional exhaustion—can also be framed in more theoretic terms. In explanation, most discussion of burnout can be subsumed under a model having three major elements:

- *Job stress*, which represents some balance between the demands of work and the resources the worker can bring to bear. Note that job stress can have two general sources: overload deriving from too much stimulation and challenge, and/or lassitude deriving from too little stimulation and challenge

- *Experienced job-derived strain*, which can be reflected in irritability and fatigue

- *Coping*, which can be either constructive, as in seeking a detached concern (Lief and Fox, 1963), which manages job stress by creating some "distance" for the actor without psychological removal; or counterproductive, as in emotional disengagement and withdrawal, cynicism, or rigidity

Similar models that have been generated (for example, Shinn, 1979; and Cherniss, 1980b) permit a definition of burnout "as a process in which a previously committed [organization member] disengages from his or her work in response to stress and strain experienced in the job" (Cherniss, 1980b, p. 18).

Relying on the three MBI dimensions, let us illustrate how job stress and strain can often result in counterproductive coping by individuals. Depersonalization can be seen as a failure to develop the appropriate levels of detached concern (Lief and Fox, 1963) that can be useful in many work settings. Detached concern seeks a precarious balance: being accessible to others and being concerned about them, but in ways that permit substantial degrees of objectivity and skill in situations that might otherwise immobilize. That this balance is often realized only to an imperfect degree gets convincing support from the many awkward approaches to inducing some degree of distance between the service supplier and clients or others. These counterproductive approaches include the following:

- The creation of emotional distance by negative labeling (Maslach, 1978a, pp. 57-58), as seen in the tendency of professionals to see clients as "bad" persons, as variously unworthy or inferior (Wills, 1978, pp. 958-59). This has been termed "blaming the victim" (Ryan, 1971);

- Intellectualizations that variously remove the service supplier *as a person* from the work situation (Maslach, 1976, p. 18). Such withdrawal is reflected in statements such as "If I were in another setting, I'd be angry with X. But I realize he is not responding to me as a person, but as an auditor";

- Responses that get triggered by categories rather than persons—for example, "That is not a patient, that is a myocardial infarction"; and

- Use of various structuring devices, such as appurtenances of power, status, or professional standing. These include the white coats often affected by R & D personnel that distinguish them from other employees.

Why label such approaches as "awkward"? To simplify, such approaches poorly reflect detached concern, may fairly be labeled "depersonalization," and also can have a broad range of effects at the work site that decrease one's sense of personal accomplishment. Two of these effects receive attention here. Thus, people may experience a full sense of the negativism often produced in others by treating them in a depersonalized mode (Maslach, 1978b, pp. 111-14), which can impact negatively on how they do their job and on how they evaluate themselves as job performers. As Maslach (1978b, p. 113) sees the situation, this chain of effects in human-service organizations often results from a loss of concern for clients:

> ... clients are viewed as somehow deserving of their problems and are often blamed for their victimization. Consequently, there appears to be a deterioration in the quality of care or service that they receive. The staff person is unable to deal successfully with the chronic emotional stress of the job, and this failure to cope can be manifested in a number of ways, including low morale, impaired performance, absenteeism, and high turnover.

In addition to its effects on performance, the derivative negative self-evaluation can have a profound personal impact. As Maslach and Jackson (1979, p. 162) note in one instance:

> When the policeman's burnout hits the phase of negative self-evaluation, his isolation from other people becomes even more pronounced. Not only does he feel distant from his children, and either unwilling or unable to share his feelings with his wife, but he also has fewer friends and is more

likely to shun social activities for solitary ones. He may simply want peace and quiet. . . . Or he may feel that he is not working well with people and may thus want to avoid any further evidence of his ineffectiveness by minimizing the number of involving relationships.

Another mode of response can be equally distancing from others: a person can make hierarchical status *the* measure of personal achievement, and reinforce it with petty bureaucratization, or rigidly "going by the book."

When the process of depersonalization and diminished personal accomplishment has progressed to a sufficient degree—to close our mini-theoretical network—the stage is set for some tragic cycling that can escalate to deepening emotional exhaustion. Literally, persons so poised cannot win for losing. Indeed, the harder they try, and the more deeply they care about being competent, the faster matters often become worse. Excerpts from Freudenberger (1974, pp. 160-62) provide a graphic description of this self-reinforcing cyclicality:

> . . . quickness to anger and . . . instantaneous irritation and frustration. . . . Thinking . . . becomes excessively rigid, stubborn, and inflexible. . . . [The person] becomes the "house cynic" . . . blocks progress and constructive change . . . because change means another adaptation [for which] he is just too tired. . . . [The person spends a] greater and greater number of physical hours [at work], but less and less is being accomplished. . . . [The person desperately needs support and caring but, often because of intensified preoccupation with work and lengthening hours,] "has just about lost most of his [or her] friends."

Freudenberger (1977, p. 27) describes this downward spiral as "an unending cycle of accelerating effort and decelerating reward. The burnout victim is on a treadmill of his or her own choosing, even though he or she ascribes it to external forces."

Norms for High and Low

This line of research has consistently distinguished high from low scores on the three MBI subscales, a convenience that at once raises questions and also provides research opportunities. The questions will be considered here, while a discussion of the research opportunities will be reserved for a later chapter.

The pilot study, at Site A, initially used median scores as cutting-points to distinguish High from Low scorers (Golembiewski, Munzenrider, and Carter, 1983). However, Site A had only several hundred employees, employment was highly valued and compensated, and the organization was in several different ways considered a "good employer." Hence, the median scores for the three MBI subscales might not be useful cutting points for "true" High versus Low scores.

Percentile rankings of the three sets of raw MBI subscale scores at Site B provide an empirically grounded estimate of High versus Low. The distribution of

raw scores by percentiles—not reprinted here, but available elsewhere (Golembiewski, Munzenrider, and Stevenson, 1986, pp. 24–25)—suggests three cutting
points for High scores, or those greater than the median: 18, 26, and 22, for
Depersonalization, Personal Accomplishment (reversed), and Emotional Exhaustion, respectively.

The pilot study at Site A had cutting points of 15, 22, and 20, respectively,
for the three subdomains of burnout.

Assignments of Individuals to Burnout Phases

A simple decision rule generates an 8-phase model of burnout. That is, emotional exhaustion is considered most characteristic of advanced phases of burnout, and depersonalization is considered least virulent. Three subscales, each
presented in terms of high and low, generate the progressive phases of burnout:

	Progressive Phases of Burnout							
	I	II	III	IV	V	VI	VII	VIII
Depersonalization	Lo	Hi	Lo	Hi	Lo	Hi	Lo	Hi
Personal accomplishment (reversed)	Lo	Lo	Hi	Hi	Lo	Lo	Hi	Hi
Emotional exhaustion	Lo	Lo	Lo	Lo	Hi	Hi	Hi	Hi

Detailed analysis establishes that the scoring conventions generate subpopulations that meet expectations, with but a single exception. The numerous
paired-comparisons of phases all but unanimously reflect the expected differ-
ences/similarities associated with the phase model. To illustrate, Phase I total
score should be lower than for all other phases; but (for example), Phase II total
probably will not differ from those for Phases III and V, since all three have one
High subscale score. The analysis is not reproduced here to conserve space, but it
relies on the *Least Significant Difference* test, as modified to take into account
differences in the size of subpopulations (Nie et al., 1975). All total-score-paired-
comparisons expected to be significantly different attain the .05 level; and no
deviant cases are encountered in the cases where nonrandom differences only are
expected on paired-comparisons of total scores. For the 48 paired-comparisons
of the three subscale scores on which significant differences are expected, all
cases attain the .05 level. To illustrate, Phase I depersonalization should be lower
than for Phases II, IV, VI, and VIII in any robust example of the phase model,
and that condition exists. Moreover, only one deviant case occurs in the paired
comparisons of those 36 cases involving subscale scores where no differences are
expected—a statistically significant difference on depersonalization for Phases I
and VII, which are both assigned low cases but whose subpopulations nonetheless
differ.

The phase assignments are quite orderly in a statistical sense, and—although some may see the exercise as artifactual—it does establish the robustness of the structure of the phases. Hence, the phase assignments facilitate search for organizational covariants of burnout that, in turn, will help test the assumptions underlying this research.

Reliabilities of Subdimensions and Phases

No test-retest reliabilities are available for Sites A or B, but perspective on this central methodological feature comes from five observations at another setting over a seven-week interval. The population is the direct-care staff of a life-care retirementment community, with N = 111 at outset and N = 71 at seven weeks (Golembiewski, Deckard, and Rountree, 1987). Changes in N mostly reflect availability of individuals at testing times rather than turnover or refusal to participate.

The results probably provide a conservative estimate of test-retest reliability, since measurement error as well as "real change" are involved, and also because Phase IV and V (as evidence will show in chapter six) seem transitional. In any case, the congruence of scores on each of the three subdimensions can be estimated by ten correlations between MBI administrations at five points in time. The coefficients average .58, .55, and .72 for Depersonalization, Personal Accomplishment, and Emotional Exhaustion, respectively. These coefficients imply that the several scores share 33, 31, and 52 percent of their variance, respectively, for Depersonalization, Personal Accomplishment, and Emotional Exhaustion.

As for the phases, they also reflect a substantial congruence at the five points in time. Knowing the initial phase assignment of an individual is powerful in predicting subsequent assignments. On average, compared to chance, the *gamma* statistic (Mueller et al., 1970, pp. 279-92) implies that knowledge of a person's initial assignment reduces one's error in predicting subsequent assignments by about 55 percent. Significantly, also, *gamma* seems to vary little between comparisons of proximate vs. distal administrations. Thus the four most-proximate observations (I vs. II, II vs. III, and so on) have a *gamma* X = .5423, while the four most-distant observations average .5395.

Advantages of the Phase Model

Even at this point, major potential advantages of the phase model seem clear, especially for practical applications. Basically, the phase model promises a way to measure burnout in large aggregates, as well as to classify individuals in terms of the virulence of their particular cases. In addition, the phases point up individual differences that would be disguised in the mid-ranges of total scores. The phases also highlight the specific contributors to a person's particular level of burnout, and this permits a more accurate targeting of ameliorative interventions. For example, a person high on depersonalization obviously would not profit from the same intervention as the individual with advanced emotional exhaustion.

The phases point up such differences and—as will become clear—sometimes with such surprising effects that in some cases they contraindicate the common wisdom. No other way of measuring burnout allows for such flexibility or has such potential use for both research and practical intervention.

However, note what the phase model does not propose to do. It neither proposes nor requires that individual cases of full-term burnout progress in order through each of the eight phases. That would be psychologically awkward or impossible, as in movement from Phase II to III. Consider also a case of acute onset, when an individual in a low phase has his or her coping skills and attitudes overwhelmed by a trauma, with the attendant emotional exhaustion only later generating (for example) a reduced sense of accomplishment. This analysis seeks only to test whether the phases are progressively virulent whenever they occur.

THE SUBSEQUENT STEPS

Demonstrating the usefulness of the phase model constitutes the next step. Specifically, chapters two through five begin the job. They relate several measures of burnout to features of the work site, to physical symptoms as well as, tentatively, to some features of blood chemistry, and to performance appraisals and productivity. Special attention is given to replications—e.g., in chapter three— to reduce the probability that artifactual results at Site B merely lead us on. These chapters suggest the particular usefulness of the model in isolating regular and robust differences, phase by phase, in three sets of significant indicators. In general, as the phases progress from I to VIII, the three classes of variables worsen. This not only suggests the usefulness of the phase model, but implies the profound personal and social costs of burnout.

A second cluster of two chapters seeks to "learn from the phase model," based on the demonstration of how the phases relate in reasonable and substantial ways to the three clusters of personal and organizational variables. Chapter six provides some perspective on the severity of burnout, with special attention being given to sequence, incidence, and persistence. Chapter seven explores diverse loci for burnout, especially for the phase model. The focus is on the "maze of causality," with attention to several personal and group perspectives on the factors that facilitate or may even be said, with some reservation, to "cause" burnout. These two chapters have obvious theoretical and practical significance. Indeed, although this exploration has only been begun in this book, results thus far strongly support two basic conclusions. Burnout is "pretty bad" in organizations, but it seems to inhere far more in organizational and group features that are potentially changeable, rather than in personality features that pose far greater challenges to change. This suggests some bad news and some good.

The two final chapters make bold to build on the descriptive usefulness of the phases, as well as on what has been learned about them. Thus, chapters eight and nine focus on three classes of initiatives derived from the phase model:

research challenges; specific practical directions for intervening so as to ameliorate burnout; and the details of a design for intervening to reduce burnout as well as the consequences of that design.

So, in general, the approach that follows has a stark profile, despite a few details that may occasionally veer toward the arcane and byzantine. Research sets the character of the challenges to be met by effective interventions, and public policy should both reflect and support study and practice.

2. ORGANIZATIONAL FEATURES AT SITE B ASSOCIATED WITH BURNOUT: WORK SITE DESCRIPTORS AND THE PHASE MODEL

Judging from the clinical literature on burnout, its covariants include a broad and noxious range, personal as well as organizational (Cherniss, 1980b; Freudenberger, 1980; Maslach, 1982a, b). In sum, the quality of working life may well contribute to the level of burnout, and the character of the work site will no doubt be adversely affected by persons in advanced phases of burnout. But we will never be able to determine the validity of these generalizations, nor estimate the magnitudes of their effects, unless we have a meaningful measure for burnout.

The phase model proposes such a bottom-line measure of burnout, and the merits of this proposal need proof. Hence the challenges attending this book begin to get earnest attention in this chapter, through testing the generalizations about burnout, assessing the validity and reliability of the phase model, and gaining perspective on the direction of causal arrows.

How to begin? The sections below identify a set of features commonly used to assess the quality of a work site, and they also predict the expected associations of these variables with the phases of burnout. Once that is done, several tests will assess whether the apparent covariants of the phases in fact "map" them in the expected ways. Site B will get sole immediate attention; and chapter three will review three replications to add credibility to Site B results.

Note that this approach to assessing concurrent validity does double duty, as it were. If the selected variables vary regularly and expectedly with the phases of burnout, such a pattern will support the present approach to progressive burnout. Moreover, while building on the insights of clinicians dealing with individuals presenting aspects of advanced burnout, the tests that follow also can add depth to our knowledge by focusing not only on individuals with advanced symptoms but on large collections of people arrayed across the full range of burnout phases. The validity of analyses drawn from extreme cases, then, can be tested for consistent effects across all degrees of burnout, for many respondents, in specific work sites whose main features are known. This kind of effort remains in short supply and provides the basic motivation for the following analysis.

SELECTED ORGANIZATIONAL COVARIANTS AT SITE B

One can envision a very large panel of organizational covariants of burnout, and with compelling justification. Our initial approach seeks a *media via*: a sufficient range of variables to permit some confidence that the tests are not myopic, and yet not so large as to discourage an analysis that is still at early levels of development.

The key initial test of the phase model took place at Site B—which is described in chapter one—and focuses on 16 variables. All based on self-reports, these variables selectively profile the work sites of respondents in several particulars thought to be relevant by most observers.

These variables are discussed here briefly, along with expectations about their likely relationship with burnout. Note that all variables are referred to as work site descriptors.

Variables at Site B

A panel of 16 variables generates data about work site conditions at Site B. These are introduced in two classes. One class consists of *Assorted Scales*, of which all but one should decrease as burnout progresses through the several phases. Inverse associations should be expected for five variables:

- Trust in supervision (Roberts and O'Reilly, 1974)
- Trust in fellow employees (*ad hoc*)
- Job involvement (White and Ruh, 1973)
- Willingness to disagree with supervisor (Patchen, 1965)
- Participation in decisions re work (White and Ruh, 1973)

An additional scale should show an increase for advanced phases of burnout: Job Tension (Kahn et al., 1964).

The *Job Diagnostic Survey*, or *JDS*, measures satisfaction with ten facets of work (Hackman and Oldham, 1980), all of which should decrease as burnout progresses. They include:

- Meaningfulness of work
- Responsibility for results
- Knowledge of results
- General satisfaction
- Internal work motivation

- Growth
- Job security
- Compensation
- Coworkers
- Supervision

Certain theoretical reasons support the selection of these particular scales, but they will not be dwelled on here. Note, however, that Hackman and Oldham (1980) provide substantial and convincing justification for the JDS. The mini-networks of theory underlying the Assorted Scales are both general and obvious. Consider here only Job Tension, which taps several important classes of stressors—for example, those related to role ambiguity and conflict—that should impact on the burnout phases, more or less directly. Significant moderators of this direct relationship have been isolated (for example, by French and Caplan, 1973), but these are not measured in the present host organization and remain obvious subjects for fine-tuning this kind of analysis, if the phase model proves generally serviceable.

Findings Concerning Work Site Descriptors

Five points contribute to the conclusion that a regular and robust pattern of association links burnout and the 16 work site descriptors used at Site B. First, note that all the possible covariants have acceptable measurement properties, Thus, Cronbach's alphas for the variables average .79, and in only two cases fall below .70—specifically, .68 and .69. (See Table 2.1.)

Second, all 16 cases contain nonrandom variance somewhere in each variable arrayed by phases, as determined by one-way analysis of variance. Note also that all observed trends are in the expected directions: Job Tension increases, phase by phase, and all other variables decrease. In short, the several organization features "map" appropriately on the phases of burnout.

Third, the paired-comparisons of variables X phases support expectations impressively, indeed, massively. See Table 2.1 and, especially, Table 2.2. To summarize, phase by phase, analysis of all possible paired-comparisons indicates that over 90 percent of the differences (404 of 488) are in the expected directions; over 55 percent of all differences (248 of 448) attain statistical significance; and only 2 differences of 448 are in an unexpected direction and statistically significant. No precise guidelines exist, but 20 percent of statistically significant differences in any set of paired-comparisons are considered noteworthy. By this criterion, the phases obviously isolate clear and consistent patterns in the 16 work site descriptors in Tables 2.1 and 2.2.

We can be more specific about the association of the phases with the panel of self-reports detailing the character and quality of Site B. Eta^2 permits quite a precise estimate of the variance accounted for by phases X work site descriptors: 17.1 percent, on average, for the 16 variables detailed in Table 2.1. Again, this qualifies as robust *and* regular, given that the most marked relationships in the social sciences—such as many of these involving socioeconomic status—may account for as much as a quarter of the variance in a range of variables.

Fourth, the data suggest that most or all of the phases discretely map significant differences on the target variables. The record for significant paired-comparisons suggests the point, of course, and focusing on the "distance" between

TABLE 2.1
Covariation of Phases of Burnout and Target Variables via One-Way Analysis of Variance, Site B

| | Alpha Score | Progressive Phases of Burnout | | | | | | | | F-Ratio * | F-Probability |
		I LoLoLo N=352	II HiLoLo 107	III LoHiLo 193	IV HiHiLo 124	V LoLoHi 107	VI HiLoHi 176	VII LoHiHi 109	VIII HiHiHi 367		
Assorted scales											
Participation	.79	17.8	16.3	15.2	14.9	16.2	14.9	13.5	13.0	46.793	< .001
Job involvement	.86	34.7	32.9	31.8	29.7	30.9	29.8	25.4	24.7	72.227	< .001
Trust in supervision	.77	15.9	14.4	15.1	13.1	14.6	12.7	12.2	12.2	23.196	< .001
Trust in employees	.79	19.6	17.7	17.6	17.0	17.4	16.1	15.0	14.7	32.726	< .001
Willingness to disagree with supervisor	.79	14.6	15.6	13.7	14.6	16.4	15.3	15.0	14.9	2.996	< .01
Job tension	.85	17.0	19.1	18.2	19.9	21.0	22.2	22.0	23.1	49.240	< .001
Job Diagnostic Survey (JDS) Scales											
Meaningfulness of work	.80	23.0	21.2	20.9	19.4	20.1	19.5	17.7	16.4	64.940	< .001
Responsibility for results	.68	36.4	33.6	33.9	32.1	33.6	31.9	30.2	29.1	51.462	< .001
Knowledge of results	.70	23.0	21.5	21.9	20.4	21.2	19.8	20.3	18.9	32.840	< .001
General satisfaction	.80	28.4	26.4	26.0	24.2	23.1	22.2	19.9	19.2	97.183	< .001
Internal work motivation	.69	35.7	33.7	33.2	31.9	34.4	32.9	31.1	29.9	37.987	< .001
Growth satisfaction	.86	23.1	21.5	20.7	19.3	20.0	18.6	16.4	15.5	73.738	< .001
Satisfaction with security	.78	10.9	10.5	10.6	10.3	9.7	9.2	9.2	8.6	21.085	< .001
Satisfaction with compensation	.88	10.4	10.1	10.2	8.7	8.7	8.4	8.6	8.2	18.987	< .001
Satisfaction with coworkers	.75	18.3	17.5	17.1	15.9	17.6	16.0	15.5	13.9	76.314	< .001
Satisfaction with supervision	.91	17.1	15.7	15.9	14.1	14.7	13.5	12.5	12.2	38.385	< .001

*Degrees of freedom = 7, 1526.

35

TABLE 2.2
Statistical Significance of Paired-Comparisons of Burnout Phases × Target Variables, Site B

	I vs. II	I vs. III	I vs. IV	I vs. V	I vs. VI	I vs. VII	I vs. VIII	II vs. III	II vs. IV	II vs. V	II vs. VI	II vs. VII	II vs. VIII	III vs. IV
Assorted scales														
Participation	X	X	X	X	X	X	X					X	X	
Job involvement		X	X	X	X	X	X					X	X	
Trust in supervisor					X	X	X						X	X
Trust in employees	X	X	X	X	X	X	X					X	X	
Willingness to disagree with supervisor														
Job tension	X		X	X	X	X	X				X	X	X	
Job Diagnostic Survey (JDS) scale														
Meaningfulness of work	X	X	X	X	X	X	X				X	X	X	
Responsibility for results	X	X	X	X	X	X	X				X	X	X	X
Knowledge of results	X	X	X	X	X	X	X				X	X	X	
General satisfaction	X	X	X		X	X	X		X	X	X	X	X	
Internal work motivation	X	X			X	X	X			X		X	X	
Growth satisfaction		X	X	X	X	X	X		X		X	X	X	
Satisfaction with security			X	X	X	X	X		X	X	X	X	X	
Satisfaction with compensation			X	X	X	X	X		X	X	X	X	X	X
Satisfaction with coworkers	X	X	X		X	X	X				X	X	X	X
Satisfaction with supervision		X	X	X	X	X	X				X	X	X	X

	III vs. V	III vs. VI	III vs. VII	III vs. VIII	IV vs. V	IV vs. VI	IV vs. VII	IV vs. VIII	V vs. VI	V vs. VII	V vs. VIII	VI vs. VII	VI vs. VIII	VII vs. VIII
Assorted scales														
Participation		X	X	X				X		X	X	X	X	
Job involvement		X	X	X				X		X	X	X	X	
Trust in supervisor	X						X		X		X			
Trust in employees			X	X			X			X	X		X	
Willingness to disagree with supervisor	X													
Job tension	X	X		X		X	X	X			X			
Job Diagnostic Survey (JDS) scale														
Meaningfulness of work		X	X	X		X		X		X	X	X	X	
Responsibility for results		X	X	X		X		X		X	X	X	X	
Knowledge of results		X	X	X		X		X			X			
General satisfaction	X	X	X	X	X		X	X		X	X	X	X	X
Internal work motivation		X	X	X		X		X		X	X		X	
Growth satisfaction		X	X	X		X	X	X		X	X	X	X	
Satisfaction with security	X	X	X	X		X		X			X			
Satisfaction with compensation		X	X	X				X			X			
Satisfaction with coworkers	X	X	X	X	X			X	X		X		X	X
Satisfaction with supervision		X	X	X				X		X	X			

Note: X indicates a paired-comparison of differences on a variable that attains or surpasses the .05 level, based on the Least Significant Difference test, as modified for unequal size of subpopulation.

37

TABLE 2.3
Four Measures of Covariation of Target Variables, by Distance between Pairs of Phases,
Site B (percent; absolute number of observations in parentheses)

	Overall % of cases	Distances +7	+6	+5	+4	+3	+2	+1
Expected direction	90.2%	94 (15/16)	97 (31/32)	96 (46/48)	98 (63/64)	95 (76/80)	90 (87/96)	78 (87/112)
Expected direction and statistically significant	55.1%	94 (15/16)	94 (30/32)	92 (44/48)	78 (50/64)	58 (46/80)	41 (39/96)	20 (23/112)
Contrary direction	9.4%	6 (1/16)	3 (1/32)	2 (1/48)	3 (1/64)	5 (4/80)	9 (9/96)	21 (24/112)
Contrary direction and statistically significant	0.5%	0	0	2 (1/48)	0	0	0	1 (1/112)

phases highlights it. Thus, Phases I vs. II, II vs. III, and so on are +1; Phases I vs. III and II vs. IV illustrate +2; and so on. The usefulness of the full 8-phase model will be supported by large proportions of expected and statistically significant differences, more or less evenly distributed among the seven possible distances.

Table 2.3 provides summary data concerning distances between phases, and these data demonstrate that neighborly as well as remote phases tend to map discrete segments of the ranges of all target variables. This conclusion holds most clearly for the five most distant pairs of phases (+3 to +7)—where over 76 percent of the paired differences are in the expected direction *and* attain statistical significance. Moreover, even distances +2 and +1 generate 41 and 20 percent records of significant differences. This suggests that even very close neighbors in phase assignments can be described in terms of significantly different degrees of 16 work site descriptors.

In sum, the data in Table 2.3 imply the usefulness of most or all of the phases, a significant demonstration. To explain, Phases I and VIII reflect the lowest and highest MBI total scores, and hence +7 results might be interpreted as a total-score effect. But pairs of phases of proximate distance can have either similar or significantly different total MBI scores, and yet they map on the target variables in quite distinct ways.

Fifth, the 16 target variables do not merely measure the same domain in multiple ways. The factor analysis (Varimax rotation) in Table 2.4, indeed, implies three major domains, which are provisionally labeled there. One factor accounts for the 45 percent of the common variance on the initial statistics, to which the other two factors add some 16 percent. Twelve of the 16 work site descriptors load on the first factor greater than .3; the second factor seems distinguished by its focus on supervisors versus peers, and by security versus job contributors to satisfaction; and the third factor suggests an emphasis on satisfaction with a good-paying job paired with a willingness to raise contentious issues with supervisors. The multi-dimensionality of the target variables suggests that they do not simply measure the same domain over and over again.

In addition, this factor analysis also supports the concurrent validity of the phase model. In general, the phases should covary indirectly with the three factor scores, although the case is weakest for Factor III. To illustrate, as the phases progress from I through VIII, Factor I should trend negatively. One-way ANOVA indicates significant variation in all three factor scores, with over 76 percent of the paired-comparisons being in the expected direction and nearly 40 percent attaining statistical significance. Three of 84 cases in an opposite direction also achieve the .05 level, which approximates 4 percent. See Table 2.5. This is similar to the record for the 16 individual scales, the reader may recall.

In addition, the pattern of covariation of phases × work site descriptors is even more robust for the first two factors, which Table 2.4 details. In sum, nearly 95 percent of those paired-comparisons are in the expected direction, and over 57 percent of those pairs attain the .05 level. In contrast, none of the

TABLE 2.4
Factors in Panel of 16 Target Variables, by Varimax Rotation, Site B

	Factors Suggesting Differences in Work Site Descriptors			
	I. High Energy, Positive Job Factors, Peer-Oriented	II. High Trust, Supervisor-Oriented, Positive Security, Tension-Avoiding	III. Active, Upward Feedback	H²
Assorted Scales				
Participation	.49	.47	.30	.55
Job Involvement	.72			.62
Trust in supervisor		.79		.72
Trust in employees	.36	.72		.66
Willingness to disagree with supervisor			.49	.24
Job tension	-.31	-.57		.42
Job Scales				
Meaningfulness of work	.81			.71
Responsibility for results	.71			.58
Knowledge of results	.40	.34		.30
General satisfaction	.76	.36		.73
Internal work motivation	.66			.48
Growth satisfaction	.73	.41		.76
Satisfaction with security		.40		.25
Satisfaction with compensation		.41		.33
Satisfaction with coworkers	.68	.31		.56
Satisfaction with supervisors	.30	.83		.79
Initial Statistics				
Eigenvalue (unrotated)	7.46	1.52	1.11	
Percent common variance	46.6	9.5	7.0	
Percent cumulative variance	46.6	56.1	63.1	

<u>Note</u>: Shows only loadings > .30.

TABLE 2.5
Summary Data on Factor Scores × Phases

	F-ratio	F-Probability	Pairs in Expected Direction	In Expected Direction and Statistically Significant	Pairs in Contrary Direction	In Contrary Direction and Statistically Significant
Factor I	79.5	< .0000	96.4%	71.4%	3.6%	0
Factor II	25.0	< .0000	92.9	42.9	7.1	0
Factor III	3.7	< .0005	39.3	3.6	61.7	10.7
Totals			76.2%	39.3%	23.8%	3.6%

5.4 percent of the comparisons falling in an opposite direction attains statistical significance.

IMPLICATIONS FOR THE PHASE MODEL OF BURNOUT

The data from Site B provide strong initial support for the usefulness of the eight-phase model—that much seems clear. Tables 2.2 and 2.3 are most persuasive on the point, indicating as they do that even proximate phases tend to differ robustly as well as regularly on the 16 work site descriptors. As the phase model requires, the eight phases show progressive deficiencies or deficits in the way employees see their organizations. Tables 2.4 and 2.5 reinforce this conclusion, establishing as they do that the work site descriptors do not merely measure one dimension in multiple ways.

The evidence in this chapter both adds support for, as well as derives momentum from, earlier analysis. No doubt the most significant recent addition to knowledge about the phase model comes from evidence about the congruence in several populations of the three MBI subscales, details about which appear in Table 1.2. In sum, individuals in very different contexts "see" essentially the same dimensional structure in the MBI items. This elemental but critical datum substantially reinforces the persuasiveness of the Site B findings, and adds weight to the review of the several replicatory studies to be reviewed in chapter three. The burnout subscales are not statistical will-of-the-wisps, but quite consistently solid psychologic structures that individuals tend to hold in common.

Nonetheless, the Site B data may be artifactual, even as they get the analysis of the phase model off to a promising start. The pattern of phases X work site descriptors may be unique to Site B, for example, or to the particular panel of work site descriptors employed there.

Chapter three begins the long process of testing for these and other possible contributors to the artifactuality of the Site B findings. Three replications get direct attention there, and they not only involve different sites but also use different sets of work site descriptors. The several variations should provide a meaningful test of the ability to generalize from the Site B associations between the phases and estimates of the quality and character of work sites. In turn, successful replications will add substantially to the evidence supporting the validity and reliability of the phases.

3. REPLICATIONS OF THE SITE B PROFILE: A BASIC PATTERN AND SOME DIFFERENCES

The profile of the association of work site descriptors with the phases of burnout at Site B can stand alone, but enhanced credibility requires replication. This chapter contributes two emphases to the argument of this book: it details the results of three replications; and it summarizes the implications of the basic study at Site B, as reinforced not only by the replications described here but also by other available studies.

ORGANIZATIONAL COVARIANTS OF BURNOUT AT THREE SITES

The profile of Site B covariants has been replicated a number of times (e.g., Burke, 1987; Burke and Deszca, 1986; Burke, Shearer, and Deszca, 1984; Deckard, 1985; Deckard, Rountree, and Golembiewski, 1986; Golembiewski, Munzenrider, and Carter, 1983; Golembiewski, Hilles, and Daly, 1987; Golembiewski and Rountree, 1986), all pretty much to the same effect. As the phases progress I through VIII, in sum, work site deficits or deficiencies increase.

This basic pattern of results *strongly supports the phase model*, of course. The basic pattern of covariants is found in *all* studies, but that pattern varies in its sharpness and magnitude. Three replicatory studies will be detailed below in support of this bold if qualified conclusion, as well as to illustrate the range of variables that have been studied. The three studies involve:

- a business organization, N = 292, previously described and referred to as Site A
- one region of a national corporation of life-care retirement communities, ten locations, all direct-care employees, N = 942, or Site C

43

- a corporate chain of life-care retirement communities, 23 locations, all direct-care employees, N = 2,123, or Site D

Organizational Covariants at Site A

Site A provides data about 22 work site descriptors—the 16 dealt with in the earlier discussion of Site B, and 6 variables from the Job Descriptive Index, or JDI (Smith, Kendall, and Blood, 1969). The JDI variables parallel several of the JDS scales, at least superficially. They measure satisfaction with five facets of work:

- Work
- Supervision
- Coworkers

- Promotion
- Pay

In addition, these five facets of satisfaction generate a total satisfaction score.

Three sets of expectations apply to Site A data. First, no significant differences seem likely on the two measures of satisfaction with pay/compensation, given the generous policies of the employing organization. Second, the previous chapter details expectations for 15 other Site B variables. For the six additional variables, third, direct expectations seem appropriate. As burnout increases, reduced satisfaction on all six measures seems reasonable, even though the two concepts are seldom considered simultaneously. As Jayaratne and Chess (1983, p. 129) conclude: "One distinction between these two sets of literature is that the job satisfaction research tends to be empirical, while the burnout literature (with a few exceptions) tends to be comprised primarily of case studies and studies that are qualitative in nature."

Site B Pattern Replicated

The Site A data trend dominantly in expected directions: individuals classified in Phase I of the eight progressive phases of burnout report the most favorable profile of work site descriptors, and those in Phase VIII the worst.[1] For details, see Golembiewski, Munzenrider, and Stevenson (1986, pp. 39-43). In sum, all but one of 22 cases meet expectations. The two pay/compensation variables show only random variation when arrayed by phases of burnout, as expected. Statistical analysis reveals that in 19 of the 20 cases in which significant effects are expected, nonrandom variance across the phases is of such magnitude and consistency that chance factors can be all but ruled out. Eta^2 indicates that over 13 percent of the variance is accounted for, on average.

Less Robust Site A Variant

The 20 overall significant cases do not show the robustness of the Site B pattern, however. Nearly 85 percent of the paired-comparisons are in the expected directions, and only 1 percent of the comparisons falling in unexpected

TABLE 3.1
Distance Between Phases and Their Sensitivity to Differences
in Target Variables, Site A

	Percentages of Statistically Significant Paired-Comparisons, by Distances Between Phases						
	+7	+6	+5	+4	+3	+2	+1
Expected direction and statistically significant	74	61	54	25	8	7	0.0

directions achieve statistical significance. But only 16.4 percent of the pairs achieve statistical significance *and* fall in the expected direction, following Table 3.1. If one accepts the notion that 20 percent represents a proportion of statistically significant paired-comparisons substantial enough to support the differentiating power of a phase, Table 3.1 implies that 5 phases are required to encompass the variation in the 22 target variables at Site A. But that table does not support the need for all eight phases, given the same assumption. See also the discussion concluding this chapter.

Organizational Covariants at Site C

A second replication involves a very different kind of population than Site A. Site C provides services rather than products; the population is substantial (N = 942); and respondents come from several locations. It is like Site A, then, only in that both are profit-seeking enterprises.

Specifically, Site C encompasses one region of a national corporation in a new and rapidly-growing health and social service industry—life-care retirement communities. Ten facilities are represented, with total employment of 1,239, of whom 76 percent participated in the survey. Most of the uncaptured cases involve part-time employees not scheduled for work during the periods when the survey administrations took place. A comparison of demographics implies that the responding population adequately represents total employment (Rountree and Deckard, 1983).

Each of the Site C facilities is structured bureaucratically, with five major departments: General Administration, Plant Maintenance, Dietary, Housekeeping and Laundry, and Resident Care. The population is 75 percent female, with a mean age of 33 years.

TABLE 3.2
Factor Analysis of Index of Organizational Reactions, Site C

Sub-scales/Items	Cronbach's alpha	Rotated Factors† I	II	III	IV	V
Supervision	.88					
Add to success		.79				
Feel satisfied		.78				
Encourages extra effort		.76				
Work habits		.74				
Influence attitude		.72				
Treated differently		.63				
Kind of Work	.86					
Things you enjoy			.81			
Feel about/like			.76			
Encourages my best			.73			
Acomplish worthwhile			.71			
Stirs up enthusiasm			.70			
Influence attitude			.66			
Financial Rewards	.87					
Amount of money				.86		
Costs to live				.85		
Needs satisfied				.79		
Way pay handled				.71		
Influence attitude				.67		
Coworkers	.76					
Generally feel satisfied					.79	
Friction among					.70	
Influence attitude					.69	
Example encourages hard work					.62	
Add to success					.55	
Amount of work	.80					
Workload						.75
Feel satisfied						.71
Influence way you do job						.69
Influence attitude						.68
Eigenvalue		8.5	2.5	2.1	1.6	1.4
Percent of variance		32.6	9.7	8.0	6.1	5.3
Percent of cumulative variance		32.6	42.4	50.3	56.4	61.7

†Displays only loadings > .30.

Variables at Site C[2]

Data from this third site use different operational measures of similar conceptual dimensions, and provide yet another test of the common patterning of covariants of the burnout phases. Site C employs the Index of Organizational Reactions, or IOR, and several work-related measures of the Psychological Sense of Community, or PSOC.

IOR is designed for use at all organizational levels and has been applied extensively within Sears, Roebuck and Company (Smith, 1976; Smith, Roberts, and Hulin, 1976). Item content extends beyond affective reactions and also covers the perceived relationship between job features and work performance. For example, item 23 asks whether pay practices encourage or discourage hard work. All items have a response stem of five equal-appearing intervals, scored 1-5, and these items generate five subscale scores. In all cases, high IOR scores indicate a positive reaction of the respondent to the indicated facet of organizational experience. Three IOR subscales are not used here.

Factor analysis supports reliance on five IOR subscales (Rountree and Deckard, 1983), which Table 3.2 identifies in terms of the items that most heavily load the subscales. Cronbach's alpha also suggests the scales have acceptable measurement properties for present purposes, although one school of thought may see those coefficients as "too high."

As for PSOC, numerous observers (e.g., Klein and D'Aunno, 1986) cite the importance to work of various aspects of what may be called the "psychological sense of community"—a worker's sense of membership, collaboration, participation, sharing, interdependency, and identification with work or a work-related group.

Three recently developed scales are included here for the purpose of tapping the presence of work-related aspects of community (Deckard and Rountree, 1984). Each of the three may be considered complementary to the others. Specifically, Primary Work Group Cohesion assesses the extent to which workers belong to an immediate work group in which the relationships between members are characterized by comfortable interdependency and tight bonds, as well as by a shared sense of accomplishment and pride in the job itself. The conceptual significance of cohesion should be patent. Generally, it derives from the long-standing work on cohesiveness (e.g., Golembiewski, 1982, pp. 149-70 and 265-70), as well as from recent work targeted on burnout that implies the immediate work group is the primary locus of burnout (e.g., Rountree, 1984). Why is the immediate work group so central? The literature on small groups provides chapter-and-verse, of course (e.g., Golembiewski, 1962). To be harshly selective here, Price (1984, p. 7) observes that "a sense of community itself is a source of social support to reduce, or buffer stressful work demands," which echoes the careful summary by House (1981).

Two additional subscales complement Primary Work Group Cohesion by attempting to ascertain the extent to which individuals derive social and emotional

TABLE 3.3
Factor Analysis of Work-Related Psychological Sense of Community Subscales, Site C

Sub-scales/Items	Cronbach's alpha	Rotated Factors[†] I	II	III
Primary Work Group Cohesion	.85			
Enjoy working together		.80		
Comfortable relationship		.79		
Tight bonds		.75		
Tight-knit group		.73		
Sense of pride		.69		
Depend on one another		.55		
Supervisor Social and Emotional Support	.87			
Supervisor source of support			.90	
Sticks up for staff			.86	
Free to discuss problems			.78	
Coworker Social and Emotional Support	.81			
Turn to when need help				.81
Really care what happens				.70
Coworkers source of support		.31		.77
Eigenvalue		5.2	1.6	1.2
Percent of variance		43.4%	13.6%	10.1%
Percent cumulative variance		43.4%	57.0%	67.1%

[†] Displays only loadings > .30.

support from their supervisor and their coworkers, respectively. For example, one item on the former scale asks if "the supervisor really sticks up for staff," and an item on the latter asks if "there are people within the immediate work group that can be turned to when you need help."

Table 3.3 summarizes several measurement properties of the three subscales tapping Psychological Sense of Community, or PSOC. The factorial structure seems quite robust, with only a single item loading more than one subscale at greater than .30. Moreover, the *alphas* imply no problems with unreliability.

Strong Support for the Phase Model

The results at Site C require no major modification of prior research concerning the deficits or deficiencies associated with progressive phases of burnout. Summary attention will be directed first at the five IOR subscales and then at the three subscales tapping Psychological Sense of Community, or PSOC.

Tables 3.4 through 3.7 strongly support the view that advancing burnout covaries directly with how employees see their work site. The authors do not here argue that work site features "cause" burnout, but the environmental model underlying most theorizing in the behavioral sciences points in the direction of such main effects. So does other evidence to be reviewed below.

Table 3.4 shows that all five IOR subscales decrease significantly as the phases advance, with $P < .001$ in all cases for the one-way analysis of variance. Moreover, as expected, about 84.3 percent of all paired-comparisons are in the expected direction. For example, the employees' reaction to IOR Supervision is less positive for Phases II than I, for III than II, and so on.

Paramountly, the paired-comparisons from Site C indicate that the IOR differences are robust, as well as regular, phase by phase. Specifically, Table 3.5 indicates that half of all paired-comparisons differ in statistically significant degree, with $P < .05$ by Least Significant Difference Test, as modified for unequal subpopulations. Indeed, 51.4 percent of the paired-comparisons are

TABLE 3.4
One-Way Analysis of Variance[†] for Index of Organizational Reactions on Burnout Phases, Site C

IOR Sub-scales	Burnout Phases							
	I	II	III	IV	V	VI	VII	VIII
Supervision	4.17	3.66	3.97	3.57	3.29	3.38	3.38	3.20
Kind of work	4.28	4.03	3.98	3.63	4.07	3.77	3.58	3.33
Amount of work	3.94	3.63	3.64	3.60	2.95	3.18	3.01	3.10
Coworker	4.09	3.72	3.92	3.64	3.78	3.56	3.63	3.35
Financial Rewards	3.26	3.08	3.01	2.93	2.50	2.61	2.62	2.62

[†] $P < .000$ for all ANOVAs

TABLE 3.5
Pair-wise Comparison Map of Index of Organizational Reactions Across Burnout Phases,[†] Site C

	I vs. II	I vs. III	I vs. IV	I vs. V	I vs. VI	I vs. VII	I vs. VIII	II vs. III	II vs. IV	II vs. V	II vs. VI	II vs. VII	II vs. VIII	III vs. IV
Supervision	X		X	X	X	X	X						X	X
Kind of work		X	X		X	X	X		X			X	X	X
Amount of work			X	X	X	X	X				X	X	X	X
Coworker	X		X	X	X	X	X						X	
Financial Rewards				X	X	X	X			X	X	X	X	

	III vs. V	III vs. VI	III vs. VII	III vs. VIII	IV vs. V	IV vs. VI	IV vs. VII	IV vs. VIII	V vs. VI	V vs. VII	V vs. VIII	VI vs. VII	VI vs. VIII	VII vs. VIII
Supervision	X							X						
Kind of work		X	X	X	X			X		X	X		X	
Amount of work		X	X	X	X	X	X	X	X					
Coworker		X	X	X				X			X			X
Financial Rewards	X	X	X	X										

† X designates a paired-comparison in which $P < .05$.

51

TABLE 3.6
One-Way Analysis of Variance for Work-Related Psychological Sense
of Community on Burnout Phases,† Site C

PSOC Sub-Scales	Burnout Phases							
	I	II	III	IV	V	VI	VII	VIII
Primary Work Group Cohesion	5.63	5.11	5.11	4.92	5.49	4.86	4.72	4.50
Supervisor Social and Emotional Support	5.71	4.81	5.11	4.71	4.10	4.76	4.13	4.24
Coworker Social and Emotional Support	5.89	5.10	5.10	5.81	5.15	5.12	4.90	4.66

† P < .000 for all ANOVAs.

both in the expected direction and statistically significant. Only two significant cases—or about 1.4 percent—fall in an unexpected direction.

In sum, the IOR subscales support the earlier research, the bottom line of which is that the burnout phases regularly and robustly vary with deficits or deficiencies in work site descriptors.

The three PSOC subscales provide a less striking replication of earlier patterns of association of the phases, at first glance. However, it is not yet clear whether the pattern of support is merely less marked than for IOR or whether the results imply a broader message. See the following subsection—Basic Support, and A Qualification.

Two tables provide the necessary data for PSOC × phases. Table 3.6 shows that all three one-way analyses of variance attain statistical significance, and a simple count shows that 78.6 percent of the paired-comparisons are in the expected direction. These results do not differ markedly from the IOR results, obviously.

However, Table 3.7 reveals that substantially fewer paired-comparisons achieve statistical significance for PSOC than for IOR. Specifically, 29.8 percent of the cases in Table 3.7 attain significance and also fall in the expected direction. About 1.2 percent of the paired-comparisons fall in the unexpected direction and achieve significance by the LSD test, as modified.

TABLE 3.7

Pair-wise Comparisons of Work-Related Psychological Sense of Community Across Progressive Burnout Phases,† Site C

PSOC Sub-scales	I vs. II	I vs. III	I vs. IV	I vs. V	I vs. VI	I vs. VII	I vs. VIII	II vs. III	II vs. IV	II vs. V	II vs. VI	II vs. VII	II vs. VIII	III vs. IV
Primary Work Group Cohesion		X	X		X	X	X						X	
Coworker Social and Emotional Support	X	X		X	X	X	X							
Supervisor Social and Emotional Support	X		X	X	X	X								

TABLE 3.7 (continued)

PSOC Sub-scales	III vs. V	III vs. VI	III vs. VII	III vs. VIII	IV vs. V	IV vs. VI	IV vs. VII	IV vs. VIII	V vs. VI	V vs. VII	V vs. VIII	VI vs. VII	VI vs. VIII	VII vs. VIII
Primary Work Group Cohesion				X						X	X			
Coworker Social and Emotional Support														
Supervisor Social and Emotional Support	X		X	X										

[+] X designates a paired-comparison in which $P < .05$.

54

Basic Support, and a Qualification

In sum, both IOR and PSOC subscales provide support for the notion that at Site C the progressive burnout phases are associated with regular and robust variations in all eight of their subscales. Thus, anything greater than 20 percent statistically significant paired-comparisons would indicate noteworthy covariation, and PSOC generates nearly 30 percent and IOR over 50 percent of such cases. Moreover, the number of deviant differences that attain the .05 level of significance–1.2 and 1.4 percent, respectively–does not require modification of the basic view that the burnout phases seem reliable and valid. The measure of this reliability and validity is the consistent and reasonable "mapping" of the phases on several panels of variables to whose number this section adds eight new variables.

But one possibility requires note, which may only point up the obvious but also may relate to a subtle artifact in the results that masks the expected association. That possibility: high PSOC scores may be critically dependent on Low Depersonalization scores and such low scores occur only in Phases I, III, V, and VII. In this view, the expectation of differences between the two clusters of phases *Low* vs. *High* on Depersonalization–I, III, V, and VII vs. II, IV, VI and VIII–is more reasonable than a linear decrease in scores for Phases I through VIII.

The data in Tables 3.6 and 3.7 do not discourage such a surmise, although there is no foolproof way to establish this Depersonalization effect with the PSOC data. Comparing the two clusters of phases *High* vs. *Low* on Depersonalization, the *Low* cluster averages almost 36 percent statistically significant paired-comparisons, while the *High* cluster generates only 19 percent. Although double-counting is involved, the average suggests that the three PSOC subscales are differentially engaged by *High* vs. *Low* Depersonalization. In the *High* cases, for example, Primary Work Group Cohesion will tend to be low, whatever the scores on the other two MBI subscales and hence a lower proportion of paired-comparisons × phases will achieve significant differences.

Organizational Covariants at Site D[3]

This section seeks not only to replicate the pattern confirmed at Sites B, A, and C, but also to extend the analysis in significant ways. Specifically, at Site D, not only does a large organization host the research, but the character of the work environment will be assessed via two panels of variables–one common to Site C and the other an addition to the research with phases. All three features help test the generality of the regular and robust associations observed elsewhere between burnout phases and work site descriptors.

All data come from the employees of a corporate chain of life-care retirement communities, working at 23 locations. Each local station has five major organization units: General Administration, Plant Maintenance, Dietary, Housekeeping and Laundry, and Resident Care. The overall response rate approximates

TABLE 3.8

Progressive Phases of Burnout and 18 Work Site Descriptors, Site D

	alpha	Phases of Burnout						F-Ratio	F-Probability
		I	III	IV	VI	VII	VIII		
		N=435	365	252	447	347	277	(df=5, 2117)	
I. Work Environment Scale									
Involvement	.72	6.94	5.99	6.10	4.09	5.24	5.19	76.41	<.000
Peer Cohesion	.76	6.32	5.83	5.78	4.72	5.31	5.52	38.41	<.000
Supervisory Support	.78	6.03	5.45	5.46	3.58	4.30	4.32	66.61	<.000
Autonomy	.80	5.31	4.88	4.86	3.99	4.31	4.61	24.75	<.000
Task Orientation	.69	7.09	6.74	6.61	5.68	6.26	6.37	25.33	<.000
Work Pressure	.79	4.24	4.18	4.29	5.72	6.07	5.99	69.32	<.000
Clarity	.71	6.94	6.45	6.34	4.83	5.58	5.49	57.54	<.000
Control	.73	7.04	6.95	6.81	6.74	7.01	6.71	2.33	.04
Innovation	.69	4.44	4.28	4.34	3.82	3.84	3.94	5.66	<.000
Physical Comfort	.63	6.74	6.33	6.29	5.08	5.77	5.67	35.53	<.000
II. Index of Organizational Reactions									
Physical Working Condition	.69	4.07	3.82	3.94	3.40	3.62	3.69	54.11	<.000
Identification with Company	.69	3.84	3.63	3.71	2.94	2.30	3.17	88.41	<.000
Personal Future with Company	.81	3.91	3.57	3.73	2.98	3.35	3.25	95.16	<.000
Rewards	.71	3.13	2.98	3.02	2.55	2.67	2.65	36.28	<.000
Co-workers	.81	3.96	3.75	3.73	3.26	3.58	3.56	59.04	<.000
Supervisor	.82	4.01	3.71	3.79	3.10	3.40	3.36	73.82	<.000
Kind of Work	.85	4.25	3.77	3.92	3.17	3.73	3.71	109.41	<.000
Amount of Work	.81	3.79	3.72	3.80	3.04	2.98	3.09	120.55	<.000

90 percent, with the usable N = 2,123. No significant differences exist between response rates at the several sites; and virtually all missing cases are part-time help or those who for various reasons were not at work during the hour or so when data were gathered at each local site.

Variables at Site D

The 18 variables in the two present panels come from two sources: the ten components of the Work Environment Scale, or WES (Insel and Moos, 1974; Moos, 1981); and the eight scales of Smith's (1976) Index of Organizational Reactions (IOR). For an IOR application, see Smith (1977).

Brief attention to the 18 scales suffices. IOR was introduced in the previous section, of course. In addition, the IOR scales from Site D have alphas that average .77. A factor analysis, not reported here in detail, generates a structure that sharply reproduces five of the scales identified in Table 3.8, but not the other three. Nonetheless, conveniently, the eight IOR scales are retained here. Table 3.8 presents the distribution of respondents by phases. Despite the substantial population, two of the phases have no entries. This surprising absence will be discussed later in this chapter.

As for WES, the variable labels in Table 3.8 sufficiently indicate their conceptual reach-and-grasp. Moreover, considerable information is available about the useful measurement properties of WES (Moos and Insel, 1981), and two sources of additional evidence support their use here. Thus the Cronbach alphas for WES average .73, as Table 3.8 shows, with only a single coefficient as low as .63. Moos also cites evidence of the usefulness of all ten WES scales even as he acknowledges that they do not factor neatly, which is also true in the present case. Also supporting the multi-dimensionality of the ten WES scales, in addition, over half of their intercorrelations are 0.3 or lower, and about three-quarters do not surpass 0.4. While all but two of the 45 total intercorrelations attain the .05 level, this reflects the size of the present population. The mean R^2 implies that about 11.7 percent of the variance is shared by the WES scales.

The rationale for including these work site descriptors in the Site D replication is quite direct. The panel contains many (but certainly not all) of the work site features that could well become common stressors generating the strains on individuals whose resultant effects are estimated by the phase model. The present panel also complements some of the work site descriptors in other studies (Golembiewski, Munzenrider, and Carter, 1983; Golembiewski and Munzenrider, 1984a), but the panels of scales are not replicas. Several of the variables in Table 3.8 cover conceptual territories similar to those of measures utilized at Sites A and B—e.g., Job Involvement, and the five facets of satisfaction at the end of the list in Table 3.8. However, several of the variables in the present panel have no clear analogs in the panels used at Sites A, B, or C—e.g., Innovation, and Future with Company.

Consistent with the conceptual undergirdings of the phase model, as well as with the results of the three studies reviewed here and in chapter two, the phases and work site descriptors at Site D should covary in a uniform way—the descriptors will worsen by progressive phases. Because of differences in scoring, specifically, two patterns of scores will meet expectations:

- scores on two variables—Work Pressure and Control—will *increase*, phase by phase;
- scores on the 16 other descriptors will *decrease*, phase by phase

The basic statistical procedures are the same as in the three other replicative studies. One-way analysis of variance tests for overall nonrandom variation in each of the variables X phases. The Least Significant Differences (LSD) test, as modified for unequal subsample sizes, will test for significant differences between all possible pairs of scores on each variable.

Strong Support for Phases

The pattern of results for Site D has both regular and robust qualities. As Table 3.8 shows, all but one of the work site descriptors attain and usually far surpass the .05 level. The scale Control constitutes the sole exception, and it appears neither regular nor robust. Moreover, as Table 3.9 indicates, the paired-comparisons dominantly support the expected pattern. Specifically, 80.7 percent of all pairs fall in the expected direction, and nearly 59 percent of all comparisons involve differences large enough to be considered statistically significant. Relatedly, less than 9 percent of the paired-comparisons fall in a direction contrary to predictions and also attain statistical significance.

One further point deserves highlighting—the two "empty" phases at Site D, II and V. Given the substantial N, there is no certain explanation of the two empty phases. Nonetheless, speculation may be useful and, in any case, it will detail some additional properties of the phase model.

Conceptually, as noted earlier, the phase model is taken to tap both *chronic* and *acute* onset. The chronic flight-path is assumed to be $I \rightarrow II \rightarrow IV \rightarrow VIII$.

TABLE 3.9
Summary of Paired-Comparisons, in Percent, Site D

In Expected Direction	Statistically Significant and In Expected Direction	In Contrary Direction	Statistically Significant and In Contrary Direction
80.7%	58.9%	18.5%	8.9%

Descriptively, in this variant the individual moves to *High* on Depersonalization, then to *High* on Depersonalization and Personal Accomplishment (Reversed), and finally adds a *High* on Emotional Exhaustion.

A family of acute flight-paths also are taken to exist. For example: Phases I → V → VIII. This pathway could describe the sudden loss of a mate, which precipitously swamps the individual's coping mechanisms and creates a substantial emotional deficit (V). Short of quick recovery, one can easily imagine that such an individual might soon experience problems at work as well as withdrawal from others (VIII). Under the same condition, an initial II might experience this pathway: II → VI → VIII.

Right now, we have little firm or extensive data about such alternative pathways (e.g., Golembiewski and Munzenrider, 1985, 1986). Those individuals tested, however, for the most part seem to reflect chronic onset. Consistently, populations contain only small proportions classified in Phases IV, V, and VI; and Phases IV-V seem to be transitional, with about 90 percent of the occupants being classified elsewhere after a year's interval. In contrast, the vast majority of all I-III and VI-VIII assignments persist over the same interval. See chapter six.

Given that these hints do not prove the prevalence of chronicity, Site D may be dominantly chronic, operating in an environment that forces quick and lasting assignments to the extreme phases. Basically, the character of most of the work may be such that II is an unlikely assignment. High scores on PA (Reversed) are common, and hence III for almost all may be the next best assignment after I. If so, moreover, acute onset for most people in this system might well precipitate them from III or even more advanced phases to VII and perhaps VIII, rather than into V or VI (as in the examples above).

This approach does *not* explain the absence of V entries, because acute onset for a I might precipitate a V. But the speculation does imply that V and VI will have far fewer entries in the present host than in organizations presenting a more attractive environment to their employees. Only longitudinal studies can explore such features of alternative flight-paths between phases, and that research must be prominent on future agendas.

IMPLICATIONS FOR THE PHASE MODEL OF BURNOUT

The four sets of data discussed here and in chapter two, it seems fair to conclude, provide substantial replicated evidence of the usefulness of the phase model. The four sets of covariation in work site features and phases of burnout contain no surprises. This consistent "mapping" of the variables, phase by phase, not only reinforces the concurrent validity of the phases; more dramatically, the results suggest possible targets for conscious efforts to inhibit the development of advanced burnout, and perhaps even to reverse it.

These four reviews of replications of the descriptive usefulness of the phases support two sets of conclusions and initiatives for subsequent chapters. The first three emphases below present tentative conclusions that require further testing

TABLE 3.10
Summary of Findings at Four Sites

	Site B	Site A	Site C IOR	Site C PSOC	Site D
Percent in expected direction	89.3%	84.8%	84.3%	78.6%	80.7%
Percent in expected direction and statistically significant	55.3%	16.4%	51.4%	29.8%	58.9%
Percent in Contrary direction	10.7%	15.2%	15.7%	21.4%	18.5%
Percent in Contrary direction and statistically significant	.5%	1.0%	1.2%	1.4%	8.9%

and elaboration; and the concluding set of four emphases outline an attainable if incomplete agenda for our program of testing and elaboration.

Three Working Conclusions

The analysis can thus far bear substantial weight, which in turn encourages building upon it. Three working conclusions derived from the analysis deal, respectively, with the usefulness of multiple phases of burnout, several practical and humanist urgencies to further test the adequacy of the present multiphase model, and some issues related to covariation and causality.

Usefulness of a Phase Model

Most clearly, the data above variously support the usefulness of a model of burnout that has several progressively virulent phases. That is, the data reveal robust and regular covariation between burnout phases and panels of indicators of the character and quality of work sites. All sites reflect a basic difference within the overall pattern. The sharpness of the common pattern of covariation differs, in short, as the summary data in Table 3.10 suggest.

What accounts for the differential robustness of the four replications? Ultimately, that question now defies any complete answer. But some perspective seems possible, given a fundamental tentativeness about the matter. Here consider only two kinds of explanation: the first focuses on local artifacts, as it were; and the second seeks broader conceptual perspective.

Artifactual Features of Replication Sites

Several local contributors to the differences-within-a-pattern seem reasonable enough, even if speculative. For example, three sites involve limited ranges of jobs, while Site A encompasses all organization members, from president to porters. The narrower range of jobs and statuses at Sites B, C, and D, in effect, may reduce the effect of intervening or moderating variables operative at Site A. For example, consider only differences in income. Site A has compensation packages attractive even in its high-paying industry, while Site B respondents come from a public agency and Sites C and D have low salary scales. Income differences might buffer burnout and its covariants, either directly or by selection and socialization of individuals with greater tolerance for the demands of their work or with different expectations concerning stressors. Personal differences between respondents may also exist. For example, Social Desirability scores at Site A were very high and, despite the complexities of the analysis (Golembiewski, 1983a), this could soften the patterns of association reported at Site A.

Conceptual Focus on Taxonomies

From a broader perspective, the differences in distributions of phases in different loci should not surprise, nor should the variable robustness of associ-

ations with work site descriptors. Given the lack of a generally-accepted taxonomy for either groups or organizations, the prevalence in replications of the
basic burnout pattern of covariation constitutes the big surprise. Since the sites
of the replications loci probably differ in profound as well as incidental ways,
the regularity of the basic pattern suggests very marked associations of burnout
with work site descriptors. Excluding dumb luck in the availability of sites, we
suppose organizational and group differences would mask or distort all but dominant patterns of covariation.

So we propose that the variable robustness of burnout covariants in Table 3.10
may reflect differences between the properties of the units, which in most cases
would camouflage relationships in nature. The point is not novel (e.g., Golembiewski, 1986), and has been stated recently in compelling terms by Miller and
Friesen (1984). They focus on an ironic question: Why is it that, the more work
we devote to an area of organizational analysis, the less we seem to know? That is,
initial analysis may isolate what seem robust patterns of relationships, and a kind
of boomtown atmosphere gets generated for a while. However, replicatory studies
typically rain on everyone's parade: some replications may support or even extend the initial results but, on balance, cases of random variation and contrary
results dominate.

Miller and Friesen are not surprised (1984, pp. 15-17). Indeed, in general, it
could hardly be any other way. We not only lack reasonable typologies for
distinguishing (for example) between organizations and groups, but little interest
exists in developing such typologies. Rather, investigators tend to assume that a
group is a group, and that an organization is an organization. Even gentle "configurational analysis" reveals the fragility of such convenient assumptions, however. For example, Mintzberg (1975) distinguishes five kinds of organizations, at
a general level: simple structure, machine bureaucracy, professional bureaucracy,
a divisionalized form, and *adhocracy*. Friesen and Miller ask rhetorically about
the common failure to make such configurational distinctions (1984, pp. 14-15):
"Now assuming . . . that at least a good proportion of organizations tended to
adopt these or some other configurations of their structural parameters—what
would happen if different kinds of organizations were mixed in research samples
and then relationships gauged . . .?" One need not grope for an answer. To illustrate, a machine bureaucracy might well tend toward advanced centralization,
while a professional bureaucracy might generally favor decentralization, or even
chaotic localism. Consequently apparent contradictions in existing research
might be reconciled after differentiating organizational configurations in different data batches.

Following through on this insight will preoccupy much work (e.g., Bowers
and Hausser, 1977; Kets De Vries and Miller, 1984; Miller and Friesen, 1984),
and general orientations for guiding "configurational analysis" exist elsewhere
(e.g., Golembiewski, 1986). But noting the bare insight does useful and multiple
duty here, as four points establish:

- Burnout phases and their covariants appear dominant in nature, otherwise the failure to distinguish unit differences would distort or hide relationships.

- Burnout research ties into classical issues in the behavioral sciences, which it highlights and cannot finesse.

- But the phase model seems to provide a useful and even strategic launching platform for extensions reaching toward such classical issues as configurational analysis.

- This volume will attempt some forays in configurational analysis—conceptually and in applications—in chapters seven through nine.

Practical and Human Urgencies

The reported incidences of the several progressive phases of burnout attract attention, perhaps even provoke alarm. Even the "best" case—Site A, a business concern that is in most respects thoroughly modern and human resources-oriented—faces a substantial challenge. The "worst" case in our quartet raises the ante substantially, as the following distributions of employees by phases of burnout clearly imply:

Phase Assignments, by Percentages

	I	II	III	IV	V	VI	VII	VIII
Site A	40.9	10.6	7.7	4.7	13.9	9.1	7.3	5.8
Site D	20.5	0.0	17.2	11.9	0.0	21.1	16.3	13.1

These incidences of the progressive phases urge attention, for both practical and humanistic reasons. Using the convention that Phases VI through VIII define "advanced," the data indicate that substantial proportions of work forces report advanced phases of burnout—over 22 percent in the most benign replication (Site A), and 50.5 percent in the most extreme case (Site D). Practically, both understanding and amelioration are challenged by these magnitudes, if only because workers' compensation for disability due to "psychological burnout" is no longer rare (Ivancevich, Matteson, and Richards, 1985). The conclusion holds most strongly, patently, if Site A represents the burnout profile of "good" organizations. This possibility does not offend reason.

Note that chapter six provides further perspective on the magnitude of the burnout problem. The incidence and persistence of burnout both receive substantial attention there.

What Causes Which Effect?

The data above do not establish causality, of course. They reveal only a substantial pattern of regular and robust covariation. This reflects the limited yet profound meaning of the results detailed above, and encourages further testing of the phase model underlying this research.

Four Features of Necessary Agendas

So where to go from here? Four guides point the way, and constitute the major challenges for this volume. In turn, they deal with the need to broaden the test of possible covariants of burnout, some greater clarity re "causal arrows" or main-line effects in the general model underlying this research, an analytic convenience for summarizing observed relationships, and some sense of how to ameliorate the causes and consequences of burnout.

Extending the Search for Covariants

The four panels of work site descriptors—the "target variables" described above—suggest the usefulness of a phase model of burnout, and this point at once urges caution and inspires effort. Why caution? Those 48 variables hardly exhaust the significant covariants, and this should temper exuberance concerning the meaning of the regular and robust pattern mapped by the phases of burnout on the four panels of work site descriptors. This caution should not lead to inaction, however, but rather to a kind of informed enthusiasm to extend the range of significant covariants against which the usefulness of the phase model can be judged. This enthusiasm gets additional impetus from independent research, which associates burnout with sets of variables similar to those described above (for example, Burke, Shearer, and Deszca, 1984).

Hence, the first three chapters of this volume may be labelled "Testing a Phase Model of Burnout." A first test of the reach and grasp of the present phase model has been attempted—that dealing with features of the work site. Two following chapters will focus on other classes of significant and probable covariants of the phase model: symptoms of physical dis-ease, individual performance, and collective productivity. In their several ways, these three classes of covariants further challenge the credibility of the phase model.

Multiple-Outcomes Model and "Causal Arrows"

So far, results establish regular and robust associations between features of the work site and the degree of burnout. No "causal arrows," however, are proposed or, hopefully, even suggested.

Subsequent analysis will have to do better in suggesting the direction of various burnout associations, given that the specification of causal arrows must largely remain a task for the future. The environmental multiple-outcomes model underlying this research proposes for testing the set of main effects below, reinforced by feedback linkages that are omitted here.

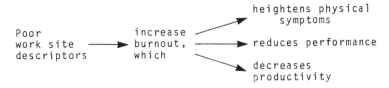

An Analytic Convenience

Perspective on the directionality and strength of associations will be sought in direct and simple ways in this book. The focus continues to be on statistically significant or nonrandom associations. The strength of associations will be estimated by the percentage of variance accounted for by pairs of covariants—by their common or shared variance. The decision rule will be simple. Consider A, B, and C, some organizationally relevant measures. A is significantly and robustly associated with B; and B is robustly related to C; but A and C have a slight if statistically significant association only. This permits speaking of possible main-line as well as reinforcing effects, if only tentatively. More tentatively, it also gives some encouragement to thinking about an "associational track," and even suggests a kind of "causal string" of covariants that implies the direction of main-line effects.

Hence the present emphasis on a weight-of-evidence approach, especially in the set of chapters four through seven, that can be aggregated under the heading "Learning from A Phase Model of Burnout." Basically, these changes provide perspective on what seem to be main-line effects, as distinguished from what are more usefully viewed as reinforcing linkages.

Causal Path Analysis Illustrated[4]

In one case, however, evidence supports the present basic emphasis on an environmental model of burnout. This illustration relies on path analysis, which not only can test a qualitatively derived model of purported causal relations but also provides quantitative estimates (path coefficients) of the relative strength of those anticipated relationships. In short, path analysis helps to clarify both theoretical and empirical relationships by providing a quantitative interpretation and test of any model (Kerlinger, 1973).

The present illustration focuses on a proposed model linking burnout, work site descriptors, and a construct labelled Emotional Agitation. In sum, based on previous analysis, this model is proposed for testing (Deckard, Rountree, and Golembiewski, 1988):

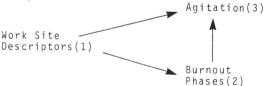

Solid lines indicate the anticipated "direct path," with both the work site descriptors and the burnout phases contributing to the variation in Emotional Agitation.

Some measurement details are necessary. Three scales from the Index of Organizational Reactions (or IOR)—Amount of Work, Kind of Work, and Financial Rewards—provide work site descriptors, based on research which highlights them as major work stressors (Rountree and Deckard, 1983). The three scales are additively combined in a composite measure of work stress. "Agitation" derives from a factor analysis of the 132 words on the Multiple Affect Adjective Check List (Zuckerman, Lubin, and Erinck, 1984) performed by Deckard (1985). The 1984 version of the MAACL builds upon an earlier and widely used set of scales (Zuckerman and Lubin, 1965). High scores on Agitation represent individuals who express strong agreement that such words characterize "how you felt in recent days": annoyed, irritated, agitated, impatient, angry, discouraged, disagreeable, and so on. For measurement details, see the section on clinically relevant affective states in chapter eight.

As expected, Agitation increases as the phases progress from I to VIII, but the association is only modestly robust in a population of 864 doing direct-service work in a retirement community (Deckard, Rountree, and Golembiewski, 1988). One-way analysis of variance indicates nonrandom variance somewhere in the distribution of Agitation scores arrayed by phases ($P < .001$). Moreover, 85.8 percent of the paired-comparisons are in the expected direction, but only 25 percent of those comparisons achieve $P < .05$ by LSD, modified.

Path analysis confirms the pattern of relationships consistent with the environmental or multiple-outcomes model. Worksite descriptors seem to impact Agitation through the phases, more so than directly. Some details will help. On the predicted direct path, work descriptors correlate .51 with the burnout phases (r_{12}), which accounts for 26 percent of the variance. The other two correlations r_{13} and r_{23} both are .27, and hence each accounts for about 7.3 percent of the variance. Moreover, as the predicted pathway requires, the two path-proofs correspond quite closely to the two other correlations (r_{13} and r_{23}). The path-proof for work descriptors and Agitation sums to .273, as compared to the .274 correlation between the two. For burnout and Agitation, the figures are .271 and .273, respectively.

In sum, this illustrative case provides both a partial proof of the environmental model underlying this research, as well as an example of a program for extensive future work.

Ameliorating Causes and Consequences of Burnout

Brief but necessary comments introduce the fourth feature of research agendas necessary to push beyond the existing beachheads. Two final chapters—eight and nine—will focus on dealing with the causes and consequences of burnout. These chapters are subtitled "Extrapolations from Phase Model Findings."

This final emphasis has a direct motivation. The first two clusters of chapters, assuming they are even moderately convincing, force the issue of doing something about what exists. That "something" will have four components in chapters eight and nine. There, some implications of the results for useful research designs will be developed; and three orientations to intervening in organizations so as to reduce burnout will be detailed, in turn.

NOTES

1. Table 3.1 uses the Hi/Lo norms developed at Site B, while earlier Site A analyses utilized a median split (Golembiewski, Munzenrider, and Carter, 1983). The results here reflect a pattern similar to, but more robust than, the results of the Site A pilot study. For a technical demonstration, see Golembiewski and Munzenrider (1983).

2. For related reports, consult Deckard (1985) and Deckard, Rountree, and Golembiewski (1986).

3. An earlier version of this section appears in Robert T. Golembiewski and Benjamin H. Rountree (1986), "Phases of Burnout and Properties of Work Environments: Replicating and Extending a Pattern of Covariants," *Organization Development Journal*, 9:25–30.

4. For a full analysis, see Deckard, Rountree, and Golembiewski (1988).

4. HUMAN COSTS OF BURNOUT: PHYSICAL SYMPTOMS AND THE PHASES

The burgeoning literature on psychological burnout suggests that noxious physiological effects will accompany high levels of strain. Thus Cherniss (1980, pp. 15-16) expects that greater incidences of a long catalog of psychophysical disturbances will be associated with increasing burnout; Freudenberger (1980) emphasizes that great personal distress is a common concomitant; and Maslach and Jackson report that their studies of burnout (for example, 1981, pp. 99-101) lead them to expect high rates of headaches, lingering colds, backaches, gastro-intestinal disturbances, and other indicators of impaired physical functioning.

A general understanding of this linkage of physical distress with burnout requires no great inferential leaps. Advanced burnout implies that an individual experiences a collection of stressors that cause so much strain that normal *coping skills/attitudes* do not suffice. Thus overextended, the individual is left vulnerable to various upsets, including those generated within the body as well as those caused by invading microbes who find that the body's normal defenses have become less than adequate to protect against internal or external attack.

The credible linkage of burnout with physical distress requires shoring up, however, because the available literature shows more agreement than detailed support. For example, most of the literature is anecdotal, involves very small populations, and does not demonstrate that the degrees of physical distress vary with the severity of burnout—all critical deficiencies. Such factors further motivate this test for the physical covariants of differential burnout in a large population, using a paper-and-pencil instrument.

BURNOUT AND SYMPTOMS OF DISTRESS

Helping to fill this central gap in the literature concerning the physical conse-quences of burnout requires several sets of details preliminary to measurement. Data come from Site B, which is described in chapter one.

The original report about physical symptoms utilizes five measures of burn-out, calculated from responses to Maslach's Burnout Inventory (MBI):

- Scores on each of the MBI subscales—Depersonalization, Personal Ac-complishment (Reversed), and Emotional Exhaustion
- A total score for all MBI items
- Assignments to one of eight phases, on the basis of High or Low scores on the three MBI subscales

The focus below will be restricted to the phases. Interested readers can consult details about the other four burnout measures (Golembiewski, Munzenrider, and Stevenson, 1986, pp. 64–75). Their patterns of association with physical symp-toms parallel the pattern of the phases. However, the other burnout measures have less robust associations with the physical symptoms, although they attain statistical significance in almost all cases.

Self-reports concerning the degree of physical well-being derive from responses to a conventional list (Quinn and Shepard, 1974; Quinn and Staines, 1979) of physical complaints. Respondents are offered four possible stems: Often, Some-times, Rarely, and Never. The response stems are used in connection with 19 indicators of well-being, with the scoring being uniform so that "Often" is coded 4 and "Never" gets a 1. The several physical symptoms are identified in Table 4.2, and a total score gets most attention.

Findings Concerning Physical Symptoms

In general, all measures of burnout covary in regular and predictable ways with self-reports about physical symptoms. The association of the phases with symptoms gets elaborated below, and the section concluding the summary of results relates the symptoms to the work site descriptors.

Symptoms and Burnout Phases

Although the magnitude of their patterning varies between individual symp-toms and clusters of them, the phase model reflects the most marked pattern of association between burnout and physical symptoms. This claim of the special usefulness of the phase model depends on the full volume for support, but this chapter contributes two kinds of evidence: a one-way analysis of variance in-volving the eight phases and Total Symptoms scores; and a factor analysis of the 19 symptoms, coupled with a one-way analysis of variance of the resulting factors versus phases of burnout.

TABLE 4.1
One-Way Analysis of Variance, Total Symptoms
versus Phases of Burnout

	Phases of Burnout				
	I LoLoLo (352)	II HiLoLo (109)	III LoHiLo (193)	IV HiHiLo (124)	
Total symptoms	33.5	34.2	33.9	39.5	
	Phases of Burnout				
	V LoLoHi (107)	VI HiLoHi (176)	VII LoHiHi (109)	VIII HiHiHi (367)	F-Ratio (df=7,1537)
Total Symptoms	38.7	40.1	40.5	42.6	39.628*

Note: Figures in parentheses indicate number of respondents.
*   Indicates P < .001.

One-Way Analysis of Variance

The usefulness of the burnout phases can be suggested by aggregating all symptoms, as in Table 4.1. The data there reflect a high probability of nonrandom variation in the array of Total Symptoms versus phases. Moreover, Total Symptoms vary regularly as well as robustly, by progressive phases of burnout, as two points establish. Thus over 96 percent of all paired-comparisons vary progressively: that is, Total Symptoms for Phase I < Phase II < Phase III, and so on. In addition, 60.4 percent of the 28 paired-comparisons are statistically significant at the .05 level, as judged by the Least Significant Difference (LSD) test, modified for unequal sample sizes. For details about the paired comparisons, consult Tables 4.3-4.4 below. Eta^2 reveals that Total Symptoms and the phases share some 16 percent of their variance in common. Note also that Total Symptoms has an alpha of 0.89.

Factor Analysis of 19 Symptoms

Focusing on Total Symptoms may mislead as well as inform, however. All 19 physical symptoms vary directly with the several measures of burnout, but some do so far more than others. And it takes no extensive medical training to guess that "feeling worn out" should relate more directly to burnout than do "swollen ankles," although distal linkages can be made. Hence the reliance here on factor analysis of the 19 symptoms to seek specific clusters that may differentially covary with phases of burnout.

Factor analysis implies that the 19 symptoms do not simply elicit generalized "feel good/bad" responses from respondents. Details are omitted here, but Table 4.2 summarizes the assignment of the 19 symptoms to subscales based on factor analysis.

Three stages of exposition highlight the association of the phases with the four symptoms factors and a total score. This analysis begins with Table 4.3, which summarizes patterns of association involving the five aggregates of symptoms and the eight phases of burnout. Note that in all five cases statistically significant variation exists, overall, and especially so for two clusters of symptoms—Factor I and Total Symptoms, in that order. This establishes the differential but substantial robustness of this association: Self-reports of physical symptoms increase as burnout phases progress from I through VIII.

A substantial regularity of differences exists among all five symptom scores, phase by progressive phase of burnout. The table containing the results of these multiple paired-comparisons is not reproduced here, but 43.6 percent of all 140 paired comparisons attain the .05 level of statistical significance. Since one-in-five statistically significant cases indicates a noteworthy regularity of increases in scores, phase by phase, the present results are striking. More than two-in-five attain significance here.

This aggregate record obscures as well as reveals, however. As Table 4.4 shows, two clusters of symptoms again stand out as having the most marked associations with the phases of burnout—Factor I and Total Symptoms. In sum, over 96 percent of the comparisons of pairs increase, phase by phase, for those two clusters of symptoms; over 62 percent of those expected differences in paired-comparisons achieve statistical significance; and all 3.6 percent of the contrary cases reflect random variation only.

The other three clusters of symptoms also show a regular increase in reported symptoms, by progressive phases of burnout, but less substantially so. Directly, for Total Symptoms and Factor I, the phases account for an average of 18.0 percent of the variance. The other three factor × phase combinations account for somewhat less than 5.7 percent of the variance.

Symptoms and Work Site Descriptors

Now let us look "backward" in the general model underlying this research, for possible reinforcing or feedback linkages. This will test the strong associations between burnout and physical symptoms which, as eta^2 estimates, account

TABLE 4.2
Modified Factors, 19 Physical Symptoms

	Corrected Item-to-Item Correlation	Alpha, Item Deleted
Factor I		
(alpha 0.81)		
Stomach pains	.49	.79
Headaches	.47	.79
Cough--colds	.35	.81
Fatigue	.61	.78
Trouble getting up	.52	.79
Sweaty hands	.45	.80
Nervous	.62	.78
Worn out	.61	.78
Poor appetite	.42	.80
Factor II		
(alpha 0.81)		
Heart pain	.62	.76
Tightness in chest	.69	.72
Trouble breathing	.61	.76
Heart pounding	.57	.78
Factor III		
(alpha 0.67)		
Leg cramps	.48	.58
Swollen ankles	.36	.66
Back pain	.44	.61
Stiffness	.53	.54
Factor IV		
(alpha 0.85)		
Getting to sleep	.73	--
Staying asleep	.73	--

TABLE 4.3
One-Way Analysis of Variance, Five Aggregates of Symptoms versus Phases of Burnout

Aggregates of Symptoms	I LoLoLo	II HiLoLo	III LoHiLo	IV HiHiLo	V LoLoHi	VI HiLoHi	VII LoHiHi	VIII HiHiHi	F-Ratio (df = 7, 1537)
Total symptoms	33.5	34.2	33.9	35.5	38.7	40.1	40.5	42.6	39.628*
Factor I: General enervation and agitation	17.0	17.1	17.1	18.1	20.0	20.5	21.2	22.2	54.995*
Factor II: Cardiovascular complaints	5.9	6.2	5.9	6.3	7.0	7.1	7.4	7.5	17.134*
Factor III: Noncardiac pains	7.1	7.2	7.6	7.3	7.8	8.2	8.0	8.3	7.766*
Factor IV: Sleeplessness	3.6	3.5	3.5	4.0	3.9	4.3	4.0	4.6	15.421*

* $P < 0.001$.

TABLE 4.4
Summary of Relationships of Five Clusters of Physical Symptoms versus Burnout Phases

	Summary of Differences, in Percentages			
	In Expected Direction	In Expected Direction and Statistically Significant	In Contrary Direction	In Contrary Direction and Statistically Significant
Total symptoms	98.4	60.4	3.6	0.0
Factor I: General enervation and agitation	96.4	64.3	3.6	0.0
Factor II: Cardiovascular complaints	92.9	42.9	7.1	0.0
Factor III: Noncardiac pains	92.9	17.9	7.1	0.0
Factor IV Sleeplessness	71.5	32.1	28.5	0.0

for nearly 20 percent of the variance in two factors and for over 5 percent in the other three cases. The former two cases seem to qualify as main-line effects.

What do the data suggest about the association of work site descriptors and symptoms? In general, work site descriptors covary with all five measures of physical distress in expected ways. Simply, the "better" the descriptors, the lower the incidence of reported symptoms—on Total Symptoms as well as on the four factorial clusters of symptoms. While quite regular, however, the association is not very robust. To summarize details reported elsewhere (Golembiewski, Munzenrider, and Stevenson, 1986, p. 76), 65 percent of the simple correlation coefficients achieve statistical significance; and all of those coefficients are in the expected direction. But only a bit over 3 percent of the variance in burnout and physical symptoms is accounted for by the 70 coefficients. Guilford (1950) describes this level as "almost negligible." Hence the record of "significance" basically reflects the substantial size of the responding population. Note that only slightly greater variance—4.9 percent, on average—is accounted for by Total Symptoms and Factor I. Earlier analysis shows that these two scores are the most revealing of the five measures of physical distress, of course.

How Bad Is Bad?

But how severe are the physical symptoms reported at Site B? Two comparisons provide useful perspective on this crucial estimate. Thus, a 1972 national sample of respondents (Quinn and Shepard, 1974) provides self-reports about all 19 of the symptoms studied at Site B, and these responses can be compared to those generated at Site B. The time gap between the 1972 survey and the 1982 survey at Site B must be taken into account, however, when such comparisons are made. Fortunately, more proximate comparisons are possible on most of the 19 symptoms. A 1977 survey (Quinn and Stains, 1979) provides more current data, but only 12 of the present list of symptoms are included in this later survey.

So we take two comparative approaches to providing perspective on the central question: How bad is bad?

Comparison with 1972 National Sample

The levels of symptoms reported at Site B are markedly higher than in the 1972 survey. In all 19 cases, significantly greater proportions of Site B respondents report experiencing each symptom "sometimes" or "often." What is the magnitude of "significantly greater"? Overall, an average of 28.2 percent of the Site B respondents choose these two indicators of the frequency with which they experienced the 19 symptoms. In comparison, 19.7 percent of the 1972 national sample chose the same response stems. Statistical analysis shows that in all cases very little probability ($P < .001$) exists that the differences are random.

TABLE 4.5
Illustrative Comparison of Symptom "Feel Fatigued,"
Site B and in Two National Samples

		Percent Reporting "Feel Fatigued"			
	Number	Never	Rarely	Sometimes	Often
All respondents, Site B	1,575	32.3	39.0	21.5	7.2
Phases I-III, Site B	653	42.1	40.7	15.5	1.7
Phases VI-VIII, Site B	652	21.2	36.8	29.0	13.0
1972 National sample (Quinn & Shepard, 1974)	2,149	58.6	26.2	12.0	3.3
1977 National sample (Quinn & Staines, 1979)	1,081	58.8	25.7	12.2	3.3

Comparison with Phases and Two National Samples

For the 1977 national survey, only 12 symptoms are included. What do these 12 comparisons show, in sum? All available cases reflect much the same pattern as the example for "feel fatigued" (see Table 4.5), and the dominant pattern can be summarized in terms of three characteristics. First, the two national samples do not differ systematically or significantly over the interval, 1972-1977. No noteworthy increase in reported symptoms seems to have occurred, and both the 1972 and 1977 data provide similar bases for comparisons with 1982 data from Site B.

Second, Site B respondents report a greater incidence of all symptoms than 1977 and 1972 respondents. The example in Table 4.5 provides a comparison typical for all 12 available symptoms: over 28 percent of Site B respondents report "feeling fatigued" either "sometimes" or "often," while the comparable percentage in the 1977 national population is 15.5. Compare the first and the last rows in Table 4.5.

Third, the symptoms seem quite sensitive to differences in burnout at Site B. Specifically, only some 17 percent of the respondents classified in Phases I-III report that they sometimes or often feel fatigued. For those in Phases VI-VIII, the comparable percentage is 42, which far surpasses both national samples.

In sum, "bad" at Site B seems pretty bad indeed. Certainly, the record seems worse than in two national samples. The implication that burnout plays a noteworthy role in Site B's record of reported symptoms also seems reasonable, although not beyond all doubt.

IMPLICATIONS FOR THE PHASE MODEL OF BURNOUT

The covariation of the phases and physical symptoms adds substantial momentum to this analysis in two basic senses. The association adds urgency to learning more about the phases, with the goal of ameliorating burnout and its noxious covariants such as symptoms of physical distress. Moreover, any other results would have taken much of the wind from the conceptual sails of the phase model. All commentators emphasize that burnout adversely affects many aspects of health, and our findings and the research of others add increasingly detailed support to those clinical observations (e.g., Burke, Shearer, and Descza, 1984, esp. pp. 172–83).

Certainly, no unqualified conclusions are appropriate, but analysis does support an emerging sense of several working conclusions about the phase model, three aspects of which merit attention. In turn, the three major sections below present a schema of results to this point, detail some qualifiers of those results, and sketch two directions for future research on the phase model.

Schema of Symptoms-Related Results

Patently, the results reflect a marked pattern of covariation of physical symptoms with psychological burnout, as variously measured, and this demonstration does multiple duty. In broad perspective, the results support numerous clinically oriented expectations about the significance of burnout and its consequences (Freudenberger, 1980); and the results are also consistent with the growing empirical literature (Burke, Shearer, and Deszca, 1984; Shinn and Mørch, 1983; and Lazaro and Shinn, 1984). More narrowly, the results reinforce the usefulness of the phase approach to burnout, and also provide support for the general model underlying this research. In its most elemental form, that environmental model provides for these main-line effects:

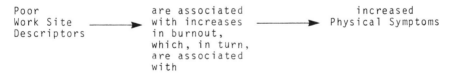

Figure 4.1 presents a schema reflecting the results thus far, using conventions that also will be relied on in other chapters to encompass progressively more comprehensive networks of associations. The figure highlights only statistically significant associations, and also estimates the strength of particular associations. "Robust" refers to an association that accounts for 15 percent or more of the variance between any two measures; and "modest" refers to about

FIGURE 4.1
Summary of Symptoms-related Associations and Their Strengths

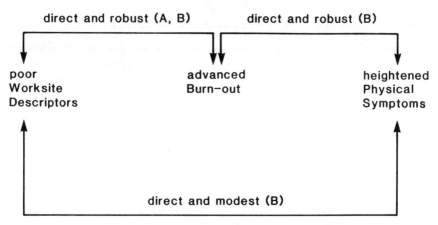

5 percent of the variance. Not applicable here are two additional estimates of the strengths of association used elsewhere in this volume. "Moderate" refers to an estimate of some 10 percent; and "slight" refers to an estimate of the variance accounted for by a statistically significant association in the range of a few percent. These rough criteria for classification should be viewed in perspective. The most solid associations in the behavioral sciences—between socioeconomic status and a range of other variables—to use a ballpark figure, commonly share 10 to 25 percent of their variance. Note that the designations in parentheses refer to whether data from Sites A or B, or both, support the generalizations sketched in the figure.

In sum, Figure 4.1 reflects basic (if partial) support for the model underlying the present research. Overall, as the model requires of its proposed main-line effects, strong linkages exist between the work site descriptors and burnout, as well as between burnout and physical symptoms. The direct but modest association between symptoms and the work site descriptors is consistent with the general model's view of these vectors as representing only reinforcing or feedback linkages. Specifically, two contrasts are instructive. Table 2.1 shows that 17.1 percent of the variance in the work site descriptors is accounted for by the phases of burnout; and the statistical analysis underlying Table 4.3 shows that 18 percent of the variance in the most useful measures of physical distress is accounted for by the phases. In contrast, work site descriptors share only a little more than 3 percent of their variance in common with the five measures of symptoms. Burnout effects dominate.

Qualifications about Symptoms-Related Results

We add two cautions to balance this optimism. First, this book and its predecessor represent an early mapping expedition—with numerous stops and starts occasioned by the need to test the burnout measuring instrument and to probe multiple associations that we authors anticipated often would be unanticipated. Hence the piecemeal and bivariate statistical analysis here.

Second, the basic pattern above suggests that burnout has economic as well as psychic costs. For example, advanced stages of burnout may well be associated with a range of conventional bottom-line indicators of illness or disease—absence from work or "sick days," compensation for health claims, and so on. Some progress has been made on encompassing such possible covariants, to be sure. A section below tentatively associates the phase model with properties of the chemistry of blood; the next chapter deals with performance appraisals; and chapter nine shows how employee turnover seems to vary with burnout phases. For the present, however, these possible physical covariants of burnout largely remain targets for testing elsewhere.

Burnout research, in short, must deal with at least two levels of reality. The data indicate that people with advanced burnout at least seem more aware of their aches and pains. Those self-reports constitute one kind of reality—a "social reality" that is important enough in itself, but still limited. Complementary data are required to test and refine associations with burnout, and these often should be more "objective" measures of bodily processes or states that are independent of the respondents in ways that self-reports clearly are not. Moreover, only longitudinal research designs can deal conclusively with the issue of the degrees to which burnout causes physical symptoms or is reinforced by them.

Before moving on to chapter five, the momentum deriving from the analysis of the phases X physical symptoms inspires two concluding points about testing the phase model. The points refer to initiatives beyond the reach of presently available data and deal, in turn, with patterns of effects and blood chemistry.

Testing the Phase Model: Three Kinds of Effects

The two sets of significant covariations established above—burnout X physical symptoms and work site descriptors X physical symptoms—need to be refined so as to permit a choice between possible kinds of effects. These include but are not restricted to the three effects illustrated in Figure 4.2. There, "growth-inducing work site descriptors" refer to: high participation in decisions at work, high job involvement, and desirable states on the other variables in the profile associated with the least-advanced phases of burnout.

The concepts of buffering and main effects have occasioned much confusion but their meanings are quite direct. To illustrate with Figure 4.2c, work site descriptors both buffer the effects of burnout on physical symptoms, and also have a main effect on them. That is, the curves representing the two qualities of work descriptors are not parallel, which indicates a buffering effect. Moreover, even when burnout is low in Figure 4.2c, people reporting growth-inducing work site descriptors have fewer physical symptoms, and this implies a main effect (House, 1981, pp. 33-34).

FIGURE 4.2
Three Patterns of Effects, Work Site Descriptors and Burnout on Physical Symptoms

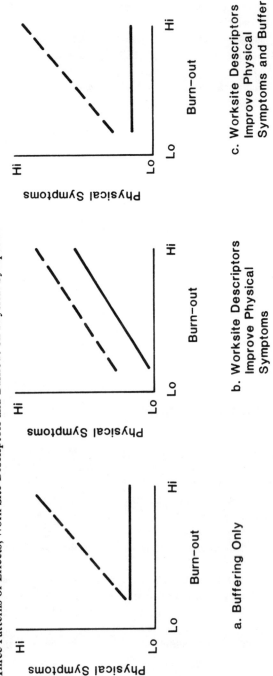

a. Buffering Only

b. Worksite Descriptors
   Improve Physical
   Symptoms

c. Worksite Descriptors
   Improve Physical
   Symptoms and Buffer

† Inspired by House (1981), p. 33

N.B. ———— Indicates Growth–Inducing Worksite Descriptors

- - - - Indicates Deficiency–Inducing Worksite Descriptors

Conclusive analysis is not available, but the present findings suggest the patterns of effects in Figures 4.2b or 4.2c. The issue of which pattern dominates is not trivial, of course. Especially for purposes of intervention, such knowledge can be critical. See, especially, chapter nine for efforts to act on the environmental model underlying this research.

Testing the Phase Model: Including Blood Chemistry, if Tentatively

If the associations of phases X physical symptoms are descriptive of relationships in nature, future research should be able to establish quite direct relationships with blood chemistry. Or, to be precise, the common wisdom suggests the *possible* association of levels of experienced stressors with:

- total cholesterol
- triglycerides
- uric acid
- HDL cholesterol
- the ratio of total cholesterol to HDL cholesterol
- the ratio of HDL cholesterol to total cholesterol

Some Stress-Related Products in Blood

Brief discussion details the nature of what medical knowledge suggests for the phase model of burnout. High levels of the first three features of blood chemistry are often considered reliable and valid indicators of manifest strain (e.g., Fried *et al.*, 1984), as well as precursors of stress-related disorders including heart disease and peptic ulcers (e.g., Smith, McKinlay, and Thorington, 1987). The fourth and fifth measures are seen as useful indicators of good health prognoses. The ratio of total cholesterol to HDL cholesterol is seen by some (e.g., SmithKline Bio-Science Laboratories, 1987) as the appropriate measure. Some researchers (e.g., Hendrix *et al.*, 1985) prefer to use the ratio HDL/Chol as their indicator of experienced strain, or an accumulation of dis-stressors as the individual subjectively perceives them. To explain, HDL cholesterol seems to help maintain the arteries, as by resisting the accumulation of the fatlike serum cholesterol that can create blockages in the arteries. Hence as the Chol/HDL ratio decreases, better health outcomes are expected; and good health outcomes are similarly associated with increasing HDL/Chol ratios.

However, research does not provide consistent support for the presumed chemical products of strain, products that are seen as precursors of serious health problems. For example, Howard and his associates (1986) question whether low job satisfaction or high role ambiguity occur along with high levels of serum cholesterol, which implies either outright rejection—or requires major

modification—of early associations of job strain with heightened serum cholesterol (e.g., Friedman, Rosenman, and Carroll, 1958).

To illustrate a very long list of explanations, three reasons provide possible
explanations of this lack of congruence between research findings and typical
assumptions about covariation. First, blood chemistry may be too subtle to
permit focusing on a few properties, which in the bargain are seldom considered
in the context of their relationships with each other or with many other hemato-
logical features. In addition, the present state of all-but-scrupulous clinical testing may leave something to be desired, or even much. Finally, measures of strain
not only vary widely, but may not have strong claims to reliability and validity.

Results with the phase model permit some confidence that it constitutes an
unusually useful estimate of experienced strain, and this motivates a pilot study
with the six measures of blood chemistry introduced above. The first run of the
research design sought to acquaint officials of a corporate wellness program
with the quality-control problems and intricacies of interfacing a clinical testing
program with behavioral research. Preliminary results have been used to justify a
full-scale effort, but the small sample size (N = 46) of the pilot study argues for a
tentative interpretation of results.

Findings of a Pilot Study

This study involves observations at two points in time. In Observation I,
respondents provide blood samples immediately after completing the MBI
form. In Observation II, about two months later, only data from the MBI are
involved. The original purpose was to gain perspective on possible leading/
lagging phenomena involving possible associations of phases × blood properties
in a large population, but management problems resulted in a bobtailed effort.

To avoid very small subsample sizes, only three clusters of phases are relied
on—Phases I-III, IV-V, and VI-VIII. This is necessary because the blood-
testing service notes that age and sex differences influence interpretations of all
four measures involving cholesterol as well as the one for triglycerides. Interpretation of uric acid levels does not require such a breakout. Separate analyses
are run for males, females, and for three age clusters—under 30, 30-39, and
over 40 years. In sum, each of the sets of phase assignments involves 26 separate analyses: one for uric acid, and 25 analyses of the other five blood measures, after differentiating respondents by five demographic categories.

Expectations are direct as well as perhaps overly simple, given what we know,
but consistent with the goal of an initial mapping of very complex territory. Improved health prospects are associated with low estimates of total cholesterol, uric
acid, triglycerides, and the Chol/HDL ratio. In addition, good health outcomes
are associated with high estimates of HDL cholesterol and of HDL/Chol ratios.

Results with Phases

As noted, the small N encourages reliance on three clusters of phases: I-III,
IV-V, and VI-VIII. Perhaps the best summary of the pilot study results is that

they trend in the expected directions, which probably understates the case because of the small subsample sizes involved, even when only three clusters of phases are used. Using one-way ANOVA for Observation I, 10 of 26 cases approach overall statistical significance $(.20 < P > .05)$ and three cases attain or surpass the .10 level. Moreover, nearly 75 percent of the paired-comparisons are in the expected direction.

The results for Observation II are quite similar.

One reason especially encourages reporting these preliminary results, small subsample sizes notwithstanding. The only similar study of which the authors are aware uses another estimate of stress or burnout, and in a large population it finds only "moderate to weak" associations with (among others) five of the measures of concern here (Anon., 1987). These results may mirror nature, or merely point to the inadequacy of the measure of stress used in that study. The present results do not establish marked and consistent associations between burnout and the measures of blood properties, of course, but they do motivate a proper test in a satisfactory population.

TWO SUBSEQUENT STEPS

The phase model, however, need not wait on promises of pie in the sky, by and by. Although we are still far short of the data required for the ideal directions just sketched for future research, even now it is possible to test the phase model—not only a bit further, but also with some additional sources of "objective," "hard," or "independent" data. This will complement the self-report data generally relied on so far, rather than supplant them. Chapter five uses quantitative and qualitative measures of performance and productivity to extend our knowledge of the phase model.

5. *SYSTEM COSTS OF BURNOUT: PERFORMANCE, PRODUCTIVITY, AND THE PHASES*

Output is a central purpose of collective life, and it may be viewed as having two major components—individual performance and collective productivity. This chapter directs attention to these two aspects of output—aggregate measures of productivity, and individual performance, as measured by appraisals. The progression of the argument is direct, although the details can be formidable. After a brief introduction, attention will be directed toward performance and then productivity measures to test the model of burnout underlying this research.

MOTIVATIONS FOR FOCUSING ON PRODUCTIVITY AND PERFORMANCE

Two factors motivate attention to performance and productivity. The burnout covariants considered earlier rely on self-reports, and therefore some observers will devalue them as reflecting only "subjective reality." This view seems overstated to the authors, and solid evidence suggests that self-reports may even be the evidence of choice in many cases (Howard et al., 1980). But the superiority of "hard data" has a broad currency; and all models need to be tested against a broad range of indicators. Moreover, if nothing else, performance and productivity are important attention-getters, and they "make the world go around" for many people, much of the time.

This chapter does not exhaust possible approaches to performance and productivity, but it provides a real test of the generality and comprehensiveness of burnout effects in organizations. Attention is directed to two questions:

- Does burnout covary with personal performance, as judged by influential others?

- Does burnout covary with differences in collective productivity, as measured by "cold numbers"?

BURNOUT AND PERFORMANCE APPRAISALS, SITES A AND B

The literature suggests three critical links between burnout and individual performance, though it adds little to enlighten us in regard to when and how often these models apply. These three alternative but not necessarily mutually exclusive links may be expressed as follows:

- High achievement has high costs, one of which is advanced burnout (Freudenberger, 1980; Maslach, 1982).

- Low achievement can have high costs, one of which is advanced burnout (Edelwich and Brodsky, 1980).

- The association of achievement and burnout is contingent—that is, it depends on the specific mixes of personal features, job characteristics, the work site's norms, and so on.

This section reviews some data relevant to these alternative views of the association of performance and burnout. This is done without pretending to resolve questions concerning which models apply and how often, but with the hope of beginning a useful dialog that provides data permitting some judgment of the relative usefulness of the three models. In any case, three emphases characterize this approach to performance. In turn, the focus shifts from notes about hosts and methods, then to some findings and, finally, to several implications of those results.

Notes about Hosts and Methods

Two data sources fuel this look at individual performance. For the most part, it uses findings taken from Site B, but with a later assist from Site A. The phases are relied on exclusively, although earlier analysis also deals with four other burnout measures—a Total Score and the three subscale scores (Golembiewski, Munzenrider, and Stevenson, 1986, pp. 88-90). Site B utilizes a panel of 16 work site descriptors (see chapter two), while Site A adds six facets of job satisfaction from the Job Descriptive Index (also see chapter three).

Findings Concerning Performance Appraisals

Several details help frame this discussion of findings. Note that one-tailed probabilities are relied upon to estimate the significance of differences on

TABLE 5.1
One-way Analysis of Variance between Self-reported Performance Appraisals and Three Classes of Variables, Site B

	Mean Scores, by Performance Appraisal Categories					
	Outstanding	Highly Satisfactory	Fully Satisfactory	Minimally Satisfactory	F-Ratio	F-Probability
A. Work Site Descriptors						
Participation	16.5	15.8	14.2	13.1	33.003	.001
Job involvement	30.8	29.9	29.1	27.7	4.942	.002
Trust in supervisor	14.9	14.5	13.0	10.3	24.179	.001
Trust in employees	18.0	17.2	16.6	13.8	13.095	.001
Willingness to disagree with supervisor	15.8	15.7	13.7	13.3	18.688	.001
Job tension	18.9	19.7	21.0	23.7	19.274	.001
Experienced meaningfulness of work	20.7	19.8	19.4	18.6	5.317	.001
Experienced responsibility for work	33.9	32.7	32.3	29.5	10.173	.001
Knowledge of results	22.0	21.1	20.3	19.3	15.072	.001
General satisfaction	24.8	23.9	23.3	20.3	9.583	.001
Internal work motivation	33.4	32.9	32.7	31.3	2.735	.042
Growth satisfaction	20.4	19.5	18.9	16.6	9.319	.001
Job security	10.1	10.0	9.7	8.4	5.829	.001
Compensation	9.6	9.1	9.1	8.4	3.037	.028
Coworkers	16.7	16.6	16.1	14.9	7.375	.001
Supervision	15.7	14.8	13.9	10.8	22.339	.001
B. Symptoms Scores						
Total symptoms	37.2	37.3	37.7	41.1	2.618	.050
Factor I: General enervation and agitation	19.0	19.2	19.3	21.3	3.415	.017
Factor II: Cardiovascular complaints	6.5	6.5	6.7	7.5	3.097	.026
Factor III: Noncardiac pains	8.0	7.5	7.7	8.2	3.041	.128
Factor IV: Sleeplessness	3.8	4.1	4.0	4.4	3.076	.027

numerous variables between two categories of performance appraisals. In effect, consistent with the general model underlying this research, we will be assessing the degree of support for the proposition that low achievement (as measured by in-house performance appraisals) is associated with high costs. Costs here are defined in terms of degrees of psychological burnout, as well as in terms of deficits in a substantial array of variables assessing the quality of the work site and individual reactions to it. Finally, remember that higher scores almost always imply more of the quality in question, whether the scale involves facets of satisfaction or job tension.

Appraisals and Work Site Descriptors

Available data permit a dual test of most associations at both Sites A and B, albeit with some measurement differences. Basically, performance appraisals at Site A come from organization records, while those at Site B are based on respondent self-reports. Overall, any misreporting probably would "sweeten" recollections at Site B, and hence dilute any associations there with other variables.

Findings at Site B

Findings at Site B reveal modest association between work site descriptors and performance appraisal, as measured by self-reports rather than agency records. Table 5.1 provides the results. All 16 of the cases achieve statistical significance, with all the descriptors worsening as performance appraisals shift from "Outstanding" through "Minimally Satisfactory." In addition, 99 percent of the paired-comparisons are in the expected direction, and over 62 percent of those differences achieve statistical significance as determined by the Least Significant Difference test, modified for unequal subsample sizes.

The pattern is more regular than robust, however. Eta^2 calculations indicate that an average of 2.5 percent of the variance is accounted for.

Findings at Site A

The association has a pattern and magnitude similar to Site B (Golembiewski, Munzenrider, and Stevenson, 1986, p. 91). This reinforces the conclusion that work site descriptors are distal covariants of performance appraisal, rather than main effects.

Appraisals and Burnout Phases

And what can be said of the association between performance and the phases? As before, Sites A and B are considered separately.

Findings at Site A

Table 5.2 provides relevant data for Site A, which associate high levels of burnout with poorer performance appraisals. As a necessary preliminary to reviewing the data, note two technical points. Due to the small size of several

TABLE 5.2
Phases of Burnout and Two Performance Appraisals, Site A

| | Individuals by Phases of Burnout | | | | | | |
	I-III	IV and V	VI-VIII	Number	Chi^2	P	Cramer's V
Day 1 burnout and Appraisal I							
Excellent	71	23	15	109	8.029	0.02	0.22
Good or lower	37	6	18	61			
Day 1 burnout and Appraisal II							
Excellent	50	12	10	72	7.365	0.03	0.24
Good or lower	32	3	16	51			
Day 365 burnout and Appraisal II							
Excellent	68	7	14	89	8.029	0.02	0.22
Good or lower	34	9	15	58			

cells, the eight burnout phases are collapsed into three categories. This is not ideal. In addition, two sets of appraisals are available. Appraisal I was made in the six months or so centering around the first survey at day 1. Appraisal II data come from a similar interval around day 365, when the second survey was administered. Some individuals are appraised twice, and a few do not get appraised in either period. Moreover, not all individuals are classified into burnout phases at days 1 and 365. Consequently, the total Ns in Table 5.2 vary.

Two points suffice to highlight the relationship observed at Site A between burnout phases and performance appraisals. First, all three cases in Table 5.2 show statistically significant associations. The more advanced an individual's phase of burnout, in short, the poorer the performance appraisal. Three chi-square values support the point that lower performance has its psychological costs and/or that more advanced burnout impacts negatively on performance, as perceived by supervisors. Of course, nearly two-thirds of all employees get "Excellent" appraisals at Site A. But only a bit over 45 percent of those in the three most advanced phases do so, while the percentage increases to nearly 70 percent for those in the other phases. Looked at from another angle, those with "Excellent" appraisals are four or five times more likely to be in Phases I-III than VI-VIII. For lower appraisals, the ratio drops to 2:1, approximately.

Second, the association is regular but only moderate in strength. Cramer's V, loosely interpreted, indicates that only approximately 5 percent of the variance is accounted for, on average, in the three cases, which reflects a noteworthy association but not a dominant one.

The point is speculative, but the substantial if diminishing "grade inflation" at Site A might well dilute any association between burnout and performance appraisals. In this sense, Table 5.2 may present a conservative estimate of the degree of association. Management had begun to address the problem, but "false positives" no doubt abounded.

Findings at Site B

Data from Site B also suggest an inverse association between performance appraisals and phases of burnout, on balance, but the interpretation here must be cautious. The one-way analysis of variance only approaches statistical significance ($P = .078$), and the data are not reproduced here to conserve space. Eta^2 indicates that about 1 percent of the variance is accounted for.

These associations of burnout and performance appraisals at Site B may be conservative. Appraisals there came from self-reports rather than organization records, and inaccurate recollections may have a "sweetening" effect that dilutes appraisal differences between the least and most advanced phases of burnout.

Appraisals and Physical Symptoms: Findings

Again, the present data permit only a qualified test of the association of performance appraisals and a crucial covariant—physical symptoms. Appraisals from company records are available at Site A, but no profile of physical

FIGURE 5.1
Summary of Performance-related Associations and Their Effects

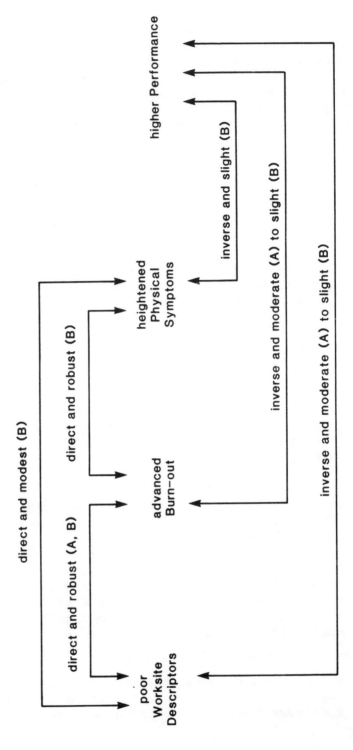

symptoms was developed there. At Site B, where data concerning symptoms do exist, appraisals rely on self-reports.

Data from Site B show a regular and inverse pattern of association between self-reported performance appraisals and the five measures of physical symptoms, as Table 5.1 reflects. All five of the measures attain statistical significance, and over 87 percent of the paired-comparisons show that physical symptoms increase as performance appraisals deteriorate. Moreover, 30 percent of the differences between pairs are large enough to achieve the .05 level of statistical significance.

Despite this regular pattern of association, however, it must be considered slight. Eta^2 indicates that only about 1 percent of the variance is accounted for, on average.

Implications of Performance for the Environmental Model

Two sections will develop the significant point that the results thus far continue to support the environmental model underlying this research, although some important qualifiers require acknowledging. A first section presents a summary schema of the results, and a second emphasizes several qualifications. Both sections relate to the same general model, which proposes, as will be recalled, these main-line effects relevant at this point:

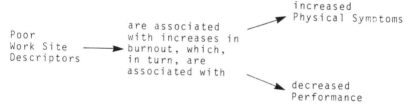

Schema of Performance-Related Results

Figure 5.1 presents a summary of results in a simple schematic. It summarizes all the regular patterns of association observed, with "regular" here reflecting statistically significant cases only at Sites A or B. How robust are these nonrandom cases? That is a separate issue, and one often neglected in research. Here strength of the associations is estimated via simple indicators, as before. "Robust" refers to cases with 15 or more percent of the variance being accounted for; "moderate" refers to 10 percent or so of shared variance; "modest" implies about 5 percent common variance; and "slight" refers to 1 percent or so of the variance being accounted for by statistically significant associations.

A few details outline the evidence supporting the schematic. Those details suggest—but do not establish—the critical causal sequence assumed by the multiple-outcomes, or environmental, model. In short, regular and robust associations suggest direct causal pathways, and lesser regularity and robustness imply either more distal points on such a pathway, or feedback linkages. One can "see" such main-line and reinforcing effects in Figure 5.1, although closure needs to be stoutly resisted. Earlier chapters establish that the work site descriptors are robustly associated with burnout differences, for example, and especially with the phases. Eta^2 calculations reveal that over 17 percent of the variance in the phases is shared with work site descriptors, in fact. Variables more distal in the model have less regular and/or weaker associations. Thus, work site descriptors have regular but weak associations with physical symptoms and with performance appraisal, where the variance accounted for is in the 1–5 percent range.

Qualifications about Performance-Related Results

Although the data support the usefulness of the general model underlying this research, five points qualify this tentative conclusion. The vehicle for highlighting both the qualifiers and the conclusion is a simple schema adapted below for performance-related outcomes. Recall that no modifications of the general model are required in chapter three, which deals with physical symptoms.

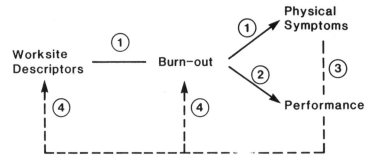

First, the data suggest—but could be far stronger at critical points in supporting—the multiple-outcomes model. Strong linkages seem to exist at ①, as required by the general model. But the linkage at ② does not seem robust, which could be explained in part by the variable quality of performance appraisals. Moreover, the slight relationship observed at ③ is consistent with the multiple-outcomes assumption, but was tested only at Site B, at which no independent performance measures are available. Finally, the strengths of several linkages ④ support their proposed status as feedback loops rather than main-line effects. Of course, other interpretations of the ④ linkages are possible, as chapter six will show in a more comprehensive summary of observed linkages.

Second, on definite balance, the results support the view that low achievement has high costs. However, both sites doubtless contain cases in which high achievement is associated with advanced burnout.

Third, the "grade inflation" concerning appraisals at both sites does not provide an ideal test of associations with burnout, but this inflation does not seem to invalidate the effects reported here. Indeed, that inflation probably dilutes any associations, rather than exaggerates them.

Fourth, relatedly, performance appraisals are generated by evaluation processes whose participants, character, and quality can vary across a broad range.

This variability might create spurious associations, of course, but the authors propose that dilution of associations is by far more likely. In either case, the appraisals have a patent salience in the organizational lives of those appraised—in terms of income, self-esteem, and so on. So, appraisals are significant, whatever the way at which they are arrived.

Fifth, no data on physical symptoms are available for Site A respondents. This precludes a test of the relative strength of the associations of independently-assessed performance appraisals with self-reported burnout and physical symptoms.

BURNOUT AND PRODUCTIVITY AT SITE B

Site B provides an additional source of bottom-line data to test the reach-and-grasp of the present approach to psychological burnout. Note that the effort is rare, if not unique. The burnout literature seldom deals with measures such as those of interest here.

Notes About Host and Method

Site B encompasses a national network of 50-plus work stations, and seems representative of public social service agencies. Employees of the agency experience all of the stimuli of federal public service, and in addition deal with clients in situations that often involve strong emotions—anger, rage, fear, greed, and so on. Such factors may well contribute to the high levels of burnout reported by division employees.

When it comes to measuring productivity, Site B departs from stereotypes about public agencies. The division has a strong interest in such measurement, with much time and energy being devoted to accumulating and disseminating a broad range of data on productivity. This point is usefully amplified in the next three sections. Two introduce quantitative and qualitative measures of productivity, and the third elaborates several of their limitations.

Six Measures of Qualitative Productivity

The agency reports several qualitative measures of productivity, which will be utilized here to gain further perspective on burnout. The focus is on evaluations generated by management as well as by clients.

Headquarters Ratings of Management and Quality

The national headquarters staff of the division performs a yearly review of each of the work stations, and this activity is used here to generate three measures of the quality of performance—management, quality, and a combined rating.

The staff produces and widely reports two qualitative measures. Omitting details, management and quality at each work station are rated as "Excellent," "Favorable," or "Needs Improvement." For present purposes, these staff-produced ratings are coded as 3, 2, and 1, respectively, for each of the two measures.

This analysis also uses a third qualitative measure—combined rating. For each work station, this measure is the sum of management and quality codes, and hence can range from two to six.

Clients' Criticism Scores

Three other measures of the quality of productivity come from division clients. Independently of the work stations, headquarters solicits the reactions of samples of clients concerning the character and quality of the services provided.

The details of this arduous data-gathering procedure need not detain us here. For present purposes, overall, three aspects of these reactions are included under the general rubric of clients' criticism scores:

- "Poor" ratings, or percent of respondents rating assistance or service as poor, on a set of stems also including "Excellent," "Good," or "Fair"
- "Not courteous" ratings, or percent of respondents noting that division employees were discourteous to clients
- "Poor" plus "Not courteous" ratings, combined

Measures of Quantitative Productivity

Each month all division stations provide headquarters with data about numbers of individual services performed, as well as the total man-hours required to do the station's work. An automated system churns out various indices for each station, primary among which are measures of overall productivity and direct-labor effectiveness. The results of this number-crunching are widely disseminated. for all to see and for some to explain.

Both key ratios rest on an engineering approach to work. All direct services are enumerated—let us say there are 46 of these activities, such as "initial screening interview." And each of these several services has a "standard time" associated with it. To illustrate, answering each incoming phone call is assigned a standard time of four minutes. Simple but laborious calculations convert activities × standard times into "standard man-hours" (SMH). For each of the division's work stations across the country, the frequencies with which the various services are performed during a month are multiplied by the appropriate standard times. The sum of these several multiplicands generates standard man-hours for each work station, which provides a measure of the total work accomplished.

The calculation of overall productivity makes one use of standard man-hours. SMH is divided by "total available hours" to generate a ratio. The question it asks is direct: how much did you do with all the time resources allocated to a station?

Direct-labor effectiveness uses the same numerator, SMH, but seeks to remove all "indirect" hours from the denominator. Direct hours include total available hours *minus* supervision, clerical overhead, leave, and so on. The central question this second ratio seeks to confront is: how much did direct-service providers do with the time resources available at a station?

Major Concerns about Productivity Measurement

The present productivity data are not ideal (Golembiewski, Munzenrider, and Stevenson, 1986, pp. 104-109). Attention here is limited to three major concerns about productivity measures at Site B.

Convention for Estimating Work-Station Burnout

All measures of productivity relate to work stations, some with over 100 employees. Other data—such as those on burnout and physical symptoms—come from individuals and are about individuals.

How to deal with these different levels of analysis? Our prime accommodation to recalcitrant realities involves estimating the level of burnout of individual work stations. Work stations are assigned to one of four classes, based on the degree of burnout reported by employees at each work station:

- Low stations, where 50 percent or more of the respondents are classified in Phases I through III;
- Bipolar stations, where 40 percent or more of the respondents are classified in each of the two sets of extreme phases—I through III or VI through VIII;
- Mixed stations, where respondents are more or less equally distributed among the three major clusters of phases—the two sets of extreme phases as well as IV plus V; and
- High stations, where 50 percent or more of the respondents are classified in Phases VI through VIII.

All but two work stations are classified in this way. The headquarters group is excluded, because no productivity data are available for it, and the low proportion of respondents to the survey eliminates a second station. In summary, the four major classes of work stations have these distributions of employees in the three clusters of phases:

		Percent of Employees, by Phases		
Work Station Burnout	Number	I-III	IV and V	VI-VIII
Low	14	58.8	13.6	27.6
Bi-polar	15	43.2	12.6	44.2
Mixed	5	31.8	34.5	33.6
High	19	23.6	15.4	61.0

Note that these classes differ from an earlier effort (Golembiewski, Munzenrider, and Stevenson, 1986, pp. 110-15). Although the formal criteria do not differ, the present judgments focus on the extreme phases. Earlier judgments attempted to do some fine-tuning to accommodate cases close to the cutting-points, but reanalysis convinced the authors that several arbitrary assignments resulted. The present classification avoids such judgments.

Failure to Isolate Immediate Work Groups

This convention for aggregating individual data at the level of work stations presents several obvious difficulties, but one little-recognized issue may be most troublesome. Two lines of independent inquiry (Golembiewski, 1983b; Rountree, 1984) support the view that the immediate work group—the cluster of first-reports of any supervisor—constitutes the most relevant unit of analysis in burnout. However, all work stations include several groups of first-reports: the smallest stations most closely approximate *a* group, but some stations have over 100 employees. Consequently, our aggregating convention lacks precision. To illustrate, consider a work station with 60 percent of its members classified in Phases VI-VIII. Assuming four immediate work groups of equal size in this station, many distributions of advanced burnout could result in a 60-percent record for the entire work station. Such differences cannot be distinguished in the present data.

Such considerations have many implications. Most probably, the present aggregating convention disguises or dilutes any interaction with productivity measures. Hence, any observed regularities may well represent a conservative estimate of effects.

Possible Ceiling Effects

Agency publications emphasize that a station can rank too high as well as too low on the two quantitative measures—overall productivity and direct-labor effectiveness. Any variances greater than ±10 percent of the "national average over a period of several consecutive months should be investigated or analyzed," an agency bulletin in effect announces a ceiling as well as a floor for productivity. Although this policy has been changed, it remained in effect throughout the period of data-gathering.

If ceiling effects do exist, of course, they would serve to moderate any associations between productivity measures and other variables. Ceiling effects would set limits on the probability that different levels of energy and motivation will translate directly into differences in productivity.

Findings Concerning Productivity

So what can be said about the covariants of productivity at Site B, given the chilling effect of the several limitations of the present approach? The next four sections summarize these findings as they relate, in turn, to work site descriptors, burnout, physical symptoms, and performance.

Productivity and Work Site Descriptors

Boldness seems quite appropriate concerning both the pattern and magnitude of the associations of work site descriptors and quantitative productivity measures. Only 1 of the 64 correlation-coefficients achieves statistical significance, and three or four other cases may be said to approach significance. The data are reported in *Stress in Organizations* (p. 111).

Productivity and Burnout

The association of burnout and productivity poses real problems. To take the easiest hypothetical case, high degrees of burnout among major proportions of a work station suggest low productivity. That is, high burnout implies little slack in a person's coping capacities, and perhaps deficits in them. So high work stations—defined earlier as having 50 percent or more of their memberships in Phases VI-VIII—pose no great problems for prediction. All other things being roughly equal, they should be characterized by low productivity, as variously measured.

Low burnout in a work station poses more of a challenge than it first appears to. In most cases, low work stations might be expected to have the highest productivity, given the energies assumedly not committed to dealing with high levels of strain. As noted, however, ceiling effects may exist, and immediate work groups cannot be identified here. Moreover, other research suggests that perhaps one-fifth of the individuals in Phases I-III have a low activity level comparable to that of most of those individuals in Phases VI-VIII (Golembiewski and Munzenrider, 1984a). Evidence also suggests that one-fifth or so of the employees low on burnout have supervisors with laissez-faire characteristics, which might well adversely affect productivity. This evidence suggests two modes of low burnout: mostly an active mode, but also a passive one in a noteworthy proportion of cases. See also chapter nine.

Hence productivity levels in low work stations—as defined above as having at least 50 percent of their membership in Phases I-III—defy easy prediction. Productivity effects may be diluted, but the initial expectation of high productivity will be retained as a best-guess. Given the small number of cases, only illustrative efforts will be made to differentiate the low work stations.

By more direct ideation, bi-polar stations—those with 40 percent or more of their employees classified in both Phases I-III and VI-VIII—are expected to be intermediate in productivity.

The remaining work stations—the mixed—pose the greatest difficulties. On the one hand, mixed stations suggest low levels of productivity. With approximately one-third of their employees in each of the three clusters of burnout phases, the potential for deflecting energy from work seems substantial. Moreover, their high proportions of members in Phases IV and V—high for this and all other populations studied—suggest transitional dynamics that could be major energy-absorbers. Other evidence suggests that persons in Phases IV and V will

TABLE 5.3
Means of Ten Productivity Measures, Arrayed by Three Categories of Work Station Burnout
(N = 48)

Productivity Measures	Low (14)	Bi-Polar (15)	High (19)	F-Ratio	F-Probability
Overall productivity					
First quarter, 1983	83.4	82.5	81.2	0.390	0.67
Fiscal 1982	80.1	79.9	77.8	0.805	0.42
Direct-labor effectiveness					
First quarter, 1983	113.1	113.0	110.1	0.405	0.67
Fiscal 1982	107.1	107.5	104.9	0.554	0.57
Headquarters rating, Fiscal 1982					
Management	2.6	2.2	2.2	2.422	0.09
Quality	2.5	2.2	2.2	2.027	0.14
Combined	5.1	4.4	4.4	3.406	0.04
Clients' criticism scores, Fiscal 1982					
"Poor" ratings, percent	1.9	2.0	2.2	0.054	0.92
"Not courteous," percent	0.2	0.3	0.5	1.273	0.29
"Poor" and "not courteous" combined, percent	2.1	2.3	2.7	0.226	0.79

shift phases in major ways in about 90 percent of the cases, over a period of a year, while the two clusters of extreme phases will remain stable in about seven of ten cases (Golembiewski, 1984a). On the other hand, mixed stations admit many combinations of burnout in their groups of first-reports, none of which can be distinguished here.

Given such indeterminacies-in-opposition, plus their small N (5), mixed stations are not considered in detail below. Brief comments on their analysis will be provided, however,

The present expectations for testing work-station burnout and productivity are tentative, then, and seven stations will not be included in the detailed analysis to follow. The excluded units include five mixed stations, the management group, and one unit with a very low response rate. Productivity expectations are:

Work Station Burnout	Expected Productivity
Low	High
Bi-polar	↕
High	Low

Work-Station Productivity and Burnout

Table 5.3 summarizes a one-way analysis of variance testing these expectations about productivity and burnout in 48 work stations. Six points highlight aspects of those data, and they all suggest—but do not establish—definite but diluted associations between burnout and productivity.

First, the productivity measures worsen as burnout increases. Specifically, low burnout work stations score lowest on all three of the clients' criticism scores, where "low" is favorable; and they also score highest on six of the other seven measures of productivity where "high" is "good." Overall, 86.7 percent of the paired-comparisons are in the expected directions, although the differences are small in many cases.

Second, the differences are not robust. Two of the ten cases achieve $P < .10$; and two additional cases attain $P < .30$. The first two cases refer to Management and Combined ratings by the headquarters staff, and those cases explain about 14 percent of the variance.

Third, no paired-comparisons achieve statistical significance in the one case of $P < .05$. This may be due to small Ns and unstable variances.

Fourth, as expected, the quantitative measures show higher productivity in the first quarter than in the preceding fiscal year. This may reflect ceiling effects in the yearly data.

Fifth, the high work stations tend to have the lowest productivity. This is true in seven of ten cases, and the high stations tie for lowest productivity in two of the three other cases. None of these differences are statistically significant, however.

TABLE 5.4

Correlations between Physical Symptoms and Ten Productivity Measures, Work Station Level, Site B (N = 55)

Productivity Measures	Total Symptoms	Factor I: General Enervation and Agitation	Factor II: Cardiovascular Complaints	Factor III: Norcardiac Pains	Factor IV: Sleeplessness
Overall productivity					
First quarter, 1983	.27*	.18	.33*	.24*	.30*
Fiscal 1982	.17	.09	.22*	.18	.19
Direct-labor effectiveness					
First quarter, 1983	.27*	.16	.34*	.25*	.28*
Fiscal 1982	.17	.07	.25*	.19	.19
Headquarters ratings, fiscal 1982					
Management	.29*	.29*	.15	.20	.35*
Quality	.06	.08	-.02	.06	.13
Combined	.22*	.24*	.09	.19	.32*
Clients' criticism scores, fiscal 1982					
"Poor" ratings, percent	-.13	-.17	-.05	-.03	.12
"Not courteous," percent	-.17	-.18	-.13	-.08	-.14
"Combined, percent	-.15	-.19	-.07	-.05	-.14

*Designates a correlation coefficient that attains or surpasses .05 level.

Note that an analysis including mixed stations leads to very similar conclusions. The data are not reproduced here, to conserve space.

Sixth, active and passive modes seem to exist for all phases (Golembiewski and Munzenrider, 1984a), and failure to distinguish modes can dilute productivity differences. Using a median split on job involvement as a surrogate for active/passive modes, to illustrate, the comparison of the high units suggests a useful line for future research:

	High/Active (14)	High/Passive (5)	F-Ratio	F-Probability
Overall productivity				
First quarter 1983	87.2	79.1	2.839	.11
Fiscal 1982	77.2	78.0	.042	.84
Direct-labor effectiveness				
First quarter 1983	119.0	106.9	2.584	.13
Fiscal 1982	105.4	104.7	.017	.90

In sum, three of the four cases are in the anticipated direction, and two of them approach statistical significance (P = .11 and .13). The difference on the deviant case—Overall productivity, Fiscal 1982—is almost certainly random.

Productivity and Physical Symptoms

The covariation of the productivity measures with physical symptoms excites interest and perhaps surprise as well. The expectation-for-testing proposes that productivity and symptoms are inversely associated, for obvious reasons. Workers experiencing health problems probably would not work at optimum levels.

Table 5.4 provides the relevant data, and three points direct attention to the highlights. First, the pattern of coefficients violates expectations for the first seven measures. Physical symptoms and productivity are *directly* associated: high productivity is associated with high rates of symptoms. In sum, 34 of the 35 coefficients in Table 5.4 trend in this direction.

Second, none of the 15 correlations for clients' criticism scores attain the .05 level. Hence, their almost unanimous direction must be interpreted with caution. Note, however, that 14 of those 15 correlations imply that better outcomes are associated with high rates of symptoms. Specifically, work stations with higher symptoms scores tend to have lower rates of criticism from their clients.

Third, for the first seven measures the pattern is not only regular but has a substantial robustness. To begin, consider the two first-quarter productivity measures, which probably are least influenced by possible ceiling effects. The record? Eight of their ten correlations in Table 5.4 attain statistical significance, and account for almost 8.3 percent of the variance, on average. The other five of the first seven measures of productivity in Table 5.4 support a similar interpretation, although less markedly so. In sum, 8 of the latter 25 correlations attain the .05 level, and on average they explain over 7.6 percent of the variation in productivity X symptoms scores.

Productivity and Performance Appraisals

At Site B, it is possible to estimate the association between performance appraisals and the ten measures of productivity, but methodological concerns require tentative interpretation. That is, productivity data are available at the work-station level and performance appraisals are self-reported by individuals. This difference between levels of data requires a major accommodation to permit a consciously-hedged comparison. The agency utilizes five appraisal

TABLE 5.5
Correlations of Self-Reports about Performance Appraisals and
Ten Measures of Productivity, Site B (N = 55)

Productivity Measures	Simple Correlation
Overall productivity	
First quarter, 1983	.01
Fiscal 1982	.05
Direct-labor effectiveness	
First quarter 1983	-.04
Fiscal 1982	.01
Headquarters ratings, fiscal 1982	
Management	.02
Quality	-.23[a]
Combined	-.12
Clients' criticism scores, fiscal 1982	
"Poor" ratings, percent	.20[b]
"Not courteous," percent	.11
Combined, percent	.21[b]

[a] $p < .01$, one tailed.

[b] $p < .05$, one-tailed.

categories which are aggregated and averaged for each work station, and these aggregate means are then correlated with the ten measures of work-station productivity.

Table 5.5 reflects the expected pattern, but not robustly. Six of ten coefficients have the expected signs, which—because of the coding convention utilized—are predicted to be negative for the first seven measures and positive for the three others. Three of the six cases with expected directions attain the .05 level, in addition, and account for nearly 4.6 percent of the variance, on average.

Implications of Productivity for the Environmental Model

The results concerning productivity constitute an important test of the general model underlying this research, and two sections highlight its mixed results. A first section schematizes the productivity-relevant results, and a second isolates several senses in which those results must be hedged. Again, the two sections relate to the basic model underlying this research—which can be labelled an environmental model of burnout or, taking another perspective, as a multiple-outcomes model. These two sections will move this analysis forward to include a greater variety of covariants than in the two previous reviews of the findings. One of these efforts has already been described in chapter five, and the earliest summary was presented in chapter four. The model's main-line effects may be sketched this way:

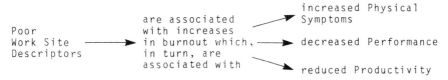

Schema of Productivity-Related Results

Figure 5.2 provides an overview of the results detailed above, relying on earlier conventions. As an aid to memory, all associations referred to are statistically significant; and their strength is estimated as slight where approximately 1 percent or so of the variance is accounted for, modest for approximately 5 percent, and moderate for approximately 10 percent shared variance. All associations are labelled A or B to distinguish the two basic research sites.

The findings in this chapter do not require abandonment of the general model underlying this research, but some modifications clearly are in order. Moreover, future research will be necessary to provide closure on several features, to which some preliminary attention will be given below.

FIGURE 5.2
Summary of Productivity-related Associations and Their Strengths

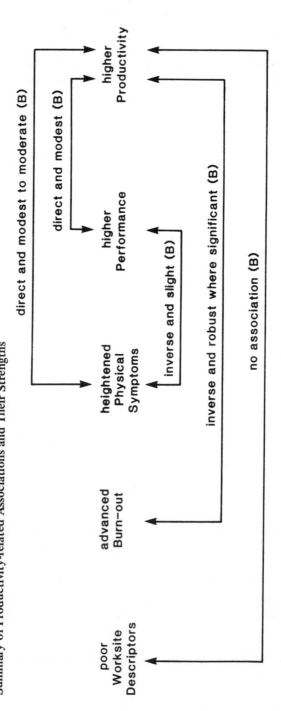

IMPLICATIONS FOR THE PHASE MODEL OF BURNOUT

The findings concerning performance appraisals and productivity provide only general support for the phase model, but two aspects in particular discourage any negative conclusions at this time. Paramountly, the several tests of association trend in expected directions, and there is strong reason to suspect that conditions at both Sites A and B are such as to disguise or distort regularities rather than to induce spurious ones. Thus, performance appraisals tend to be lower for those in advanced phases of burnout, even though a kind of "grade inflation" at both sites should operate to distort the pattern of association. Relatedly, productivity at Site B tends to decline with higher distributions of advanced phases in work units. And this occurs in spite of a kind of measurement double-whammy—agency policy mandates a ceiling as well as a floor on productivity, and Site B provides neither measures of individual behavior nor identification of immediate work groups.

It should be added that we incline toward a benign view of the present results because of data that cannot be shared with the reader. In another study, an important objective indicator of performance mapped very regularly and robustly with the phases in one large population. For understandable but lamentable reasons, the host decided to exercise a contractual provision for confidentiality not only concerning the specific locus and phase X productivity covariation there, but even about the general economic sector in which the study took place.

In any case, the phase model still stands in clear need of testing against better measures of performance and productivity. This injunction is not only general, but relates specifically to Site B evidence that higher quantitative and qualitative productivity are paid for in terms of heightened symptoms of physical dis-ease. This evidence stands in opposition to the ideation underlying the general model, and the relative strength of the association suggests that physical symptoms may constitute more of a main-line effect with respect to productivity than a feedback or reinforcing loop. The next section provides some conceptual detail on this central point, but empirical closure must wait on future investigations.

Thumbnail Research Design and Four Conceptual Approaches

From one point of view, the failure reflected above to improve on the productivity-relevant findings over a two-year period may seem unexceptional and understandable. In more detailed form, that is to say, the bulk of the materials above were published earlier (Golembiewski, Munzenrider, and Stevenson, 1986, chapter five). Researchers in all areas of organizational inquiry have pointed up the difficulty of studying productivity, and especially in the public service sectors (e.g., Yeager, 1987, p. 417; Smith, 1984, pp. 93–103). A long litany of explanations has been offered. For example, we are told that many organizations do not measure productivity or, if they do, data are available only for such large categories of employees that it becomes difficult and at times even impossible to assign direct responsibility for effects. Moreover, others argue that performance appraisals have great political relevance but are made in such unstandardized and even subterranean ways that interpreting them is hazardous (Longenecker, Gioia, and Sims, 1987). Finally, but only for present purposes, it might be very embarrassing for some organizations to make available certain productivity data as to the accuracy of which they have little doubt. Death rates in hospitals for various classes of surgical procedures seem to fall into this category, constituting a kind of ultimate measure of staff performance.

In principle, designs for estimating burnout X productivity interaction pose no deep difficulties. Take health services, for example, which observers see as posing difficult measurement issues but where real research opportunities exist (e.g., Golembiewski, 1987a). Take lifetime, chronic-care services in retirement medical communities, with multiple field units that differ basically only in physical locus. Demographics could help eliminate the alternative hypothesis that individual differences contribute to any observed effects. Moreover, over the long-run, there would be little reason to expect major differences in future presenting symptoms or in morbidity levels of those individuals qualifying for membership. Morbidity rates then could be observed over time, for the purpose of testing for associations with differences in the distributions of burnout phases in the several loci. The cards seem nicely stacked in favor of a relatively clean test of such associations, for small units in organizations seem to have an affinity for extreme phases of burnout. Chapter six, in particular, provides data on this central point. Roughly, all organizations of any size seem to have, in the aggregate, a substantial number of individuals assigned to both the most and least advanced phases of burnout. But individual work units within organizations seem tilted toward low *or* high burnout, on very definite balance (Golembiewski, 1984; Golembiewski, Munzenrider, and Stevenson, 1986, pp. 182-85). Such an effect was suspected at Site B, as discussed above, but researchers were allowed to disaggregate the total organization only to the regional level, which could involve populations of 100 or so. Hence, possible burnout X phases interaction may be disguised.

Practical issues bedevil such a design, of course, but strong conceptual reasons encourage someone to transcend the difficulties, either in a chronic-care setting or some similar site. Why might (for example) an association of morbidity X phases occur? At least four possibilities exist. First, and perhaps the least significant, associations or effects might derive from what the French describe as "going to work with one buttock." Evidence reviewed in chapters one through three, especially, supports such a view of withholding one's self from work because it is considered need-depriving, if not just "dumb." People in advanced phases report lower satisfaction with work, higher job-related tension, lower involvement in the organization, and so on. Performance and productivity effects might be expected.

Second, advanced burnout seems consistent with an increased preoccupation with self. The association of physical symptoms and the phases, for example, supports such a view. Credibly, such a preoccupation with self could be associated with lower quality control at work. This would particularly be the case, of course, under the condition that seems to obtain—that work units have an affinity for those persons in one or the other of the two classes of advanced phases of burnout. In health-care settings, the dominance of advanced phases might well heighten the incidence of negative outcomes, even serious negative outcomes. Relatedly, outcomes might well improve where the employees cluster in the least-advanced phases.

Third, high proportions of a work unit in advanced phases might well create a generally negative emotional tone or climate that could impact adversely on (let us say) medical outcomes. Two conceptual pathways can be distinguished, at least. Thus, attitudes among staff certainly could affect what services are provided, when, and with what style. More generally, the emotional quality of a site might impact upon how clients respond to the several crises likely to face them as they approach the ends of their lives. Such a wholistic view has gained a greatly-increased currency, of course, even though the evidence for it seems essentially anecdotal (e.g., Cousins, 1983).

This book includes some support for such a view. Chapters eight and nine, especially, provide data that tie burnout to group properties as well as to clinically relevant affective states. But detailing their association with productivity in health-care settings, as well as with the phases, remains a job for the future.

Fourth, conceivably, burnout effects could be so extreme as to encourage malfeasance in health-care settings. Some evidence of this kind already exists (Jones, 1981), but one can only speculate whether the range of negative effects extends to morbidity in settings like chronic-care retirement communities. In contrast, the three previous perspectives imply less-direct associations between the phases of burnout and ultimate health-care effects.

6. THE MAGNITUDE OF THE BURNOUT PROBLEM: PERSPECTIVES ON SEQUENCE, INCIDENCE, AND PERSISTENCE

The recent flurry of attention to burnout leaves numerous questions unanswered, even as it raises the consciousness of many about what seems one of the contemporary work site problems—perhaps *the* major concern. Here the focus is on a single question, which requires a very complex response as a working approximation to an answer.

HOW BAD IS BURNOUT?

An answer to this key question does not come easily; however, at the present stage of development, the phase model helps. The evidence suggests that, all in all, things are pretty bad, in the following ways:

- Burnout does not seem rooted in exotic causes, but seems rather to be basically triggered by events rooted in the character and quality of features ubiquitous to the work site.
- Burnout seems to have a high incidence in organizations. Many people seem to have "it" in advanced degrees.
- Burnout seems to have a high persistence. It seems to last for extended periods in most organizations.

Possible Precursors and Consequences of Burnout

What say the data about the usefulness of the environmental model of burnout underlying this research? Figure 6.1 provides the broad context. The figure sketches the overall pattern of results, with the usual conventions applying. Thus A and B refer to the two primary research sites. "Robust" refers to estimates of

FIGURE 6.1
Overall Summary of Burnout Associations and Their Magnitudes

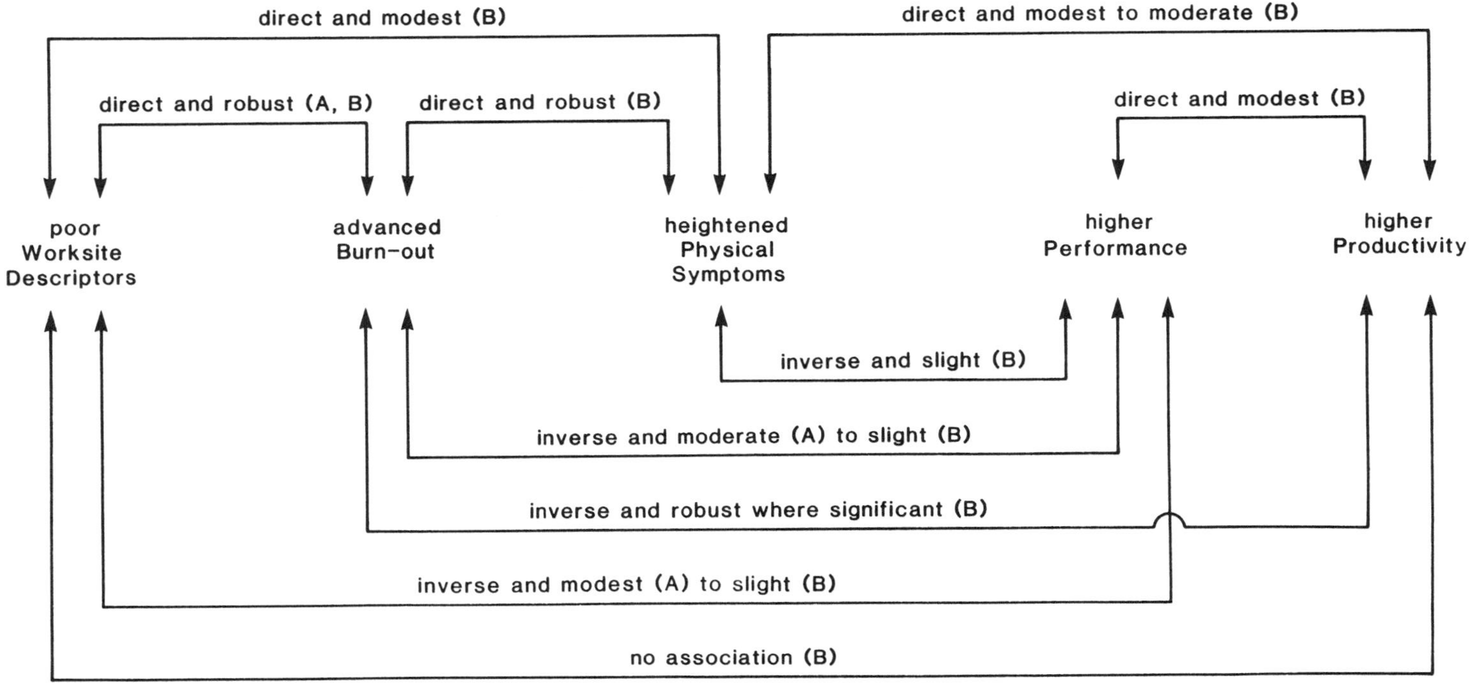

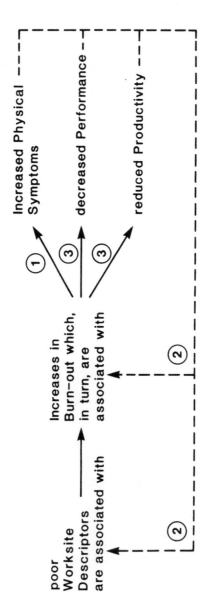

Case I: Environmental Model

shared variance at the 15 percent level or greater; and the labels "moderate," "modest," and "slight" target the 10, 5, and 1 percent levels, respectively. All the associations referred to attain statistical significance, so the labels refer to the robustness of associations that are unlikely to reflect chance variation.

Figure 6.1 supports two broad conclusions. The front-load or input components of the general model underlying this research seem quite consistent with the available data. Two of the outcomes proposed by the model, however, demand further research. Brief attention goes to each point, in turn.

Clarity about Front-Load Components

Relatively strong evidence suggests the usefulness of the front-load components of the general model, which involve the linkages of three variables. Witness the robust association of work site features with the phases of burnout, along with progressive burnout's strong and direct linkages with physical symptoms. These contrast with the modest if still direct association between symptoms and work site features.

The pattern attracts attention for several reasons. The pattern suggests a temporal or causal linkage of work site descriptors to burnout and then to physical symptoms, with a secondary or reinforcing linkage between symptoms and work site features. In addition, that pattern suggests that a longish tradition of research and applied effort has been on the right track. Specifically, the results reinforce the long-standing efforts to improve the work site, and the findings also motivate even more forceful efforts of this kind (for example, Golembiewski, 1982). Most of this work follows an environmental model, and sees awkward outcomes at work as reasonable reactions to need-depriving policies, procedures, practices, and structures.

Questions and Outcomes

Complicated by measurement problems, the data provide support for at least two possible interpretations of the other two major proposed burnout outcomes—performance and productivity. Case I does not require rejecting the model underlying this research, *if* interactions among the three outcomes are set aside for the moment. A skeletal schema helps target the three main points for discussion. Interpretively, as the environmental model requires, ① symptoms are robustly linked with burnout; and, consistently, the several linkages between the three outcomes and work site features, ②, have magnitudes that are modest, at best. In addition, though performance and productivity, ③, are seldom robustly associated with burnout, all associations are in the direction proposed by the environmental model. Moreover, measurement problems may well dilute any associations and, if that is the case, the present results reflect conservative estimates.

Case II concentrates on the associations *between* outcomes, one pair of which has significant implications for both theory and application. The relatively strong *and* direct linkage between symptoms and productivity is not only unexpected but—given the reasoning sketched in the previous chapter—may be a conservative estimate because of the unresolvable issues with productivity measurements at Site B. There, high quantity and quality of productivity seems associated with heightened physical symptoms.

Two outcome stems can be retrofitted to account for this association; these will be distinguished as Case IIA and Case IIB. Only the dominant effects are sketched here, in the interests of simplicity and convenience.

Case IIA suggests the common, trade-off view of work. In this model, physical symptoms play a central role in the sequence of effects rather than being one of the direct multiple outcomes of burnout. Case IIA takes this form:

Case IIA
Trade-off Model

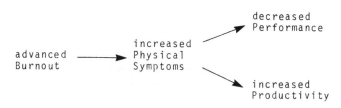

Here, management maintains some balance between illness or symptomology with productivity and performance. Some such notion underlies much of the industrial medicine approach, for example, which adopts a kind of inoculation strategy to increase a person's resistance to physical illness or symptoms—by diet, exercise, meditation, and other stress management techniques—but with little focus on changes in the work site.

Better productivity measures than the present set may strongly support Case IIA, but the fit with present data is ragged at a few spots. Thus, the data indicate that performance appraisals have an inverse association with physical symptoms, as well as a direct linkage with productivity, which Case IIA does not nicely encompass.

Case IIB fits a bit more comfortably with the present result, and also merits emphasis because of its incongruence with the "corporate wellness" view that has such a contemporary prominence. Case IIB proposes a "long line" of sequential outcomes of burnout, in this form:

Case IIB
Long-line Model

Here, the employing organization pushes for productivity at any cost, and discards those unable or unwilling to comply.

Neither the body of behavioral research nor the present data permit a choice between these two versions of Case II, and questions come far more easily than even tentative answers. For example, the productivity data come from a single organization, which happens to be in the public sector. This suggests two interpretive possibilities. The narrower one proposes that the relationship between physical symptoms and productivity derives from the specific ways that Site B manages its affairs and does its business. More expansively, Site B is a public-sector organization, often a political storm-center, and that raises the issue of possible differences between public and business sectors.

So this analysis proceeds with a mixed gait—call it tentative optimism or exuberant constraint. Whatever the descriptor, the following sections—dealing with the incidence and persistence of the phases—urge that this analysis *must proceed*, problems or no. The situation seems too serious to justify any other course.

Incidence of Burnout in 33 Settings

Despite its clear salience and despite alarums from all points of the compass, *no* studies deal directly with the incidence of burnout in organizations. We know many kinds of people get it—helping professionals (Maslach and Jackson, 1981), students and teachers, as well as NFL football coaches, *inter alia*. We lack data, however, on what proportions of various professions get it, and no firm data inform us of the degrees to which people in various organizations experience it.

This lacuna is no mystery, of course. It reflects the unavailability of a valid and reliable measure of strain, conveniently applicable to numerous organizations. And it is this critical gap that motivates the development of the phase model.

Clearly, the guidelines for public policy in this area are ill-informed in important particulars. For example, if extreme cases of burnout are widely distributed, strategies for dealing with this dis-ease would differ profoundly from those appropriate if (as many propose) only certain smallish subpopulations are at risk. Thus Maslach (1982) writes of burnout as an affliction of "those who care," while Freudenberger (1980) sees its greatest impact on the gifted and competent whom he describes as more likely to be idealistic.

Expectations about Incidence: Humanist and Realist Views

Is burnout an affirmative action dis-ease, or one substantially restricted to some elites or professions? The question is crucial, patently.

Before introducing the data, consider what the common wisdom says about the incidence of burnout. Several hundred managers were asked about the distribution of phases of burnout they expect to find in their organizations, and also about the distribution they find tolerable. These "actual" and "ideal" distributions almost universally take on a "one-hump" shape, but with an interesting difference between two clusters of informants.

The two clusters of managers might be described as "organizational humanists" and "organizational realists." The humanists constitute the smaller cohort, and they want to shift their normal curve decisively toward the least-advanced phases with the goal of eliminating all (or almost all) cases of advanced burnout. The organization realists constitute the far larger group of managers, and their one-hump curves for ideal and actual distributions of the phases are similar in shape to those of the humanists, but trend more toward the advanced phases. The realists observe that organization membership requires doing uninteresting or difficult things, at awkward times, for almost all members, at least some of the time, and for many members much or all of the time. The realists locate 20 or more percent of their employees in Phases VI through VIII and, given various (to them) intractable realities, place their realistic ideal at perhaps 10 percent.

Both realists and humanists see too much burnout and both desire to shift their bell-shaped curves toward the less-advanced phases. The humanists see less of Phases VI-VIII in practice, however, and their goal is to see more of Phases I-III than the realists acknowledge.

Notes on Hosts and Methods

The methodological posture for gathering data about the distribution of burnout is quite flexible, as befits this "natural history" stage of inquiry and as is necessitated by the brief period for data-gathering allotted to us by most of the organizations. An *ad hoc* network of observers[1] sought hosts in several countries, with the unit of analysis being defined in general and wholistic terms—all employees of a small oil-exploration firm, the total enrollment in an undergraduate course, all employees of a U.S. chain of nursing homes, and so on. No rigorous measurement was attempted of the collective features of the populations—their cultures or climates, structural arrangements, and so on. Refined analysis can hardly be so cavalier.

The hierarchical status of respondents also was determined, when appropriate. Four classes of respondents are distinguished:

- executives, or those who manage middle-managers
- middle-managers, or those who manage supervisors
- supervisors, or those who manage service-providers or workers
- service-providers or workers

Data on Incidence of Burnout

The summary descriptions and hopes of both realists and humanists are substantially off-the-mark. Basically, the distribution of employees by phases in most organizations is bimodal, with most employees clustering in the most- or least-advanced phases. Moreover, few organizations approximate the "actual" estimates, and almost all organizations have a much greater proportion of VI-VIII employees than even the realists acknowledge. Finally, reaching

TABLE 6.1
Incidence of Phases of Burnout in Selected Populations, Absolute Numbers and Percentages (N = 33)

	N =	I LoLoLo	II HiLoLo	III LoHiLo	IV HiHiLo	V LoLoHi	VI HiLoHi	VII LoHiHi	VIII HiHiHi
							Phases of Burnout, in Percent		
1. Stratified sample of managers cross-matched by sex and hierarchical level who were volunteer respondents from a number of Canadian firms and public agencies	244	79 32.4%	42 17.2	35 14.3	20 8.2	15 6.1	22 9.0	0 0.0	31 12.7
2. Site A, Day 1, a business division of a multinational firm with highly attractive conditions of employment but experiencing major market pressures	296	121 40.9%	31 10.6	23 7.7	14 4.7	41 13.9	27 9.1	22 7.3	17 5.8
3. Site A, Day 365, after a comprehensive effort involving a shift in management style from "loyalty" to "competence"	229	84 36.7%	21 9.2	42 18.3	6 2.6	20 8.7	17 7.4	17 7.4	22 9.6
4. Chartered Canadian accountants serving their several firms in personnel roles; who met for a specialized training program	36	9 41.7%	3 11.1	4 8.3	2 8.3	2 5.6	4 2.8	3 0.0	9 22.2
5. A division of a U.S. federal agency, whose employees often have intense experiences with clients	1535	352 22.9%	107 7.0	193 12.6	124 8.1	107 7.0	176 11.5	109 7.1	367 23.9
6. All operating and supervisory employees of a chain of nursing homes, generally considered the "Cadillac" of their type	2389	694 29.1%	0 0.0	0 0.0	337 14.1	0 0.0	442 18.5	227 9.5	689 28.9
7. Salespersons and supervisors from a small mid-American hardware firm	64	5 7.8%	7 10.9	23 35.9	17 26.6	3 4.7	3 4.7	0 0.0	6 9.4

115

TABLE 6.1 (continued)

Phases of Burnout, in Percent

	N =	I LoLoLo	II HiLoLo	III LoHiLo	IV HiHiLo	V LoLoHi	VI HiLoHi	VII LoHiHi	VIII HiHiHi
8. MBA students, Canadian university	20	5 25.0%	0 0.0	1 5.0	1 5.0	0 0.0	6 30.0	0 0.0	7 35.0
9. Men and women enrolled in Ontario, Canada, Police College	424	78 18.4%	32 7.5	69 16.3	17 4.0	31 7.3	38 9.0	24 5.7	135 31.8
10. Total employees, Canadian oil exploration firm	132	71 54.0%	27 20.0	2 1.5	1 0.8	8 6.1	19 14.0	2 1.5	2 1.5
11. Total enrollemnt, undergraduate OB course, Canada	114	15 13.6%	40 35.1	0 0.0	3 2.6	7 6.1	40 35.1	1 0.9	8 7.0
12. Total enrollment, undergraduate business policy course, Canada	102	23 22.5%	15 14.7	1 1.0	1 1.0	19 18.6	35 34.3	1 1.0	7 6.9
13. Total corporate Human Resources professional staff	31	6 19.4%	0 0.0	1 3.2	1 3.2	7 22.6	7 22.6	3 9.7	6 19.4
14. Executives and mid-managers of a local probation office	53	16 30.2%	10 18.9	4 2.5	7 13.6	1 1.9	2 3.8	3 5.7	10 18.9
15. Male and female police in an educational setting, Canada	708	165 23.3%	50 7.1	103 14.5	35 4.9	52 7.3	84 11.9	56 7.9	163 23.0
16. All employees in one region of a corporation of life-care retirement communities	864	195 22.6%	59 6.8	126 14.6	70 8.1	76 8.8	80 9.3	83 9.6	175 20.3
17. Top three executive and managerial levels, medical specialties firm	36	6 16.7%	2 5.6	2 5.6	5 13.9	3 8.3	3 8.3	4 11.1	11 30.6
18. Clerical section in a municipal government, Canada	58	11 19.0%	4 6.9	5 8.6	5 8.6	1 1.7	5 8.6	10 17.2	17 29.3

	N =	I LoLoLo	II HiLoLo	III LoHiLo	IV HiHiLo	V LoLoHi	VI HiLoHi	VII LoHiHi	VIII HiHiHi
19. Clerical section in munici-pal government, after layoff announcement, Canada	78	18 23.1%	2 2.6	9 11.5	2 2.6	12 15.4	2 2.6	6 7.7	27 34.6
20. Laborers in a municipal govern-ment, Canada	25	6 24.0%	2 8.0	4 16.0	2 8.0	1 4.0	5 20.0	2 8.0	3 12.0
21. Laborers in a municipal govern-ment, after layoff announcement, Canada	38	5 13.2%	1 2.6	6 15.8	5 13.2	3 7.9	2 5.3	4 10.5	12 31.6
22. All professional personnel, Italian consulting firm	10	2 20.0%	1 10.0	1 10.0	2 20.0	0 0.0	3 30.0	1 10.0	0 0.0
23. All dentists, group dental practice A	17	14 82.4%	1 5.9	1 5.9	1 5.9	0 0.0	0 0.0	0 0.0	0 0.0
24. All dentists, group dental practice B	16	4 25.0%	3 18.8	4 25.0	2 12.5	1 6.3	1 6.3	1 6.3	0 0.0
25. All employees of a non-profit, denominational, full-service hospital, excluding doctors	772	227 29.4%	85 11.0	105 13.6	81 10.5	59 7.6	64 8.3	32 4.1	119 15.4
26. All employees of a non-profit, denominational, full-service hospital, excluding doctors	637	190 24.8%	61 9.6	69 10.8	71 11.1	41 6.4	68 10.7	33 5.2	104 16.3
27. All employees of a full-care community hospital in Can-adian regional center in rural area, excluding doctors	399	92 23.1%	20 5.0	87 21.8	32 8.0	22 5.5	36 9.0	29 7.3	86 20.3
28. All employees in Midwestern U.S. medical clinic	111	15 13.5%	9 8.1	5 4.5	18 16.2	14 12.6	11 9.9	4 3.6	35 31.5
29. Hospital administrators, from numerous locations at develop-ment programs	94	17 18.1%	17 18.1	7 7.4	11 11.7	3 3.2	17 18.1	2 2.1	20 21.3

Phases of Burnout, in Percent

TABLE 6.1 (continued)

| | N = | Phases of Burnout, in Percent | | | | | | | |
		I LoLoLo	II HiLoLo	III LoHiLo	IV HiHiLo	V LoLoHi	VI HiLoHi	VII LoHiHi	VIII HiHiHi
30. All employees in Midwestern chronic health-care setting	89	19 21.4%	6 6.7	10 11.2	10 11.2	4 4.5	16 18.0	3 3.4	21 23.6
31. All employees of a full-care, regional hospital in Canadian agricultural region, excluding doctors	196	46 23.5%	13 6.6	30 15.3	20 10.2	15 7.7	19 9.7	20 10.2	33 16.8
32. National U.S. chain, life-care retirement communities, all direct-care employees	2,123	435 20.5%	0 0.0	365 17.2	252 11.9	0 0.0	447 21.1	347 16.3	277 13.1
33. Officers from Illinois State Police	91	29 31.9%	12 13.2	6 6.6	8 8.8	1 1.1	15 16.5	2 2.2	18 19.8
	N = 12,031	3,054 25.4%	683 5.7	1,343 11.2	1,183 9.8	569 4.7	1,716 14.3	1,051 8.7	2,432 20.2

the "ideal" distribution of phases represents a major challenge—for both realists and humanists, and even in the "best" organizations.

Table 6.1[2] presents data on the distribution of the phases of burnout in 33 organizations of various kinds, with the total number of respondents exceeding 12,000. Note that Table 6.1 reflects convenient targets rather than a scientific sample. Openness to inquiry alone distinguishes the cases in the table, and one can interpret this openness as characteristic of "better" organizations or, perhaps, of those in deep trouble. The authors incline to the former view, but acknowledge the latter.

Table 6.1 suggests four classes of conclusions. They relate to: the overall distribution of assignments of unit members by phases, the ranges of distributions of extreme phases, the ranges of assignments to intermediate phases of burnout, and the effects of hierarchical status.

Overall Distribution by Phases

No firm conventions apply for summarizing the distribution of phase assignments, but one general pattern seems obvious. Looked at in the most simple way, roughly a quarter of the cases fall in each of the most extreme phases (I and VIII). Using an aggregating convention that has proved useful for other purposes (e.g., Golembiewski, 1984), alternatively, Phases I-III encompass 42.3 percent of all respondents and Phases VI-VIII include 43.2 percent.

Two conclusions leap from such elementary summaries. Assignments tend to cluster in the extreme phases, not only overall but, typically, within particular organizations or discrete systems. This rejects the common wisom, flatly. The distribution of phases is not a "normal curve," but a determinedly bimodal one. Moreover, burnout seems far more of a problem than either realists or humanists acknowledge.

Ranges of Extreme Phases

Despite the general tendencies, the 33 cases do reflect substantial ranges of proportions of members classified in the extreme phases. Consider the summary in Table 6.2. It focuses on two clusters—the three most and three least advanced phases of burnout.

Table 6.2 reflects a strong tendency to bimodalism. For example, less than 1 percent of all respondents are in units that do not have at least 20 percent of their members classified in both of the two clusters of extreme burnout phases. Looked at another way, the simultaneous clustering in two sets of extreme phases is reflected in two facts. Over seven in ten of those in Phases VI-VIII will be in units having between 40 and 60 percent of their members in those three advanced phases. The corresponding proportion for those in Phases I-III? Over five in ten persons classified in I-III will be in units 40-60 percent populated by persons in those three phases.

This bimodality may seem puzzling but can be explained by the apparently great salience of burnout in relation to the qualities of the group of first-reports—

i.e., those people in organizations reporting directly to some supervisor or manager (Golembiewski, 1983; Rountree, 1984). Put another way, the total organization does not appear to be the behaviorally relevant unit for analyzing burnout. The group of first-reports has that distinction among those studied so far. In the aggregate, knowing the phase of burnout of an individual permits the best prediction of the phases of at least a majority of all other members of that individual's immediate work group (Golembiewski, 1983; Rountree, 1984).

Bimodality is a central finding because it does not support the strong contemporary claims about the potency of *a* macro-organizational culture (e.g., Peters and Waterman, 1983). The present view inclines far more to the position that the *multiple* cultures of numerous immediate work groups influence differences in burnout and some research directly associates degrees of burnout with patterns of significant differences in the specific group properties of micro-units. See chapters seven and eight for some details about group and cultural properties.

Ranges of Intermediate Phases

With the exception of three units (Cases #7, #13, and #28), as bimodalism requires, the present populations have a narrow range of members classified in the two intermediate or "interval" phases—IV and V. Overall, Table 6.1 shows

TABLE 6.2
Proportions of Respondents in Two Extreme Sets of Phases

	Phases I - III		Phases VI - VIII	
	No. of Units Within Range	% of All I - III Respondents	No. of Units Within Range	% of All VI - VIII Respondents
0-10%	0	0	1	0
10.1-20	0	0	3	0.7
20.1-30	5	14.7	6	8.1
30.1-40	7	18.5	7	15.6
40.1-50	10	44.2	11	27.8
50.1-60	5	13.9	4	47.6
60.1-70	4	6.5	1	0.3
70.1 or greater	2	2.3	0	0

TABLE 6.3
Proportions of Respondents in Intermediate Phases

Range of Those Classified in Phases IV and V	No. of Units Within Range	% of all IV-V Respondents
5% or less	1	0.1
5.1 - 10	4	1.7
10.1 - 15	12	57.4
15.1 - 20	11	36.5
20.1 - 30	4	3.2
30.1 or greater	1	1.1

that Phase IV contains 9.8 percent of all assignments, and Phase V has 4.7 percent. Looked at another way, about 70 percent of the units have 10–20 percent of their members in Phases IV and V combined, and these 23 units encompass over 94 percent of all individuals in the two intermediate phases. See Table 6.3.

Effects of Hierarchical Level

In the applicable cases, hierarchical level is not a major covariant of the phases of burnout. This reinforces other findings (e.g., Golembiewski and Scicchitano, 1983), and stands apart from the literature that implies the significance of status in so many particulars (e.g., Golembiewski and Munzenrider, 1977).

Implications of Data on the Incidence of Burnout

Three caveats help frame several significant implications suggested by the data in Table 6.1. Paramountly, the adequacy of the High/Low norms for the three MBI domains is critical in any interpretation of the data. The present norms are based on Site B data, and seem conservative because the norming population probably sets a stiff standard for High scores. Opinions on this central point can differ, and future research may undermine the present judgment. But the norms stand for the present, at least.

In addition, the one-shot data here permit only tentative conclusions about a central distinction underlying the phase model of burnout—chronic versus acute onset. *The* chronic sequence for progressive burnout seems to be: I → II → IV → VIII. Many acute flight-paths might be envisioned—e.g., I or II → V → VIII. In the acute cases, an individual is precipitated (from I or II, let us say) into a situation beyond comfortable coping limits. Emotional Exhaustion can increase suddenly (V) and, subsequently, an individual's work performance and personal relationships might deteriorate (VIII). The unexpected death of a central person, such as a spouse, might induce this flight-path. Only longitudinal analysis will permit specificity concerning several significant questions about the phase model in connection with chronicity and acuteness of onset which, in turn, will have profound implications for treatment. See also chapters eight and nine.

The third and final caveat also relates to the one-time observations relied on in the present design. Entrance to, and exit from, the advanced stages cannot be distinguished here. Since good reasons encourage the suspicion that entrance may have covariants that differ from exit, at least in degree, the failure to distinguish the directionality of phase assignments no doubt confounds the interpretation of present results. This may be a conservative effect, however, in that interphase differences may well be "blurred" by aggregating exit/entrance cases.

These three caveats must discipline interpretations of Table 6.1, to be sure, but six points seem worth making. They involve: the magnitude of the problems posed by the proportion of individuals classified in advanced phases of burnout; the desirability or acceptability of the reported incidences of the phases; the bimodality of phase distributions; the implications of the observed distributions for chronic and acute onset; a brief discussion of cases that differ from the central tendencies in the panel; and a final emphasis on the broad impact of the findings concerning the incidence of the phases.

Burnout Seems a Substantial Problem

It may be dramatic to write of the incidence of advanced phases of burnout in epidemiological terms but, given the covariants analyzed in chapters two through five, Table 6.1 justifies considering burnout as a substantial problem. Specifically, at the unit level of analysis, only 4 of the 33 populations have less than 20 percent of their members classified in the three most-advanced phases of burnout, and these four cases are small populations. More ominously still, 16 of those 33 units have 40 percent or more of their responding members in Phases VI-VIII. The picture does not appear brighter at the individual level of analysis; over 43 percent of all respondents are classified in the three most-advanced phases.

Substantial proportions of all populations tested, then, will suffer the consequences of these apparent covariants of advanced burnout: poor attitudes concerning the character of the work site; high levels of physical symptoms; poor performance appraisals; and lower productivity.

One cannot be certain that the units in Table 6.1 are representative but one can argue cogently that, if anything, they underrepresent the "worst" organizations. Presumably, organizations with very high concentrations of the most-advanced phases would be less open to researchers than the present panel. So Table 6.1 may reflect a conservative view of what exists in the world of organizations.

Burnout Incidence Seems Unacceptable

Table 6.1 in its several stages of evolution has been reviewed with several managerial populations and few consider acceptable even its very lowest incidences of advanced phases of burnout. Most estimates of "tolerable levels" cluster in the 5--10 percent ranges for Phases VI-VIII, and the ideal is in the 5 percent range. The most favorable incidences reported in Table 6.1 are two to four times higher than those tolerable levels, while the average incidence approximately quadruples the 10 percent estimate of "tolerable."

Hence, Table 6.1 reflects not only empirical data but also raises a serious normative challenge. What levels of burnout should be associated with the desirable organization?

Phase Distributions Seem Bimodal

In most of the 33 populations, the "normal curve" does not serve as a useful representation of the distributions of phases. A two-humped curve serves far better. Specifically, 29 of the 33 cases have at least 20 percent of their members in each of the two clusters of the three extreme phases, and 15 cases approximate 40 percent in each of those clusters of phases. Generally, in addition, the larger the unit, the closer the proportions approach 55 percent in VI-VIII and 40 percent in I-III.

The prime implication for managerial action and policy seems direct. One should not think, in general, of a single thrust that will accommodate to the situations of most organization members with regard to burnout. Most members of most macro-organizations will cluster in the two sets of extreme phases of burnout. And management policies must relate to employees where they are.

The present view contrasts sharply with common managerial views, which typically assume that normal distributions dominate in nature—i.e., that most cases of burnout fall somewhere in the middle phases. This myopia encourages visualizing some single set of policies and procedures relevant to burnout that "imply the greatest good for the largest number."

The burnout distributions in Tables 6.1 and 6.2 suggest the need for a portfolio of starkly-opposed policies and procedures to deal with a two-humped reality. Oppositely, perhaps the dominant managerial metaphor, the ideal for many, suggests a "smoothly running machine" or a "well-integrated team." In sharp opposition, the two-hump distribution of burnout phases suggests two clusters of ships passing in the night; and at least for a substantial proportion of those ships, the seas may be very stormy.

The point is also at substantial odds with those observers led by Peters and Waterman (1982)—who focus on an organizational culture and applaud its alleged salubrious effects. Bimodality of burnout supports the long-standing concept of multiple and interacting sub-cultures (e.g., Shils, 1951). Indeed, growing evidence implies that the immediate work group is the prime locus of burnout, not the macro-organization. Independent studies (Golembiewski, 1983; Rountree, 1984) show a very strong affinity of groups of first-reports for one or the other of the two clusters of extreme phases—with some 70 to 80 percent of all respondents coming from immediate work units that have at least a majority of their members classified in either clusters I–III or VI–VIII. See also chapter seven.

Two powerful possibilities or probabilities inhere in this basic bimodality. Presumably, local supervisory practices and policies impact most on member burnout, in opposition to the impact of an intergroup culture. This does not surprise (e.g., Shils and Janowitz, 1948), but it poses complex analytical and practical challenges. Moreover, it follows that most burnout, as measured by the phase model, is chronic. Hence, it relates to persisting features of work, rather than to acute onset associated with traumatic life events.

Phase Distributions and Chronic or Acute Burnout

Despite the nonlongitudinal character of Table 6.1, it permits some speculation about chronicity and acuteness. Consider the low proportions of those classified in Phases IV and V, as well as the narrow range of those proportions. Other data later presented in a section on persistence also suggest both the infrequency and instability of assignments to Phases IV and V.

Both infrequency and instability argue for distinguishing chronic from acute burnout. Thus Phase IV is seen as central in chronic outset: I → II → IV → VIII. Whence the instability? Phase IV implies difficulties with both relationships and task, which quickly would lead to heightened Emotional Exhaustion. That is, IV soon would lead to VIII and, absent sharp improvement, Phase VIII would tend to persist. This is consistent with the raw percentages in Table 6.1 for those phases—9.8 for IV vs. 20.2 percent for VIII.

As for Phase V, it is seen as central in acute onset which, by definition, is induced by some major trauma. Such traumatic life events probably are infrequent, with Phase I or II often serving as the take-off point for sudden movement to V. Moreover, remaining at Phase V for extended periods seems unlikely. Absent quick recovery to Phases I or II, the prototypic flight-path might well be: I or II → V → VIII. The low incidence of Phase V (4.7 percent) in Table 6.1 is consistent with the line of thought both in connection with the rarity of traumatic onset as well as with the probable transiency of Phase V assignments.

"Deviant" Firms

Two firms—Cases #7 and 10—seem to differ most from the overall profile for all units and their deviancy can be credibly explained, at least at a general level. Firm #10 has a management style that inclines toward Likert System IV, other data tell us, and to boot is a prosperous exception to the crippling recession that plagues Canada's "oil patch." Firm #10 has the highest individual proportion of employees classified in the least-advanced phases of burnout and also has twice the overall proportion in Phases I–III. Those sharp differences can be explained by the relative absence of two classes of stressors—those stressors that other evidence associates with directive or authoritarian management styles and policies, and those stressors that seem reasonably inferred from very hard economic times in comparable firms.

Firm #7 stands out because it has over 60 percent of its employees classified in Phases III and IV which, in Table 6.1, account for less than 18 percent of all cases. Somewhat conjecturally, Firm #7 specializes in unchallenging sales-work—employees are "order-takers," and disgruntled ones at that—and the initial managerial response to low satisfaction and job involvement has been an effort to "turn the screws." This helps account for the poor scores on Personal Accomplishment and Depersonalization that characterize Phases III and IV. At the same time, the work is slow-paced and management is not demanding. Both features probably would inhibit the onset of the most-advanced phases, but management sees the present state as undesirable and has begun to seek ways out of the present lose/lose situation.

Challenges in "Worst"–Perhaps Most–Organizations

It may be that the 33 cases represent "better" organizations and, if so, the implied challenges assume awesome proportions. Consider only one point, which rests on the assumption—as seems credible (Carpini, Siegel, and Snyder, 1983)—that conditions at work have powerful effects on the character and quality of the polity. The traditional formulation holds that people *will be free*, given appropriate systems at the macropolitical level. The present data raise a different possibility. If the negative organizational influences associated with advanced burnout also inhibit effective freedom and political performance—which certainly seems reasonable—the data in Table 6.1 do not imply sanguine outcomes for our polity.

Persistence of Burnout

Data are similarly lacking on another aspect of *the* question—how bad is burnout in organizations? This related concern deals with how long burnout lasts, with whether burnout seems chronic or acute, in convenient medical terminology. Burnout would be worse were it generally chronic, in introductory précis. Were burnout generally acute, in contrast, the conditions inducing advanced stages would be episodic and variable. And this would constitute relatively good news.

Notes on Hosts and Methods

What say the available data? Several brief preliminaries are necessary before perspective can be provided on whether burnout is chronic or acute. Data come from five sites. Voluntary surveys were conducted at Site A over an interval of about 12 months, with response rates approximating 75 and 67 percent, respectively. Detailed demographic comparisons strongly imply that the two responding populations constitute close replicas of the total population (Golembiewski, Munzenrider, and Carter, 1983). Site A's experience is reviewed in Case V in

TABLE 6.4
Persistence of Phase Assignments at Five Sites, in Percentages

Kind of Stability	I. N = 71 (2 months)	II. N = 28 (5 months)	III. N = 76 (7 months)	IV. N = 89 (1 year)	V. N = 113 (1 year)	N = 377 Grand Means
A. No Change	38.0%	46.4%	32.9%	25.8%	38.9%	35.0%
B. No Change and ± One Phase	46.5	43.6	47.4	43.8	57.5	49.1
C. Stability within Phases I-III	78.6	66.7	64.7	57.1	81.1	71.8
D. Stability within Phases VI-VIII	73.5	71.4	64.3	72.5	52.0	67.4
E. Stability within Phases IV-V	26.1	37.5	20.0	28.6	14.3	24.6
Site Description	life-care retirement community	corporate Human Resources group	consumer products firm	medical clinic	product division of multi-national business (Site A)	

Table 6.4, which also summarizes data from four other sites. Together, the five sites permit some comparisons of tendencies in persistence.

Expectations about Persistence

The literature reflects no clear sense of the persistence of burnout, and this impoverishes attempts to describe, predict, and ameliorate. Pines (1983, p. 161) reports the test-retest reliability of one burnout measure as .89 for a one-month interval, .76 for two months, and .66 for a four-month interval. The differences in correlations reflect measurement error as well as true change, of course, and suggest a substantial persistence of burnout effects as well as the reliability of the measuring instrument. Except for her work, the literature remains moot on persistence, although it reflects the general sense that burnout typically persists over extended periods and, hence, is more chronic than acute, in conventional terms.

Findings about Persistence of Phases

Sparse data suggest that time does not heal burnout, whatever other good offices it may provide. Table 6.4 deals with phase assignments in five settings at two variably distant points in time. Five kinds of "stability" are estimated, comparing the two assignments. Since all assignments here include both measurement error and "natural change," all estimates are no doubt conservative measures of stability.

Four points summarize the data in Table 6.4 and some underlying features as well. First, phase assignments remain quite stable over intervals from two months to a year. Thus, 35 percent of the assignment, on average, do not change at all (Case A). Looked at another way, in Case B, nearly 50 percent of the assignments change no more than a single phase. In 49.1 percent of the assignments, that is, an individual rated a II on Day 1 would later be a I, II, or III.

Second, substantial variation exists *between* phases in their rate of change over time, and that variation at once implies that the management of burnout will be both facile in some senses and difficult in others. The eight phases seem differentially stable, that is, with the extreme phases being the most stable, and Phases IV and V being the most dynamic. Specifically, individuals assigned initially to Phases I-III retain that assignment in nearly 72 percent of the cases. The corresponding percentage for Phases VI-VIII is 67.4 percent. In contrast, IV and V assignments remain stable in only 24.6 percent of the cases in a later assessment.

Third, on balance, it is equally probable that, when a change in assignment does occur, it will be for the "better" or the "worse." "Better" here is defined as movement to a lower phase, such as an original IV being assigned later to a I. For Site A, 26 percent of the assignments are "better," 35 percent are "worse," while (as noted) 39 percent remain identical.

Fourth, assignments on the three MBI subscales do not seem to change, either radically or at significantly different rates. A person initially rated high on any of the subscales, in general, probably also will be rated high later. Specifically, for Site A, the probabilities that there will be no major change on the three subscales—68, 71, and 75 percent, respectively, for Depersonalization, Personal Accomplishment, and Emotional Exhaustion—obviously do not differ much.

Well, Does Time Heal All Wounds?

As for the bottom-line question, "Will time heal burnout?"—the answer seems clear. One should not count on it.

Overall, the data on persistence incline toward the conclusion that, to use the convenient medical terminology, burnout is more chronic than acute. This reinforces some earlier conclusions, but hardly settles matters, since chronic burnout implies some relatively persistent stimuli in the individual and/or in the employing organization or immediate work site. Later analysis will suggest that personality factors do not dominate in burnout, or even much influence it. And the present analysis is also consistent with an important suggestion that will be aggressively supported in the next chapter—that the properties of the immediate work group and its supervision seem most important in inducing different levels of burnout.

Acute/Chronic Onset and Exit/Entrance, Again

The raw data underlying the analysis of stability raise two immediate issues that surfaced earlier, but deserve reemphasis. Despite the progressive virulence of the phases, they clearly are not rigidly sequential. Indeed, it seems unlikely that the sequential phases chart a step-by-step pathway for progressive burnout. Consider Phases II (HiLoLo) and III (LoHiLo), for example. The data imply that those phases are progressively virulent. But one could hardly insist that those moving toward advanced burnout from Phase II would proceed to Phase III, which requires an "improvement" in Depersonalization and a "worsening" of Personal Accomplishment.

Two possible explanations can reconcile "skipping" with the view of the phase model as encompassing progressive virulence. These explanations involve entrance/exist and acuteness/chronicity.

Consider some "skips," like a quick shift from LoLoLo to LoLoHi, or Phase I → V. Credibly, such cases of entrance to advanced burnout might reflect *acute* changes in a person's life, which can be distinguished from *chronic* organizational conditions. Put otherwise, there might be at least two basic kinds of entrance to burnout reflected in the data above. Several acute varieties would not only come and go more quickly than the chronic; they also might be less common than the chronic, as certainly appears to be the case in the present data. In schematic form, one can distinguish a basic chronic entrance mode from one of several alternative acute entrance modes:

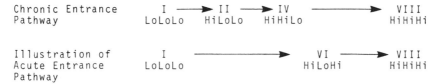

The acute illustration might involve the sudden death of a spouse who was the center of the survivor's life, the strain of which can quickly precipitate Phase VI and later lead to deterioration in performance at work as well as adverse effects in the individual's personal life (Phase VIII).

Such speculations may be attractive, but they do not settle matters. The possibilities still support the core notion of the progressive virulence of the eight phases, while permitting needed flexibility in actual flight-paths to or from more advanced phases of burnout. In chapter eight, several possible flight-paths receive our speculation, but they can only be advanced with any certainty after being tested by longitudinal research.

Exit seems to pose more complicated analytical problems. Given the strong tendency toward stability in the phases, these must wait for long-term research using very large populations.

IMPLICATIONS FOR THE PHASE MODEL OF BURNOUT

In sum, these several perspectives—on sequence, incidence, and persistence—support the general model underlying this research and also underscore the need for greater specificity in the phase model.

To illustrate, consider here only the association at Site B of heightened physical symptoms and increased productivity. This implies high costs, on the surface, but the linkage requires detailed elaboration. Directly, research may establish the generality of this linkage; or that research may find this linkage only in certain kinds of organizations, like Site B.

This specification will be eventful. The first interpretation will require a tough choice: Output may have to be traded-off for decreased symptoms of physical distress. The other alternative presents a more attractive possibility, although probably not an easy piece: changing the characteristics of organizations like Site B to reduce stressors on employees. This possibility can be exploited as we gain perspective on a central question. How can work site features like those at Site B be minimized or eliminated, thereby avoiding the dilemma posed by the first case? See chapter nine.

Urgency also seems appropriate, whatever the conclusions to which such research will contribute, because progressive burnout seems to have both substantial incidence and persistence. These constitute a dour duo and must somehow be dealt with in practice, whatever future research shows. That research may limit responses to fine-tuning within the context of a basic dilemma, or it may permit more attractive and broader choices for doing something about advanced burnout. This book takes the latter approach, while realizing it may be necessary to settle for the former.

NOTES

1. These data are provided by an *ad hoc* network of observers. They include: Gary M. Andrew (Rand McNally & Co.); Sister Marianna Bauder (St. Mary's Hospital & Medical Center); Leslie S. Boss (Brigham Young University); R. Wayne Boss (University of Colorado at Boulder); Robert Boudreau (University of Lethbridge); Ronald J. Burke (York University); Allan Cahoon (University of Calgary); Diane Carter Carrigan (SmithKline Clinical Laboratories); Sister Lynn Casey (St. Vincent Hospital & Health Center); James Michael Corbett (Aspenwood Dental Corp.); Rick Daly (Allergan Pharmaceuticals); Gloria J. Deckard (University of Missouri at Columbia); Eugene Deszca (York University); H. Sloane Dugan (University of Calgary), Mark Dundon (Sisters of Providence Health System), Jane Nelson Fine (St. Mary's Hospital & Medical Center); Terry D. Fine (Aspenwood Dental Corp.); Mike Fuller (University of Calgary); Alan M. Glassman (California State University, Northridge); Roysten Greenwood (University of Alberta), Robert B. Grimm (University of Colorado at Boulder); Alan Guerrie (Aspenwood Dental Corp.); Richard Hilles (Allergan Pharmaceuticals); Keith Hornberger (St. Francis Hospital & Medical Center); Tom Janz (University of Calgary); Brad Leach (Sheriff, Boulder County, Colorado); Joseph Lischeron (University of Calgary); Sister Ann Marita (St. Francis Hospital & Medical Center); Franca Maroino (Tesi Spa Consulting Firm); Marco V. Maroino (Tesi Spa Consulting Firm), Mark L. McConkie (University of Colorado at Colorado Springs); Wayne Montgomery (Personal Improvements Programs); Robert Munzenrider (Penn State University, Harrisburg); William M. Murray (St. Vincent Hospital & Medical Center), David P. Noffsinger (Aspenwood Dental Corp.); Sue E. Noffsinger (Grand Junction, Colorado); Michael S. Ross (University of Calgary); Benjamin H. Rountree (University of Missouri at Columbia); Julie I. A. Rowney (University of Calgary); Patrick Scott (International Trade Association, U.S. Department of Commerce); John Shearer (York University); Jerry G. Stevenson (University of Dayton); Christopher N. Tennis (University of Colorado at Boulder); David J. Voorhis (Voorhis Associates); and William D. Wilsted (University of Colorado at Boulder).

2. For an earlier version of the incidence study, see Golembiewski *et al.* (1986). It provides data on 26 cases.

7. FOUR POSSIBLE CONTRIBUTORS TO BURNOUT: EARLY RUNS OF THE "MAZE OF CAUSALITY"

The causal direction of the associations described in chapters two through six remains, for the most part, an open issue, and the time has come to chip away in earnest at it. We use the term, "chipping away at," because we cannot settle the matter with the present data and designs. Chapter two contains an effort at causal modelling, of course, but that remains more illustrative than definitive. We can, however, make an additional inroad or two here on causality, lack of knowledge about which will basically limit the theoretical and practical usefulness of the phases of burnout.

"Causality" is a topic that can paralyze, especially when taken in large doses. Of course, causality is *the* issue, but too much concern about it, at early stages of study, can inhibit later progress in dealing with it. Here, we seek to crawl before we attempt to walk, much less run. This constitutes no apology, but rather a statement of our operating bias. We seek some proximate movement, and assume the risk that we may be charged by some with merely copping-out on the issues.

FOUR APPROACHES TO EXPLORATION

How will we approach this "chipping away"? We are guided by several key questions:

- Does a Joe Btzsflk phenomenon seem to underlie burnout effects?
- Is burnout related to critical life events?
- Does immediate work-group membership affect burnout?
- Do the properties of immediate work-groups vary with the degree of burnout experienced by their members?

This agenda is neither simple nor direct, and it constitutes only one set of steps down a very long trail. For one thing, *all* four classes of determinants—and *many* more—may well contribute to progressive burnout. So, the present goal is to provide some perspective on which, if any, kinds of determinants seem to have particularly powerful effects on burnout, as measured here. The products are neither comprehensive nor definitive.

Burnout as a Joe Btzsflk Phenomenon, I?: Selected Demographics

Older readers of Al Capp's "Li'l Abner" may recall the tragicomic figure of Joe Btzsflk, and younger readers need only a little introduction to Joe. In short, it was *always* raining where Joe was. He had an omnipresent dark cloud over his head. Readers instantly got the idea that Joe was the type of character who could be counted on to snatch defeat out of the jaws of victory even on his lucky days. On most days, Joe did not have an outside chance of avoiding disaster, let alone copping a victory.

The reference to Joe encourages two questions. Do personal or personality characteristics incline some individuals to burn out? And if so, are the tendencies strong or weak? The present approach samples one wide-ranging and one narrow perspective. The former deals with a panel of demographic variables, and the latter focuses briefly on a syndrome of personal tendencies that has attracted considerable attention of late—Type A.

Burnout and 17 Demographic Variables

An important aspect of burnout involves who, if anyone, is at special risk. Is burnout a disease of young, idealistic, and talented persons who recoil at the various intransigencies of large systems (Freudenberger, 1980)? Or is burnout an affliction particularly common among helping professionals, those who really care and must labor under conditions that often trigger powerful emotions in both helper and client (Maslach, 1982a)? Or, among numerous other possibilities, do the incidence and virulence of burnout differ for the young and old, for females and males, for those high in hierarchies and their underlings?

This section provides some perspective on common and central questions about demographics, and has four emphases. First, a panel of 17 demographics is described, and their expected associations with burnout are detailed.

Second, these demographics are tested—one at a time—for associations with burnout, using Site B data. As detailed earlier, these data come from low- to mid-level employees in a division of a federal agency, and their results support other public-sector studies (for example, Maslach and Jackson, 1981 and 1984).

Third, the Site B results are confirmed by an analysis of data from Site A, a business setting. These results are noted briefly because this study also utilizes a univariate approach and generates results that differ only marginally from Site B findings. Other research in business contexts (for example, Cahoon and Rowney, 1984) confirms the broad pattern of Site A findings.

Fourth, Site B data permit a multivariate analysis of one significant demo-graphic—gender. These results test, as it were, the consistent pattern established by taking the 17 demographics one at a time. Age and ethnicity are considered along with gender, to assess their combined associations with burnout.

Selected Demographics and Expected Associations

What factors differentiate respondents at Site B? Seventeen demographics are listed below, along with the conventions used to code each variable.

Demographic Variables Studied at Site B

- Sex, coded as female and male.
- Age, coded in five classes: Under 30, 30–39, 40–49, 50–59, and 60 and over.
- Pay grade, coded in terms of self-reports on six clusters of General Schedule (GS) levels identified by management: GS 1-4; GS 5-6; GS 7-8; GS 9; GS 10-11; and GS 12 and above.
- Position, coded in seven categories: Division Chief; Assistant Division Chief; Section Chief; Unit Specialist; Clerical; Technical; and Other.
- Ethnicity, coded in conventional terms: White, Black, Hispanic, Asian/ Pacific Islander, and Other.
- Current assignment, for nonsupervisory personnel only, coded in terms of six activities that are not specified here to avoid identifying the host organization.
- Years in current assignment, coded in four categories: Last 2 years, 3–5, 5–10, and Over 10 years.
- Education, coded in terms of five categories: Some High School; High School Grad; Some College; College Grad; and Graduate Education.
- Last performance appraisal, coded in terms of five categories, from Excellent to Unsatisfactory, which are self-reports concerning agency action.
- Time since last promotion, coded in terms of five categories ranging from This Year to Never Promoted.
- Years with parent organization of which the division is a subunit, coded in six categories ranging from 2 years or less through over 20.
- Years with division, with four codes: 2 years or less, 3–5, 6–10, and 10 years or more.
- Years in present job, coded as: 2 years or less, 3–5, 6–10, or more than 10.
- Prefer assignment elsewhere in parent organization, coded as Yes, Maybe, or No.

- Marital status, coded as Married, Divorced and Separated, or Single.
- Job rotation schedule, coded as Weekly, Monthly, Not Rotated, or Other.
- Self-rated potential for promotion, coded as: Excellent, Good, Not Good, or Poor.

The 17 demographics are convenient targets but, beyond that, they seek to explore several mini-theoretical networks of possible associations with burnout. Several demographics (for example, pay grade and position) seek to tap aspects of that usually potent covariant, status. Marital status tentatively probes for differences in burnout that may be associated with the gross condition of one important social-support system. Several variables relate to possible links of frustration with burnout. These include job-rotation schedule, time since last promotion, prefer assignment elsewhere, and potential for promotion. Several demographics test for the effects of time, in what amounts to a kind of Chinese water-torture approach to burnout—for example, years in present job and years with division. Other variables can be seen as testing for the effects on burnout of formal actions such as performance appraisal, current assignment, and time since last promotion. And a few variables probe for associations between burnout and personal features—age, sex, ethnicity, and education.

Nonrandom Associations at Site B

The data reflect a mixed and weak pattern of association of demographic variables and burnout phases. Most of the demographic variables—11 of the 17, to be precise—are associated with burnout phases in nonrandom ways, as determined by the .05 level on the chi-square test. These statistically significant variables are listed below, along with brief descriptions of the character of the variation observed.

Demographic Variables Associated Nonrandomly with Burnout Phases

- Sex, with females tending toward advanced phases more than males.
- Age, with younger respondents tending toward Phases VI-VIII more than older respondents, especially those beyond age 50.
- Pay grade, with high grades being associated with lower phases of burnout.
- Position, with the highest-status positions tending to have the greater proportion of least-advanced phases.
- Ethnicity, with Hispanics reporting the highest proportion of advanced phases of burnout.
- Current assignment, with those with direct contact with clients reporting a higher proportion of advanced phases of burnout.
- Years with parent organization, with the newest employees and those

with ten years or more of service having the most favorable distributions of phases.

● Years in division, showing the same curvilinear pattern as length of service in the parent organization.

● Prefer assignment elsewhere in parent organization, where those choosing to stay have the most favorable profile of scores.

● Marital status, showing marrieds reporting the lowest incidence of advanced phases and the highest incidence of least-advanced phases.

● Self-rated potential for promotion, with those claiming the most potential having the most favorable distribution of burnout phases.

Despite the statistical significance of these 11 demographic variables, however, their degree of association with progressive burnout ranges from modest to slight. Overall, the 11 cases explain an average of only 1.3 percent of the variance, with not a single case explaining even 4 percent.

Table 7.1 illustrates the distribution of burnout scores when more than two coding categories are involved, and uses the most marked case of association between burnout phases and any demographic variable. The major contributors to nonrandom variance seem obvious to cursory analysis. Nearly 60 percent of the respondents who prefer reassignment fall in Phases VI-VIII, while only 30 percent preferring to stay put are so classified. Even more markedly, those rejecting reassignment are classified in Phases I-III more than twice as frequently as those preferring reassignment. Although these tendencies are unsurprising, the association is not very robust. About 3.6 percent of the variance is shared, according to Cramer's V.

Confirmation from Site A

The present results are consistent with an analysis of a commercial organization at Site A (Golembiewski and Scicchitano, 1983), and deserve brief mention despite the small population of Site A. The results parallel those from other business settings (e.g., Cahoon and Rowney, 1984), and also mirror the findings at Site B. A number of demographics at Site A have nonrandom association with burnout, but in all cases that association is weak-to-negligible. Specifically, the pattern of burnout relationships with demographic variables is similar to that at Site B (Golembiewski and Scicchitano, 1983, p. 441): "Only 14 of the 40 cases attain statistical significance and, even in that minority of the cases, only small magnitudes of effects are involved. Less than half of these cases account for even as much as 3 percent of the common variance."

Multivariate View of Gender

The demographics seem worthy of a more complex look, especially since the data from Site B permit analysis beyond most data batches. The focus here is on gender, age, and ethnicity, as exemplars of what can be done analytically.

TABLE 7.1
Preference for Reassignment in Parent Organization and Phases of Burnout, Site B

Preference	Phases of Burnout								Number
	I	II	III	IV	V	VI	VII	VIII	
Percent yes	12	5	10	7	8	16	9	34	329
Percent maybe	18	6	11	8	6	12	8	30	728
Percent no	32	8	15	8	7	9	6	15	479
Number	354	106	193	123	107	175	109	368	1,536

Note: Chi-square = 115.543; degrees of freedom = 14; chi-square probability < .001; Cramer's V = .19.

To begin, consider four practical motivators of this re-analysis, following Golembiewski and Scicchitano (1983). First, affirmative action issues heighten interest in demographics. If burnout is associated systematically with demographic factors, for example, could (and should) members of a particular race or sex (or whatever) be excluded from jobs whose demands put them at special risk? Second, workman's compensation and disability concerns attract attention. Sub-populations at special risk of burnout might file claims in unusual proportions or amounts, especially if their degree of risk is known but not taken into explicit account at the time of the employment decision. Third, knowledge that certain sub-groups are at special risk could target remedial interventions, especially preventive ones. Fourth, with rare exceptions (e.g., Etzion and Pines, 1981) studies look at demographic variables one at a time (for example, the results just presented).

The particular focus here is on gender. Despite the dominant research view that burnout and gender do not share noteworthy variance (e.g., Etzion and Pines, 1981; Golembiewski and Scicchitano, 1983; Maslach and Jackson, 1983), support continues to exist for the view that gender makes a real difference. Three arguments underlie this persistence, as summarized by Maslach and Jackson (1983). First, many women get a double dose of stressors, as employees and as mothers who are heads-of-family. In addition, women are more at risk of burnout because they have a stronger tendency to serve in people-helping professions—teaching, nursing, counselling, and so on—as well as to be in direct contact with clients rather than in administrative roles. Direct contact with clients and people-helping seem major contributors to burnout. The concept of burnout gained its early popularity as a description of the personal consequences of just such roles. Finally, Maslach and Jackson note that women are more likely to invest emotionally in their work, and hence may be more susceptible to burnout. Put dramatically, burnout becomes a cost of caring.

Does burnout differ by gender, taking age and ethnicity into account? Details are available elsewhere (Munzenrider, Golembiewski, and Stevenson, 1984), where multivariate analysis comprehensively tests for associations of the three demographic variables with five measures of burnout. The phases get definite emphasis, but analysis also considers the three MBI subscales as well as the Total Score.

Overall, no findings of this complex analysis contradict other studies (see Munzenrider, Golembiewski, and Stevenson, 1984, especially pp. 95–102), but the findings do add some depth and nuance to the available literature. In sum, small but persistent associations exist on most (but not all) measures of burnout in 1-to-1 tests. To illustrate with the phases and the three focal demographics, seven chi-square tests are run: four attain usually acceptable levels of significance, two closely approximate $P = .10$, and the final chi-square value indicates $P = .25$. Women also differ significantly from men on two MBI subscales—Depersonalization and Personal Accomplishment—and these differences cannot be accounted for by simple age or ethnic (white or minority) differences. In one-way analysis, however, age is a more significant covariant of the four MBI measures. For age, all four analyses are statistically significant and explain an average of nearly 4 percent of the variance. In contrast, two of the four analyses of gender attain the .05 level, and they account for about 1 percent of the variance (Munzenrider, Golembiewski, and Stevenson, 1984, p. 95).

Two-way and three-way analyses of variance also isolate some complex gender-related differences, but age differences once again are more pronounced. Certainly, women do not appear at substantially greater risk of burnout than men, at least not at Site B. We illustrate with a summary of one of the three-way hierarchical analyses of variance. All four analyses of age × MBI measures of burnout surpass the .01 level; ethnicity washes out, after controlling for age; gender achieves statistical significance in two of our cases, after controlling for age and ethnicity; and age × sex interactions are significant in two of four cases. No substantially different findings result when gender is entered into analysis first, with age subsequently being controlled for ethnicity and gender.

In sum, multivariate analysis does not support the conventional belief about burnout and gender—that women are at some greater risk of burnout. In some cross-classifications, in fact, men seem at greater risk. If we are forced to choose one generalization, indeed, white males under age 40 appear to have the greatest risk of burnout (Munzenrider and Golembiewski, 1984, pp. 96-98).

Implications for the Phase Model of Burnout

The similar patterns in both public and business contexts urge caution in accepting the popular notion that certain demographic aggregates are at special risk with respect to burnout. That notion has been persuasively argued by those who see burnout as "a disease of overcommitment" (Freudenberg, 1980), or as a result of "caring" (Maslach, 1982). To be sure, such notions may apply at a level of analysis less coarse than this one. However, the present data imply that advanced burnout will either be randomly distributed in demographic aggregates, or will account for small proportions of the variance where statistically significant relationships exist. So, burnout should not be considered a problem of only some populations at special risk. Burnout seems to be a widely distributed phenomenon.

Burnout as an Affirmative-Action Affliction

Hence, sadly, burnout may be said to be an affirmative-action affliction. Consequently, ameliorative social and organizational action will have to be broad-gauge, even if later research does isolate discrete pockets of individuals at special risk. Note that this notion is consistent with the broad theoretical underpinnings of the stress literature, which propose that the same stressor may motivate some people even as it herniates others. Hence, any stressor may, technically speaking, lead either to dis-stress or eu-stress, depending upon individuals and their specific coping attitudes and skills, their specific condition of life, the availability or scarcity of support groups, and numerous other moderating and confounding variables (House, 1981).

Despite their arguing for an appropriate tentativeness, the data also suggest several notions that may be managerially useful, in the sense that managers are well-advised to know the odds, so that they can make informed decisions about which way to lean when choices must be made under conditions of uncertainty. Five points seem most prominent, to judge from the record of statistically significant cases reviewed above. One disclaimer, however, needs to be boldly stated. Only longitudinal research can establish definite trends. Hence, when the present data show that older respondents have lower burnout, that may mean only that at Site B those who leave at earlier ages are disproportionately in the most advanced phases of burnout.

First, despite its popularity as a proposed remedy, the frequency of job rotation has only random associations with burnout at Site B. This is not surprising, despite the general neglect of the point that the character of job rotation seems far more salient than the frequency. Rotation between jobs that are just about equally noxious and stressing, with little to distinguish between them in terms of variety and other motivators, suggests no great theoretical or practical leverage for ameliorating the effects of burnout. The rotation opportunities at Site B have those qualities, and thus reflect only random associations with psychological burnout.

Second, although measures of organizational status are inversely associated with burnout phases, the relationship is not robust. That is, pay grade and position are nonrandomly associated with the phases, but each explains only about 1 percent of the variance. These data remind us that status indicators may provide only limited opportunities for manipulation without creating other problems. As experience in World War II suggests, heavy reliance on status-enhancers can backfire, even creating "relative deprivation" that is so great that it undercuts the rationale motivating the stimulation. Thus Air Force personnel were the least satisfied with the awarding of medals for heroism, despite the fact that they were by far the most likely recipients. The military police were the most satisfied, in contrast, apparently because so few of them got medals that the others suffered no great deprivation relative to their few bemedalled peers. In the Air Force, not getting a medal—or not getting enough of them—had more of an impact. Such a high proportion of its members received medals so often that not getting a medal became a very significant cause of disaffection—the very condition the giving of medals was thought to prevent, and no doubt did for some. Generally, see Stouffer and associates (1949) concerning the concept, whose applications cover a broad range (e.g., Gurr, 1970).

Third, several of the associations above suggest a respondent self-awareness that can be variously used to leverage constructive action of one kind or another—as in career planning that could lead to personal or job changes. Thus, individuals classified in advanced phases of burnout often prefer reassignment, and also see themselves as having poor chances of advancement. This does not necessarily imply any consciousness of burnout, of course, but it does reflect a sense that things are out-of-kilter, which might motivate choice and change.

Fourth, the data imply countervailing forces in organizational burnout. In the immediate future, most organizations will continue to have work forces that are aging, with a growing proportion of women at all levels. To the degree that the present data are generalizable, they suggest significant burnout effects in the near future. Women tend to be overrepresented in the advanced phases of burnout, while older employees and those with the longest service have the most favorable distributions on burnout. Over time, as most women attain longer service, these differences may moderate.

Fifth, the data suggest the managerial usefulness of focusing on time as a covariant of burnout. Tenure in both the parent organization and the division are curvilinearly related to burnout, with those with longest and shortest employment having the most favorable distributions of burnout phases. Hypothetically, this suggests a simple dynamic: young employees have a greater zest for their jobs than those with intermediate tenure; and the longest-term employees either have become reconciled to their work, or their higher-burnout colleagues have left the agency in disproportionately large numbers. These generalizations need to be qualified, however. Time served in the present job has only a random association with burnout, for example, although certain direct client-contact jobs heighten burnout. This suggests a major cross-current to the two generalizations above. Understandably, individuals may stay in unattractive jobs for a variety of reasons, but the present data suggest that these reasons do not reduce the consequences of staying.

Burnout as a Joe Btzsflk Phenomenon, II, III, . . .?: Type A and Self-Esteem

Of course, many approaches could be taken in searching for possible personal or personality covariants of burnout. The results above show that demographics can be regular covariants of burnout, but not very robust ones. Those results only begin a very long task, however, and one can wish for much further study, even though the total job has a mind-numbing magnitude.

Personality properties considered in isolation from environmental features do not seem to help much in explaining burnout phenomena (French and Caplan, 1973), so they do not have a high priority in our recent work. However, we did test our bias, in two basic ways. They involve Type A and self-esteem.

Type A: A Brief Review

Earlier analysis (Golembiewski, Munzenrider, and Stevenson, 1986, pp. 155–63) focuses on an analysis of Type A and its often neglected dimensions, and for obvious reasons. Much research seeks health-related covariants of Type A personality features (e.g., Jenkins, Rosenman, and Zyzanski, 1974; Ivancevich, Matteson, and Preston, 1982), and certainly with enough success to motivate a test for associations with the burnout phases. Moreover, this obvious target-of-opportunity has been neglected, with rare exceptions (e.g., Glass and Carver, 1980), especially in organizational settings. Paramountly, both burnout and Type A seem stress-related; and they both have been associated with major human deficits (e.g., Jenkins, Zyzanski, and Rosenman, 1979, pp. 15–16; Cherniss, 1980a,b).

Data come from Site A, a consumer-products division of a multinational firm. The focus is on the phases and five measures derived from the Jenkins Activity Survey, or JAS (Jenkins, Zyzanski, and Rosenman, 1979):

- Type A versus Type B
- Speed and impatience
- Job involvement
- Hard-driving and competitiveness

The latter three measures are Type A domains.

At Site A, the four JAS scores have regular but not robust associations with the phases. Three of the four do contain nonrandom variation somewhere in the distributions of JAS scores × the phases, and "hard-driving and competitiveness" approaches overall significance (P = .065). However, as we conclude elsewhere (Golembiewski, Munzenrider, and Stevenson, 1986, p. 160): "These evidences of covariation ... do not extend to the phase model in its entirety. Thus, none of the [four] sets of JAS scores trends in a consistent direction; and only 7 of the 84 possible paired-comparisons of the three significant JAS scores attain statistical significance."

Type A and Acute Onset?

Special attention needs to be directed at Phases III, V, and VI, which play the major role in the nonrandom variance. In fact, these three phases are involved in all but two of the significant paired comparisons.

Why special attention? In short, nonrandom associations of Type A characteristics with several of the burnout phases exist, and one can speculate about why these selective associations generally involve the phases assumed to characterize acute onset—Phase III, and especially Phases V and VI (see also chapter eight). The data suggest that Type As cope differently with acute onset than Type Bs, perhaps in being able to marshal personal resources to "fight" the trauma. Similarly, no significant overall Type A vs. B differences may appear in chronic onset: Phases I → II → IV → VIII. By definition, chronic onset involves the long-run grinding down of one's coping resources that eventually gets to most people.

This implies a role for Type A in burnout similar to that emerging in connection with heart disease. Initial research tied Type A personality to a substantially higher risk of heart disease (e.g., Jenkins, Zyzanski, and Rosenman, 1979), but serious questions about the directness of that association seem appropriate. Quite recently (*Atlanta Constitution*, 1988), the popular press highlighted a medical study also published in a ranking journal (Ragland and Brand, 1988) that found Type A men about half as likely to die of heart disease compared to Type Bs, in a panel of subjects who had all been diagnosed as having similar heart problems. Some speculate that this is because Type A men are less likely to accept or to "give in" to their disease. As for the linkage of Type A to initial heart disease, opinions differ, especially concerning whether people should try to unlearn Type A behavior to avoid heart disease. The initial research implied this unlearning, but the more recent research suggests that could be counterproductive, at least for men who have had an initial problem with heart disease.

Self-Esteem: Phases and Blood Chemistry

More recent work with self-esteem has greater attractions, although administrative problems at the field site result in what is best described as a pilot study with a small population. The pilot study uses Rosenberg's (1965a, b) 10-item measure of self-esteem, with numerous measurement details being available (Robinson and Shaver, 1973, pp. 81–83; Rosenberg, 1965a, b). Six measures of blood chemistry also are considered. For details on the latter, see chapter four.

The test for an association of the phases X self-esteem has an obvious motivation in one sense, and is less direct in another. Rosenberg's self-esteem measure focuses on liking or approving of the self and, as a dependent variable, self-acceptance reasonably might be predicted to diminish as the phases escalate. Others propose (e.g., Fischer, 1983) that self-esteem is an important intervening variable in how people respond to stressors. High self-esteem will keep one trying, but strain plus low self-esteem might result in a "worn-out" response.

This pilot study will not permit a test of these two possibilities. But the goal of some preliminary mapping is within reach (Golembiewski and Kim, 1988). Note that Cronbach's alpha for the two self-esteem observations suit research purposes: .78 and .93.

The association of phases X self-esteem is suggestive, but not definitive. Both were assessed twice, about two months apart ($N_1 = 35$ and $N_2 = 44$). Neither one-way analysis of variance test proves significant, but both approach the .05 level (P = .071 and .134). And nearly 79 percent of the paired-comparisons indicate a direct association of self-esteem with the progressive phases, as expected. On Rosenberg's measure, a low score indicates high self-esteem. The insignificant F-values do not permit a direct interpretation of the LSD test of differences in paired-comparisons but, as with Type A, Phases III, V, and VI seem most prominent in accounting for the variance shared by phases X self-esteem.

Associations of self-esteem and six measures of the properties of blood chemistry also were assessed. Those properties include:

- uric acid
- triglycerides

- total cholesterol
- HDL cholesterol
- ratio of total cholesterol to HDL cholesterol
- ratio of HDL cholesterol to total cholesterol

See chapter four for details. Here note only that all measures but uric acid are seen as specific to gender and age. So twenty-five Pearson correlations are run between self-esteem and the latter five blood properties, separately for each of five demographic categories: male, female, 29 years old or less, 30–39 years old, and 40 years old or more. And six correlations are run for uric acid: one for the total population, and the other five for the demographics. Since self-esteem is measured twice, about two months apart, 62 coefficients will be analyzed. Blood was taken only at the time of the first self-esteem estimate, but there seem no substantial differences in O_1 vs. O_2 patterns of the associations of self-esteem and blood products.

The associations of self-esteem and blood chemistry motivate replicating this analysis in a more satisfactory population. Generally, favorable chemical outcomes are associated with high self-acceptance, although causal paths are beyond this analysis. Specifically, 79 percent of the comparisons reflect a high/high pattern: e.g., higher self-acceptance is associated with favorable blood chemistry. Moreover, nearly 28 percent of these pair-comparisons attain $P \leqslant .10$, with 17.8 percent at $P \leqslant .05$. No paired-comparisons in an opposite direction attain significance, in contrast (Golembiewski and Kim, 1988).

In sum, this analysis does not settle any matters, but it powerfully attracts. Data trends suggest some covariation of phases, self-esteem, and blood properties—perhaps direct, perhaps variously buffered. The small population permits no unqualified conclusion, except that the usefulness of the phase approach will be revealed only in more satisfactory versions of the analysis just sketched.

Toward Three Situational Perspectives

So attention now turns to the three other focal questions introduced earlier. They are clearly situational in character, and include:

- Is burnout, as measured here, related to critical life events?
- Does immediate work-group membership affect burnout, as measured here?
- Do properties of immediate work-groups vary in credible ways with the degree of burnout reported by their members?

By way of preview, looking at these three questions can inform this analysis in useful ways. "Life events" can provide some guidance concerning the probably significant distinction between chronic and acute contributors to strain, and hence burnout, following the usual psychomedical distinction. The phase approach has emphasized this distinction at several points. Acute contributors might include episodic life events—the loss of a spouse, and so on—which impact on individuals and encourage fight/flight reactions (Holmes and Rahe, 1967; and Cochrane and Robertson, 1973). Given real pain, such contributors to strain may be characterized by a general cycle: impact, emotional support plus time, and then recovery (e.g., Kubler-Ross, 1981, 1982).

Relatedly, the last two sections of this chapter test aspects of the person/ environment approach consistent with present findings. They test whether chronic contributors to burnout seem to derive basically from the character and quality of relationships in the primary work group. Central variables include leadership style, degrees of participation and involvement, and the norms in the group of first-reports headed by each organizational supervisor. Concepts like "contagion," "resonance" (Chapple and Sayles, 1961, p. 89), and so on, in this view, are useful in explaining the persistence and heightening of burnout effects.

Burnout as Induced by Critical Life Events?

In the abstract, at least, one can make a reasonable argument that life events are central in inducing burnout. Hence, considerable attention over the last decade or so has been paid to a "tensile-strength view" of people. Generally, the view assumes that individuals have a "safe loading" of life events that can be carried without major compensating costs. Beyond some point, however, the weight of these events begins to strain individual carrying capacities in ways that impact on aspects of performance. As Sarason, Johnson, and Siegel note (1979, p. 131):

> During recent years, numerous studies have investigated the relationship between life stress and susceptibility to physical and psychological problems. Most of these studies have been based on the assumptions that (a) life changes require adaptation on the part of the individual and are stressful, and (b) persons experiencing marked degrees of life change during the recent past are susceptible to physical and psychiatric problems.

Most tensile-strength approaches have relied on the Schedule of Recent Events, or SRE (Holmes and Rahe, 1967), whose early results generated a freshet of interest. SRE is a self-administered instrument of 43 items that tap events in the respondent's immediate past, to which "life-change units" are attributed, corresponding to the adjustments thought to be required by specific events. The sum of these units constitutes a "total life stress" score—so many points for a marriage, for the death of a spouse, taking a mortgage, and so on. The associated generic research strategy has many similar expressions. For example, are various point totals accumulated over the period of a year associated with different rates of illness? Illustratively, some observers report a linkage between degree of life change and sudden cardiac death (Rae and Lind, 1968); and others find an association with the seriousness of chronic illness (Wyler, Masuda, and Holmes, 1971).

After the initial blushes of enthusiasm, second thoughts have come to dominate the literature on life events, especially approached via SRE. Thus, a comprehensive and influential review of life-stress literature emphasizes conflicting findings, which are traced to various methodological difficulties (Rabkin and Strueing, 1976). And others stress specific measurement problems with SRE (for example, Brown, 1974; Yamamoto and Kinney, 1976).

The weight of this revisionism tends to opposite effects. For some researchers, the gold-rush atmosphere associated with life events has diminished, or even dissipated. Mechanic (1974b, p. 88) provides a characteristic version of this reaction: ". . . it is clear that stressful life events play some role in the occurrence of illness . . . but, any statement beyond this vague generalization is likely to stir controversy." Other students seek to specify that role more clearly, as by developing alternative ways of measuring life events (for example, Sarason, Johnson, and Siegel, 1979).

Curiously, burnout research has been touched only gently by the attention to life events or life stress, perhaps because the emphasis on burnout postdates the revisionism sketched above. Indeed, we find only one relevant piece of research (Justice, Gold, and Klein, 1981).

This section will hitchhike on the measurement progress made in the analysis of life events. The specific search is for linkages of life events with burnout, the general case for which seems credible. Later attention will go to linkages with physical symptoms and type of onset.

Notes on Host and Methods

All data in this section come from respondents at Site B, from the several nationwide locations of a federal agency in the people-helping business. Details on the host appear at several points, especially in chapter one.

Life Experiences Survey

The Life Experiences Survey, or LES, seems to reflect the most satisfactory product of the revisionist work on life stress. Basically, LES seeks to improve on SRE in two significant particulars. As the LES developers note (Sarason, Johnson, and Siegel, 1979, p. 133), a satisfactory measure of life stress "should allow for ratings, by respondents themselves, of the desirability or undesirability of the events [and] it should allow for individualized ratings of the personal impact of the events experienced." SRE did not distinguish between differences in the valence of events, on the grounds that life events are stressful in themselves, independent of their desirability to specific respondents. In effect, SRE relies on group ratings of the effects of various life events in assigning standard "life-change units" (or LCUs) to specific events, with marriage arbitrarily assigned 50 LCUs as a starting point.

More specifically, LES is a paper-and-pencil instrument that asks respondents to focus on 47 life events, common to many individuals. Three blank spaces also permit respondents to indicate other events they have experienced. Many of the items are based on existing life-stress measures, particularly the SRE. Other items reflect contemporary societal changes—more women working outside the home, for example. Note also that one section of the LES form taps life changes specific to the academic arena, but those events are not used in this study.

Respondents to LES are requested to rate separately the desirability of all events experienced during the prior 12 months. Ratings are made on a seven-point scale ranging from extremely positive (+3) to extremely negative (−3). A rating of zero indicates that the event was experienced but had no impact for the individual.

Types of LES Scores and Life-Events Arenas

For present purposes, given a significant reduction in subjects deemed necessary for quality-control reasons,[1] LES responses are used to generate a complex 4 × 6 matrix of scores differentiated by both "type" and "arena." The four types of scores are listed below:

- *Absolute Change*, which arithmetically sums the absolute values attributed to all positive *and* negative events, and hence measures life change *per se*, independent of the directionality of events;

- *Positive Change*, which sums the magnitude of effects associated with all events rated desirable by a respondent;

- *Negative Change*, which sums the magnitudes of all undesirable events reported by the individual, and

- *Relative Change*, or the algebraic sum of all positive and negative experiences, which provides a resultant measure of all recent life stress.

The literature has used each of these measures of life change. Absolute Change is the traditional measure, and rests on the notion that change *per se* requires adaptation and hence is stressful, whether desirable or undesirable (Selye, 1956). Others have proposed the need to distinguish positive from negative life experiences, as people evaluate them (for example, Ross and Mirowsky, 1979; Justice et al., 1981). Hence, the calculation of Positive Change and Negative Change scores will permit testing findings such as that of Justice and associates (1981) who report that only negative events seem significantly and positively associated with burnout. In short, Justice's results do not support the Absolute Change approach, which proposes that what counts is the cumulative impact of *all* life events, whether desirable or undesirable. In addition, Relative Change reckons the balance of positive versus negative life events, which discounts desirable experiences in terms of one's undesirable experiences.

The present approach also assesses whether "life-event arenas" are usefully distinguished. A summary of the items included in the several arenas appears elsewhere (Golembiewski, Munzenrider, and Stevenson, 1986, p. 194). Briefly, six arenas are identified:

- *Financial*, an arena tapped by responses to four items relating to foreclosure and other major changes in financial status;
- *Work*, tapping five items relating to a new job, trouble with employer, and retirement;
- *Personal*, an arena defined by responses to 13 items including detention in jail, death of a close friend, and so on;
- *Family*, tapped by 16 items including illness, marriage, death of spouse, and marital separation;
- *Total Life Events*, which sums all LES items plus three possible additions; and
- *Major Life Events*, which sums selected items, including death of child or spouse, and business failure (based on Paykel, Prusoff, and Uhlenhuth, 1971).

The rationale for attention to these arenas should be transparent, and is reflected in the question: does burnout, as measured here, seem to be differentially impacted by life events in the several arenas?

A few technical details provide useful perspective. The arenas have acceptable alphas, except for Financial (.50). However, the arenas are highly correlated, with the lowest coefficient being .68, and $\bar{X} = .74$. These high intercorrelations discourage inter-arena differentiation, even as they suggest a certain validity to the Joe Btzsflk view of life. As for the four types of LES scores, their overlap varies substantially. Data are not presented here (see Golembiewski, Munzenrider, and Stevenson, 1986, pp. 169–70).

Findings Concerning Life Events by Phases

The several LES types X arenas do not vary regularly or robustly with burnout. Statistically significant associations do exist, but they either account for small amounts of shared variance or they do not generate clear patterns of paired-comparisons. The data will be reviewed here for the phases only, but an analysis of the three MBI subscales also is available (Golembiewski, Munzenrider, and Stevenson, 1986).

LES Score and Burnout Phases

As Table 7.2 suggests, the association of life events and the phases of burnout seems distal and, at most, mediated in profound ways by unspecified variables. For Positive and Relative scores, the expectation is that they will decrease as the phases progress from I to VIII. For Absolute and Negative scores, direct association is expected and those scores should increase for the most virulent phases.

LES Positive Change reflects the *most* marked pattern of association with the

TABLE 7.2
LES Positive Change Scores and Burnout Phases, Site B

	Phases of Burnout									
	I LoLoLo	II HiLoLo	III LoHiLo	IV HiHiLo	V LoLoHi	VI HiLoHi	VII LoHiHi	VIII HiHiHi		
LES Arenas	(195)	(66)	(129)	(68)	(66)	(113)	(75)	(262)	F-Ratio	F-Probability
Financial	.80	.73	1.26	.81	.77	1.04	.79	.57	2.44	.02
Work	1.48	1.14	1.69	1.49	1.08	2.20	1.31	.87	3.82	.001
Personal	3.64	4.15	4.53	3.91	3.77	5.51	3.84	2.79	2.82	.01
Family	3.74	3.49	5.98	5.77	2.62	6.38	4.60	2.62	3.01	.01
Total life events	10.02	9.97	13.54	12.44	8.49	15.64	10.63	6.98	3.64	.001
Major life events	.62	.47	1.40	.77	.33	1.23	.77	.39	3.46	.001

Note: Figures in parentheses denote numbers of respondents.

148

phases, and even there the results are mixed and of modest strength. Table 7.2 does reflect nonrandom variance, by phases, for Positive Change in each of the LES arenas. But those six arenas share only a bit over 2 percent of the variance with the burnout phases, as Eta^2 establishes. Moreover, cursory inspection— reinforced by paired-comparisons via the Least Significant Difference test— establishes that Phases III, V, and VI account for the bulk of the nonrandom variance. Indeed, *all* of the significant paired-comparisons involve those three phases. In addition, while nearly 60 percent of the paired-comparisons are in the expected direction, only about 5 percent achieve statistical significance.

In all major particulars, the other three kinds of LES change scores generate similar patterns of association in all six life-events arenas. Although they generally trend in expected directions, the degree of association is diluted or distal; Phases III, V, and VI account for all of the few cases of nonrandom variation between pairs (see Golembiewski, Munzenrider, and Stevenson, 1986, p. 174). As in the case of Type A, note that Phases III, V, and VI seem particularly associated with LES variations. The later discussion in this chapter of acute flight-paths speculates on this finding common to Type A and LES.

A Summary: Life Events and Phases

The data, then, support two firm conclusions about the association of life events and burnout. First, no dominant pattern seems to exist in the data. At best, mediated and distal relationships can be inferred. Despite expected patterns and some statistically significant cases, life events do not regularly or robustly covary with burnout. This holds for all six arenas tapped by four kinds of LES scores.

The data bring to mind a paraphrase of an earlier quotation. It seems that life events—as diversely measured, and in several arenas as well as in the aggregate— seem to have some variable but small-to-modest association with burnout. Any statement beyond this vague generalization, however, should stir controversy.

Consider a stark contrast. Conceptually, variations in LES should "cause" differences in burnout, although feedback or reinforcing linkages no doubt also will exist. The data above show no pattern of association consistent with this view. Indeed, only an average of 1 percent of the variance is explained in that 75 percent of the cases in which overall nonrandom variance exists somewhere in the distributions of LES scores X phases of the six arenas. Moreover, only about five in ten paired-comparisons fall in expected directions, and only 2 percent of those cases achieve statistical significance.

Second, LES still may be useful as a moderating or intervening variable. Site B data do not permit an ideal test, but some perspective may be gained by focusing first on physical symptoms and then on the two assumed major kinds of burnout—chronic and acute.

Findings Concerning Life Events, Phases, and Physical Symptoms

This mini-analysis dichotomizes each LES score as high or low at the median and arrays physical symptoms for both subsets in terms of the eight phases. A

TABLE 7.3
Physical Symptoms, by Phases of Burnout, for High and Low LES Positive Scores, Site B

	Phases of Burnout										
	I LoLoLo	II HiLoLo	III LoHiLo	IV HiHiLo	V LoLoHi	VI HiLoHi	VII LoHiHi	VIII HiHiHi	F- Ratio	F- Probability	Eta^2 (percent)
Low LES positive											
Total symptoms	34.07	34.03	35.20	36.76	39.71	41.30	41.59	42.92	38.97	< .0000	16.3
Factor I: General enervation and agitation	17.10	17.19	18.43	18.61	20.68	21.31	21.50	22.43	18.00	< .0000	20.66
High LES positive											
Total symptoms	34.22	35.81	34.39	36.67	39.22	41.17	40.75	44.06	38.36	< .0000	16.7
Factor I: General enervation and agitation	17.33	17.94	17.29	18.74	30.22	21.03	21.88	22.73	16.94	< .0000	20.8

major role for the phases would be signalled if physical symptoms increase by phases, for both high and low subpopulations of LES.

What say the data? Three points summarize the major features of the analysis assessing the relative strengths of the association of LES, burnout, and physical symptoms. To begin, although the data are not reproduced here to conserve space, three of the four kinds of LES scores have nonrandom associations with the two most robust measures of the symptoms reported by respondents at Site B–Total Symptoms and Factor I, labeled General Enervation and Agitation. For this analysis, only these two measures of symptoms are considered. To be specific, significantly more symptoms are reported by those who have experienced more intense recent life events as measured by Negative, Relative, and Absolute LES scores. The three significant associations, however, account for only modest amounts of variance–an average of 2.8 percent.

In contrast, Table 7.3 arrays two measures of physical symptoms by the eight burnout phases, for both the high and low subclasses of the positive LES score. Note that the illustration in Table 7.3 mirrors the pattern in the other three kinds of LES scores, a basic pattern that has two major features. For both high and low LES scores of all four kinds, the two measures of symptoms vary regularly and robustly, phase by phase. In addition, the ranges of symptoms for both high and low LES seem generally comparable, although no statistical tests are performed. Regardless of the level of the four kinds of LES scores, then, the association of phases and physical symptoms seems both dominant and of similar magnitude.

Finally, the similarity of the basic pattern illustrated by Table 7.3 can be established by a summary of some complex comparisons–for all four kinds of LES scores, each distinguished as high and low, for the two measures of physical symptoms, arrayed by the eight phases of burnout. Table 7.4 presents that summary. It indicates that over nine out of ten of all paired-comparisons are in the expected direction, and nearly four in ten of those comparisons achieve statistical significance. The average variance explained approximates 18 percent, in addition. Looked at another way, only about 6 percent of those multiple paired-comparisons are in a direction contrary to expectations, and only one of those cases achieves statistical significance.

Findings Concerning Life Events, Phases, and Kinds of Onset

The LES also can provide some perspective on distinguishing chronic from acute onset, as is suggested by the apparent sensitivity of Phases III, V, and VI to Type A and LES differences. Directly, this analysis associates those phases with acute onset. To be sure, a longitudinal design would be more useful than the snapshot at Site B, so any results must be viewed tentatively. Nonetheless, this effort seeks to shed a little light in a dark analytic corner. (See also, Golembiewski, Munzenrider, and Stevenson, 1986; Golembiewski and Munzenrider, 1986a and 1986b; Golembiewski and Munzenrider, 1987). Only negative LES scores will be used to indicate kind of onset. In general, very low negative LES scores

TABLE 7.4
Summary of Paired-Comparisons for Four Kinds of LES Scores,
Distinguished as High versus Low, by Burnout Phases, Site B
(percent)

	Total Symptoms	Factor I: General Enervation and Agitation
In expected direction	93.5	95.0
Statistically significant and in expected direction	31.1	41.1
In contrary direction	6.5	5.0
Statistically significant and in contrary direction	0.0	0.0
Average Eta^2	16.4	18.1

should indicate chronic phases, and very high negative LES scores seem more likely to imply acute onset. The probabilistic rationale is general but direct. Experiencing many undesirable life events in some time frame patently should tend to induce acute onset in a higher proportion of cases than would few or no life events of that kind. Of course, some evidence just reviewed suggests the special salience of negative LES, as distinguished from three other ways of aggregating responses of individuals to requests for catalogs of their recent life experiences.

Four emphases guide the analysis of life events, phases, and kind of onset of burnout: first, a conceptual rationale, followed by notes on method, a brief summary of results and, then, details of the limitations of this approach.

A Conceptual Rationale

Both theoretical and practical factors motivate this effort to distinguish and to contrast acute vs. chronic kinds of onset. For example, chronic onset seems likely to derive from persisting features of the work site, while acute burnout would tend to inhere in trauma like personal misfortune, illness, or the death of a loved one. The pace of onset might encourage profoundly different effects. A "bad" work site could permit out-of-field compensations, for example, as by an individual enriching nonwork experiences over time so as to achieve some balance in life. In contrast, acute onset requires sudden and *ex post facto* adjustments.

Given such features, the persistence of the two modes of burnout might well differ, as would ameliorative strategies. Chronic onset might be amenable only to a fundamental change in the inducing conditions. In contrast, acute onset might more typically have to run relatively patterned courses, as in the processes of grieving: shock, anger, a growing sense of loss that can trigger withdrawal and perhaps even depression, and then a gradual return to personal equilibrium through an acknowledgment of the death and subsequent adaptations (e.g., Kubler-Ross, 1981, 1982).

In this elemental sense, distinguishing the two types of burnout onset has practical as well as theoretical significance. Basically, amelioration effective for one type might well be contraindicated for the others. Consider the following hypothetical possibility, which at times could well be the reality. Acute onset might be helped by time, and by generous applications of what is generally called "social support" (e.g., House, 1981). In contrast, chronic onset might well be exacerbated by those two ameliorators. The passage of time might only heighten concern or even despair; and social support might have the paradoxical effect of reinforcing or even heightening the sense of strain experienced—by processes of resonance, amplification, and, perhaps, even by conformity that commonly could encourage an exaggerated profession of symptoms and hence can help amplify them in objective as well as social senses. "I knew I was over-stressed, but I believed I was a rare case, before we started to talk about it. It's much worse than I thought. Everybody I talk to is as bad off as I am, or worse."

The phase model can accommodate the two kinds of onset, at least conceptually. The empirical test has not been attempted, but the phase model proposes only the progressive virulence of the phases, not that an individual moving to the most advanced burnout will go through each of the phases. Indeed, even brief reference to the phase model suggests that such a progression would be psychologically awkward or impossible, as in the movement from Phase II to III, or HiLoLo to LoHiLo.

Specifically, two clusters of phases serve as surrogates for type of onset. Provisionally, four phases relate to full-term chronic onset:

$$I \longrightarrow II \longrightarrow IV \longrightarrow VIII$$
$$\text{LoLoLo} \quad \text{HiLoLo} \quad \text{HiHiLo} \quad \text{HiHiHi}$$

The sense of progressive building of stressors and strain should be patent in this flight-path. In contrast, several acute flight-paths might be envisioned. For example:

$$I \longrightarrow V \longrightarrow VIII$$
$$\text{LoLoLo} \quad \quad \quad \text{LoLoHi} \quad \text{HiHiHi}$$

Here Emotional Exhaustion (V) suddenly sets in after the death of a beloved spouse, who was also best friend and constant companion. The survivor withdraws from personal relations and from work. Hence VIII may quickly follow V. Less traumatic cases of acute onset might involve a new boss with whom the transition is not only very rocky but of such character as to decrease one's sense of personal accomplishment. This implies I → III movement and, absent improvement, various escalations are possible.

Notes on Method

The present operational definition seeks to isolate, as nearly as possible, three equal groupings of negative LES scores from 1590 Site B respondents. The procedure is uncomplicated, if arbitrary. A small number of cases—36—are excluded because of the extremely high scores of some respondents who report they had experienced all or most of the life events in the same degree. This suggests either respondent fatigue, if not frustration, or perhaps a gross misreading of the instructions. In addition, 155 respondents are excluded because they check *no* positive or negative life experience, which is interpreted as improbable and hence as a non-response. The remaining 1399 cases are assigned to three clusters of scores, in this way:

	Frequency	Percent	Description
NLES I, or chronic onset	400	29	0 on NLES, but some positive scores, with total absence of either positive or negative events being interpreted as a non-response to LES
NLES II	557	40	-1 to -5 on NLES
NLES III, or acute onset	442	32	-6 to -141 on NLES

Some Findings Concerning Kind of Onset

NLES III is proposed here as a surrogate for acute onset, and NLES I isolates the batch of individuals more likely to experience chronic burnout. Given several important qualifications—especially related to the adequacy of the acute surrogate—a variety of evidence suggests that the present conventions are serviceable, if only for openers (Golembiewski, Munzenrider, and Stevenson, 1986; Golembiewski and Munzenrider, 1986a, 1986b, 1987). Compared to the phases, however, differences in onset account for small amounts of the variance in patterns of association with a panel of variables that studies of several independent populations associate regularly and robustly with the phases (Golembiewski and Munzenrider, 1986b).

Since those in Phase VIII could arrive there either by acute or chronic pathways, the rough-and-ready distinction here considers Phases I, II, and IV to be "chronic," while Phases III, V, VI, and VII are "acute." Phase I also could appear in both clusters of phases, of course, but it is not included in the acute cluster because high NLES scores cover the year preceding the individual's assignment to a phase and hence any Phase I after acute onset should have moved out of that phase. No one can say with certainty whether or not in the observation interval some acute cases returned to I, of course, and any such individuals would obscure differences between types of onset.

Does the NLES trichotomy constitute a useful surrogate for kinds of onset? An affirmative answer requires sharp distinctions between the three NLES groupings on a range of variables, and early tests indicate consistent but not great differences. The appropriate tables are not reproduced here (Golembiewski, Munzenrider, and Stevenson, 1986), but their overall pattern suggests that NLES differences covary with phase assignments. Specifically, the chi-square test indicates the distribution of the three LES clusters X kind of onset almost certainly cannot be attributed to chance—chi-square = 47.72, P < .001, with the least advanced phases tending toward NLES I and the most advanced phases tending toward NLES III. Cramer's V suggests that less than 2 percent of the variance is accounted for, but the case for the adequacy of the surrogate does not require a high proportion of explained variance.

Some summary data illustrate the support for the usefulness of the present surrogate for estimating chronic onset. When VIIIs are parcelled out among the chronic and acute clusters (Golembiewski, Munzenrider, and Stevenson, 1986, pp. 115-20), the NLES differences trend in the expected directions. That is, those experiencing few negative life experiences tend toward chronic assignments, in about 6 out of 10 cases. Relatedly, those with the most negative life experiences get acute assignments, again in about 6 of 10 cases. In sum:

	Chronic Subset	Acute Subset
Of those in the three NLES groups,	the percentages assigned to Phases I, II, IV, and VIII (partial) are	and the percentages assigned to Phases III, V, VI, VII, and VIII (partial) are
NLES I	56.2	43.8
NLES II	48.8	50.2
NLES III	41.7	58.3

Limitations of the Design for Kind of Onset

As noted, these summary results are tentative, given limitations in the design. Five points highlight these limitations. First, analysis of chronic vs. acute onset requires a longitudinal design with several observations and interviews, rather than a mere LES surrogate.

Second, the single observation relied on here cannot distinguish cases of "exit" from more advanced phases with "entrance" to them. This direction of movement probably makes a difference, if only in the sense that "getting better" may induce a more optimistic and attractive mood than "getting worse" for those who are "in" the same phase but who are headed in opposite directions, as it were. Little is known about exit and entrance in the phase model.

Third, some evidence (e.g., Golembiewski and Munzenrider, 1984a) implies that "active" and "passive" adaptations exist to all phases of burnout. Those in Phase I are "active"—as estimated by above-median scores on Job Involvement, for example—in about three-quarters of all cases. In addition, those in Phase VIII are "passive" in about 7 or 8 of 10 cases. "Actives" and "passives" have similar patterns on a range of descriptors but, uniformly, actives have the more desirable pattern. That is, actives and passives both reflect (for example) lower job satisfaction and higher rates of physical symptoms, as phases progress I → VIII. But passives are for the most part "worse" than actives on these comparisons (Golembiewski and Munzenrider, 1984a).

Preliminary results support the guess that active vs. passive modes obscure differences between chronic vs. acute onset (Golembiewski and Munzenrider, 1987). See also chapter nine.

Fourth, although a reasonable case can be made, in general, we simply do not know in what cases which severities of Negative Life Events scores will trigger acute cases of onset. For example, differences in coping skills might well exist such that some individuals with even very high NLES scores might not experience acute onset. The obverse also might be true, as even low levels of NLES for some vulnerable individuals might trigger acute onset.

Fifth, the present cutting-points for NLES might not be optimal. This would blur any differences, in general.

These five limitations could obscure or confound differences between chronic and acute cases. Consequently, any observed differences are perhaps most reasonably interpreted as conservative estimates of effects.

Burnout as Induced by Group Properties?

The focus now shifts from the individual to the group, and the inquiry will proceed along two lines. The general case will focus on whether work groups seem to have an affinity for homogeneous levels of burnout. Later analysis will test for specific differences in the properties of groups whose members report different levels of burnout.

In sharp contrast with the prominence accorded psychological burnout among individuals, its distribution among work groups has received little attention. The issue is not trivial, whether for intervention or research.

Establishing a substantial association between burnout and work-unit properties would encourage a significant and neglected line of inquiry. For example, such research could trace the impact of burnout of immediate work-group features—for example, supervisory style and local practices. The lack of such integrative research is both curious and understandable. The immediate work-group has received major theoretical and empirical attention, in virtually all areas of the management literature (for example, Likert, 1977). But burnout has typically been viewed from an individual perspective. As Carroll and White note (1982, p. 41): "Unfortunately, most writers on the subject of burnout tend to overemphasize either personal variables (the need to over-achieve, . . . and so on) or environmental variables (such as noise levels . . . and environmental obstacles)."

As for intervention, information about linkages of burnout with work-unit properties seems critical in targeting prescriptions intended to ameliorate burnout. The incidence, persistence, and negative outcomes associated with burnout all put a premium on effective countermeasures, of course.

Hence, the motivation for the present effort is strong. Evidence supporting a group locus will urge major rethinking of the typical approaches to burnout, both as a target for research as well as for intervention. Heavy concentrations of advanced phases of burnout in specific work groups will be consistent with some familiar patterns, e.g., burnout induced by certain supervisory styles and practices, as moderated by personal characteristics. Such perspectives can be helpful in many areas of management of course, as well as in training and development activities.

General Case: Work-Unit Affinity for Extreme Scorers[2]

Only two organizations have been studied in sufficient detail, but immediate work-groups have an affinity for one or the other extreme set of phases. Organizations can have majority representations of those in Phases VI-VIII (e.g., Rountree, 1984); or those in Phases I-III can dominate (e.g., Golembiewski, 1983a). But immediate work-groups—that is, groups of first-reports—are typically homogeneous as to phase assignments.

To give a general sense of this affinity, Rountree (1984) isolates 186 immediate task groups in 23 settings, with N = 1393. He distinguishes three clusters of phases: Low (Phases I-III); Moderate (Phases IV-V); and High (Phases VI-VIII). He notes (1984, pp. 245-46): ". . . the affinity of work groups for extreme scorers seems substantial. . . . Consider that 87.5 percent of all [Highs] are members of work-groups having at least 50 percent of all of their members in those three most-advanced phases." Lows show a similar but less marked tendency. Less than 10 percent of all Moderates are in work-groups where they constitute a majority, consistent with incidence data reviewed in chapter six.

Golembiewski (1983a) reports a similar conclusion. Eschewing details that can be interpreted as making the affinity even stronger, he observes that over 72 percent of those classified in one or the other set of three extreme phases are in immediate work-groups, having at least 50 percent of their membership in the extreme phases. Moreover, over 92 percent of those classified in Phases I-III have at least 50 percent of their membership similarly classified.

Variability of Phases by Task

As an interesting side-note, the two sets of data suggest that task does not determine level of burnout. Rountree (1984) includes 5 types of task groups in his set of 186; and Golembiewski's (1983a) population performs a single activity at 43 locations across the United States. Typically, units performing the same task include cases from the full range of burnout distributions.

Note that the common wisdom identifies some jobs that are purported to be stressor-rich—air-traffic controllers, urban police, and so on. So some jobs also might generate higher levels of burnout than others, on average. But the phase model has not yet been applied to the broad range of occupations.

Specific Test: Group Properties and Levels of Burnout

In general, then, the affinities suggest not only a prime locus for burnout, but also a milieu for treating it. The findings suggest "contagion" or "resonance" effects, and are consistent with the centrality of intact teams in a range of areas of theoretical and practical concern, including but not restricted to Organization Development, or OD (for example, Golembiewski, 1979, vol. 2, pp. 3–32).

In general, the findings above apply just as introduced. However, specificity is required, particularly in regard to this question: do immediate work-units differ in a range of properties that relate in reasonable ways to differences in the burnout of their members?

Notes on Host and Methods

Fortunately, we can begin to approach this central issue. In the bargain, we can rely on a large number of respondents from an organization that differs in important particulars from Sites A and B, which provide most of the data on which this volume is based. Moreover, the research design was developed independently.[3]

Applicable data come from a substantial population (N = 2,393) employed at 23 locations of a corporate chain of life-care retirement communities. Each location is similarly organized, with five major departments: General Administration, Plant Maintenance, Dietary, Housekeeping and Laundry, and Resident Care. Response rates approximate 90 percent of total employment, with almost all of the uncaptured cases involving part-time help or those employees on vacation or otherwise not at work when data were gathered at specific sites.

The present host differs in important ways from Sites A and B. Although a profit-making concern, like Site A, the present host operates at many different locations at which emotionally arousing encounters are frequent in people-helping roles, like Site B. In contrast to both other hosts, particularly A, the present industry historically has low-wage rates, a low-skill profile among its employees, and high employee turnover.

Sharply-Defined Immediate Work-Units. Here the focus is on those persons who not only report to an integrative first-line supervisor or manager but who also work in the same physical, social, and task settings. Membership in these 113 groups ranges from 2 to 22 persons, and encompasses nearly 60 percent of all respondents (N = 1,393). About 42 percent of the total respondents could not be clearly associated with a single work-group, in the present meaning, and these employees are not considered further here. These excluded employees have multiple group memberships, interstitial and boundary-spanning roles, or perform in such multiple and highly variable loci as to complicate respondent descriptions of their "work settings."

Burnout by Immediate Work-Units. Present comparative purposes involve some detailed data manipulations, which can be sketched here. To begin, each of the 1,393 respondents is assigned to a phase of burnout, using Site B norms. Then, each immediate work-group is characterized by the distribution of its membership in three clusters of phases of burnout: Phases I–III; Phases IV and V; and Phases VI–VIII. This permits arraying all 113 work groups by percentage of members in three sets of phases, based on this model:

Percent of Respondents in Three Burnout Clusters

	Phases I–III	Phases IV and V	Phases VI–VIII
Work group 1	0	0	100
·	·	·	·
·	·	·	·
·	·	·	·
Work group N	100		0

The three clusters are surrogates for the eight phases. The loss in discrimination is acknowledged, but the availability of "only" 113 groups would leave several of the full eight phases with few or no entries, even in 2 × 8 analyses.

This array supports an additional convenience. Specifically, a 1-in-6 random sample of 12 high burnout (HiBO) groups is selected from those having 50 percent or more of their members in Phases VI through VIII. And 12 low cases also are selected from the smaller number of work-groups having 50 percent or more of their members in Phases I through III. Table 7.5 provides summary data about these two randomly drawn samples of 24 immediate work-groups, with total membership of 185. These seem credible surrogates for the larger collection of immediate work-groups and all responding employees.

This convenience has costs as well as attractions. Basically, the small N requires very large and consistent differences between HiBO and LoBO work groups. Otherwise, the differences will not achieve statistical significance. Thus, the present convenience of drawing random samples of work-groups in effect constitutes a conservative test of the proposed associations detailed in Table 7.6, as is introduced below.

Work Environment Scales. Form R of the Work Environment Scales (Insel and Moos, 1974) provides the present picture of the properties of the several immediate work-groups. Table 7.6 identifies the ten WES scales, clusters them in three dimensions, describes the scales, and sketches the proposed associations

TABLE 7.5
Burnout in 24 Randomly Selected Immediate Work Groups (N = 185)

Work Group	Number of Members	High Burnout Sample — Percent in Clusters of Phases			Work Group	Number of Members	Low Burnout Sample — Percent in Clusters of Phases		
		I-III	IV-V	VI-VIII			I-III	IV-V	VI-VIII
1A	11	0	9.1	90.9	1B	17	70.6	0	29.4
2A	5	0	0	100.0	2B	3	66.7	0	33.3
3A	17	0	0	100.0	3B	5	80.0	20	0
4A	6	0	16.7	83.6	4B	4	75.0	0	25.0
5A	9	0	22.2	77.8	5B	6	66.7	0	33.3
6A	15	0	13.3	86.7	6B	5	60.0	40	0
7A	4	0	0	100.0	7B	5	80.0	20	0
8A	14	7.1	21.4	71.4	8B	4	75.0	0	25.0
9A	7	0	0	100.0	9B	14	64.3	0	35.7
10A	8	39.5	0	61.5	10B	5	60.0	20	20.0
11A	3	0	0	100.0	11B	3	66.7	0	33.3
12A	11	9.1	18.2	72.7	12B	4	75.0	0	25.0

of the scales with burnout. As the predictions suggest, each WES scale is scored so that a high score indicates a greater degree of the environmental feature at issue. Specifically, each scale is tapped by nine items, each to be scored as true or false, which are coded as 1 or 0, respectively. The maximum score for any scale is 9.

Note that WES scales have measurement properties appropriate for present purposes. Information concerning both validity and reliability is presented elsewhere (Moos and Insel, 1982). In addition, Table 7.6 presents alpha scores for the present WES administration. Those scores average over .7, and no alpha is sufficiently low to discourage use of any scale for research purposes.

In effect, the WES variables permit both partial replication and extension of earlier research. The WES overlap only in part with the work site descriptors emphasized in chapters two and three, which associate regularly and robustly with burnout differences reported by individuals. Specifically, involvement, work pressure, and clarity correspond most closely to variables included among the descriptors. Several WES scores—for example, peer cohesion, task orientation, and innovation—differ most sharply from the work site descriptors employed in earlier chapters.

Findings on Work-Unit Properties and Burnout

Basically, as Table 7.7 reflects, differences in burnout seem associated with quite distinct patterns of properties in immediate work-groups. In sum, substantial evidence supports the ideation underlying this research. Burnout is significantly associated with regular variations in immediate environmental features in six of the seven cases on which major differences are expected, and an additional case approaches statistical significance. The remaining cases concern those about which qualified predictions are made, and on which the differences trend in expected directions. Four points highlight the major contributions to this conclusion.

First, six of the WES reflect statistically significant differences between the HiBO and LoBO samples. Involvement, supervisor support, autonomy, clarity, and physical comfort are significantly greater in HiBO than in LoBO, as expected. In addition, work pressure is significantly less in LoBO than HiBO, which implies few or no cases of laissez-faire supervision in the latter work-groups.

Second, a seventh WES score is in the expected direction and closely approaches statistical significance—peer cohesion.

Third, as expected, only random variation characterizes innovation. This result fits the notion that burnout can derive from understimulation as well as overstimulation, a point emphasized in chapter one but often neglected in the literature.

Fourth, two variables—task orientation and control—trend in expected directions, but do not approach significance. This may reflect the deviant

TABLE 7.6

Work Environment Scales, Descriptions, and Associations with Burnout

WES	Alpha	Scale Descriptions
Relationship dimensions		
Involvement	.67	Employee concern about and commitment to jobs
Peer cohesion	.71	Employee friendliness and support for one another
Supervisor support	.80	Management supportiveness of employees and encouragement of employee support for one another
Personal growth dimensions		
Autonomy	.66	Encouragement of employees to be self-sufficient and to make own decisions
Task orientation	.65	Emphasis on good planning, efficiency, and getting the job done
Work pressure	.71	Pressure of work and time urgency dominating job milieu
System maintenance and change dimensions		
Clarity	.71	Employees know what to expect in daily routines; explicit rules and practices are communicated
Control	.76	Management use of rules and pressures
Innovation	.65	Emphasis on variety, change, new approaches
Physical comfort	.81	Physical surroundings contribute to pleasant work environment

162

LoBO groups > Hi, with the latter having emotional
slack to devote to tasks versus personal strain
LoBO groups > Hi, reflecting impact of social
support
LoBO groups > Hi, reflecting impact of supervisor
support

LoBO groups > Hi, since latter will lack energy to
be self-directing

LoBO groups > Hi, in general but the former may
contain deviant cases -- for example, norms en-
forcing low task orientation based on greater peer
cohesion in LoBO
HiBO groups > Lo, in general, but HiBO may include
some laissez-faire variants with low work pressure

LoBO groups > Hi, as in lesser role conflict

HiBO groups > Lo, in general, in providing external
discipline for individuals; but HiBO may include
some laissez-faire supervisors
Probably no linear relationships, since HiBO can derive from both under- as well as overstimulation
LoBO groups > Hi, given fewer job stressors implied
by greater physical comfort at work site

TABLE 7.7
Work Environments under Conditions of High versus Low Burnout

Work Environment Scales	Scale Means		T-Value	Probability
	HiBO	LoBO		
Involvement	4.82	6.79	-4.25	.001
Peer cohesion	5.34	5.93	-1.42	.085
Supervisor support	4.32	5.57	-2.82	.005
Autonomy	4.48	5.02	-1.73	.049
Task orientation	6.32	6.72	-1.06	.149
Work pressure	5.54	4.69	1.87	.038
Clarity	5.70	6.60	-2.34	.014
Control	7.25	6.84	1.19	.124
Innovation	4.08	.42	-0.79	.220
Physical comfort	5.17	6.55	-2.65	.007

conditions anticipated in Table 7.6. Alternatively, the association of the two variables with burnout may not be robust.

IMPLICATIONS FOR THE PHASE MODEL OF BURNOUT

The sections above do not suggest a substantial locus for burnout in the properties of individuals. The data do contain some clues about the intervening or moderating role of personality features in several of the phases—especially III, V, and VI. But that is all.

In sharp contrast, the group-oriented analyses seem to hold far more promise, at least at the present level of development of the phase model—hence the emphasis here on four important implications of group orientations for the phase model. First, the data reinforce the hard-learned but often neglected lesson concerning the centrality of the intact work team. The results of the last two analyses can be explained—at the first level of approximation, at least—as reflecting burnout responsive to variations in the properties of the work-group setting. These properties involve styles of supervision, group atmosphere, and so on, consistent with the dominant tradition in organization analysis (Likert, 1977).

Second, the data imply the limits of "stranger" workshops for stress management. That is to say, the intact work-unit seems the more reasonable target for designs to ameliorate burnout. Moreover, workshops for individuals may have some paradoxical effects, even counterproductive ones. For example, any augmented skills in managing stress that individuals acquire in stranger work-shops may result only in making the work site *more* stressful for colleagues back home, by merely increasing the tolerance of some individuals to stress rather than reducing work site stressors. The point gains salience from the possibility—supported by experience at Site A—that those in advanced phases of burnout seem unlikely to avail themselves of opportunities to develop attitudes and skills for more successful stress management.

Third, the data also imply the serious limitations of the all-but-universal neg-lect of burnout in both organizational diagnosis and prescription. A work-unit with most members in Phases I–III would seem a likely target for the typical interaction-centered team-building design—via three-dimensional images, mirror-ing, or other confrontational techniques. Such stimulus-heightening in the serv-ice of change seems less appropriate for a work-group dominated by Phase VIII. There, indeed, stimulus overload would be a danger against which safeguards should be considered in designs related to choice or change. Low-stimulus designs seem more appropriate for such a work-group—role negotiation, flexible work hours, and so on (Golembiewski, 1984b, 1984c).

No wonder, then, about the mixed results of attempts to apply a single team-building design to a large batch of work units. Mixed results should be expected, since there is no reason to expect that groups with different distributions of burnout will respond similarly to the same team-building design. Quite the opposite seems likely, in fact.

Fourth, the preceding two emphases also provide both general and specific evidence concerning a key focus for ameliorating burnout. The present findings reflect only association, of course; they do not establish causality. At the same time, the results encourage a prudent risk. The results above support the effort to influence burnout via the direct manipulation of the properties of intact, immediate work-units, such as group cohesiveness, and so on.

Conveniently, we know much about inducing desired changes in the "inde-pendent variables" in such linkages, such as by affecting cohesiveness (Golem-biewski, 1965, pp. 101–11). Patently, this suggests a direct approach to amelio-rating burnout, whose usefulness only future research and applications will affirm or deny. Chapter nine develops this central point.

A final point concludes this summary of chapter seven by drawing attention to two credible kinds of onset in burnout. Chronic and acute flight-paths must be distinguished not only in longitudinal studies, but must also be clarified in the relationships reported here, which in general focus on a point-in-time. We hazard a guess. In the present analysis, Phases III, V, and VI seem especially sensitive to Type A and LES differences. This may well reflect the reasonably greater vulnerability to acute episodes of those individuals who have turbulent LES histories or who score high on Type A measures. Longitudinal studies alone can satisfactorily test this hunch, support for which would testify to the very sub-stantial power of the phase model.

NOTES

1. Examination of LES responses encourages deletion of some cases. The complex character of the instructions, as well as the placement of LES items at the very end of a long survey, seems to have encouraged fatigue or error by a small number of respondents.

Some respondents *obviously* did not follow instructions. For instance, some respondents score *all* items. Cases fitting this profile are excluded from analysis: that involves 36 cases.

Moreover, LES scores for some individuals are zero. Results of prior studies utilizing the LES or similar instruments indicate that it is highly unlikely that a respondent would *not* experience at least one of the numerous life events over the prior year. Negative LES scores—or 1,004 cases with less than zero scores—set one limit for including cases, since the negative score is involved in calculating two of the three other LES scores. There are 1,250 positive LES scores.

2. Previously-published results are based on median scores for the three MBI subscales at Site A, N = 290 (Golembiewski, 1983a). The present findings rely on Site B norms, which are substantially higher for each MBI subdomain.

3. The design was developed by Benjamin Rountree, then with the University of Missouri at Columbia, and various collaborative activities followed the assemblage of the data (e.g., Golembiewski and Rountree, 1986).

8. *INITIATIVES FOR RESEARCH: EXTRAPOLATIONS FROM PHASE MODEL FINDINGS, I*

The seven preceding chapters provide a kind of platform or foundation. That platform is of variable strength: some of its key supports are weak or uncertain; and no one can claim that it is complete, although some major components seem to be reasonably in place.

This chapter and the following one seek to provide a preliminary assessment of the outreach potential of the phase model via attention to research and intervention. The motivation is direct. In part, the usefulness of a construct like the phase model is reflected in its consistency with things we already know about some limited aspects of nature, or can quite directly come to learn. In addition, the usefulness of a construct like the phase model is measured by its ability to "cast a long shadow," to provide insight or motivation for encompassing a range of matters distal to the focal construct. Constructs have a variable potential for outreach, as it were—by providing credible linkages between unconnected facts or events, by focusing attention in directions that were previously less appreciated but in the construct's light deserve heightened priority, and by encouraging us to order aspects of our lives differently or with sharper locus.

One caveat should precede this overview of initiatives based on burnout phases. To paraphrase Blaise Pascal, "Compared to divinity, humankind is not much. Compared to bullrushes, however, humans are everything." So it is with the present status of progress on burnout phases. Compared to ultimate knowledge, the existing scope and methods are halt and lame. Nonetheless, the progress outlined above permits useful initiatives for research, intervening, and public policy.

THE PHASE MODEL AND FOUR INITIATIVES FOR RESEARCH

Prior discussion has emphasized the research advantages and challenges of the phase model, and four illustrative highlights will prove useful in this chapter

FIGURE 8.1
An Elemental Branching of Major Possible Responses to Stressors

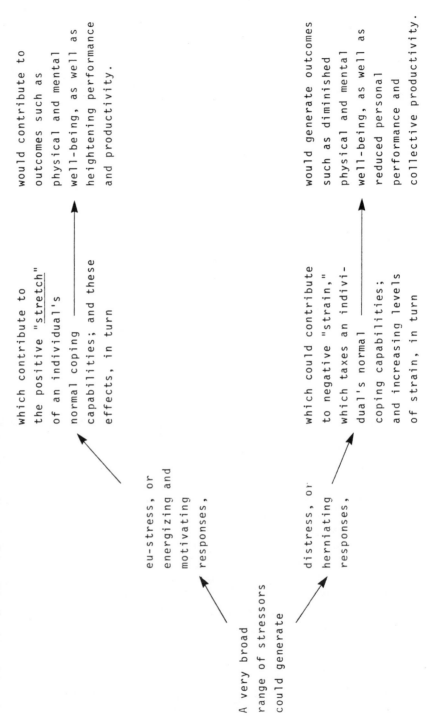

would contribute to
outcomes such as
physical and mental
well-being, as well as
heightening performance
and productivity.

which contribute to
the positive "stretch"
of an individual's
normal coping
capabilities; and these
effects, in turn

would generate outcomes
such as diminished
physical and mental
well-being, as well as
reduced personal
performance and
collective productivity.

which could contribute
to negative "strain,"
which taxes an indivi-
dual's normal
coping capabilities;
and increasing levels
of strain, in turn

eu-stress, or
energizing and
motivating
responses,

distress, or
herniating
responses,

A very broad
range of stressors
could generate

lest the major conclusions get lost in the welter of detail necessary to establish the model's credibility. The phases constitute a strategic choice for research, as a first section indicates. Moreover, exploiting that choice requires converting several stubborn challenges into opportunities—11 in number, for our present purposes, as a second section details. A third section sketches how the phase model can be anchored in the clinical literature, as one important way of estimating how "bad" are advanced phases of burnout. This third section also deals with the phases in relation to several clinically relevant affective states. Finally, a fourth and concluding emphasis shows how the phase model can serve in a critical research initiative. Here the focus is on specifying *kinds* of change when most of the literature focuses on one kind only.

Phases as a Strategic Choice

Above all, the phase approach seeks to avoid some major difficulties of the stress literature to which burnout research can trace its lineage. Directly, the strategic choice underlying much of the stress literature seems awkward, perhaps even unredemptive. So, the focus below is on how the basic choice is often made in terms that have a high probability of failure, a choice that may even be a conceptual *cul-de-sac*. The discussion also demonstrates how the phase approach to burnout may help the potential intervener avoid putting the "wrong foot forward."

The point is a critical one, so let us approach it via some historical perspective, perhaps even leisurely. Quite early in stress research it became clear that the target for analysis got complicated, fast. Initially, stress was framed in elemental stimulus → response terms. Some stressors—literally anything might serve that purpose—would trigger something in the person—a "fight or flight" response, a "General Adaptation Syndrome," or the like (Selye, 1956). The idea caught on quickly, being obviously simple and perhaps of such universal scope as to have powerful attractions for many.

Soon enough, however, that elemental $S \to R$ linkage had to be significantly modified. An elaborated model came to have features like those sketched in Figure 8.1.

So far, so good. Excellent, in fact.

But an awkward imbalance characterized the development of the basic $S \to R$ linkage. In concept but seldom in practice, the orthodoxy soon became:

Ideally, in short, both the stimulus and response sides should get attention. However, the focus usually has been on $S \to O$ or $S \to E$—although not unrelievedly. Only a little satisfactory attention has gone to:

This has proved a momentous bias, and a daunting one. Not only do extraordinarily large numbers of differences—within and between stimuli, individuals, and environments—require specification. In addition, the scale of even studies "large" by present standards is much too small to map such linkages in any satisfactory way. Moreover, the attention to R typically has a micro-focus, even in those cases where R receives close scrutiny—readings of systolic and diastolic blood pressure, levels of various hormones, and so on.

The main consequences? In the long run, this strategic approach may possibly lead to a comprehensive network of relationships. In the short run, on balance, the outcomes have been awkward. At the level of "molar outcomes" relevant to management students, no reasonably clear connections exist between classes of stressors and outcomes. In general, with rare apparent exceptions (for example, Karasek, 1981), today's regularity becomes tomorrow's random difference, or even anti-finding. One supposes this is due largely to the mass of intervening, compounding, and confounding variables in different studies. Depending on how things happen to fall in a specific batch of data, individual studies sometimes lead to sharp patterns of results in one direction, at other times reveal no consistent patterns, and in still other instances distinguish patterns in multiple or even opposed directions. At our present stage, indeed, it seems that the more elegant and rigorous the design, the more opaque the findings at the macro-level. This seems the case with the "person/environment fit" model, for example, which clearly puts the emphasis on O and E (French, Caplan, and Harrison, 1982). At the micro-level, substantially greater patterning seems to exist (Karasek, 1981), but the outcomes in such research are very different from the measures of immediate managerial relevance—estimates of productivity and performance, for example.

The phase approach to burnout deliberately takes the opposite track: it focuses on an R, a bottom-line response. Burnout is not the only R, of course, but it seems a reasonable candidate, and one proximately associatable with a range of effects of patent managerial significance. In sum, burnout places priority emphasis on a kind of bottom-line measure of the effects of stressors, which discounts an individual's coping skills and resources. The multitudinous properties of S, O, or E are not of initial concern. Rather, indeed, the present approach assumes (among other factors) that: the same S can be a nonstressor or stressor for different Os at the same time, or for the same O at different times; the coping capabilities of Os will differ profoundly (the same "amount" of the same stressor can herniate one O and inspire another to joyous achievement); and complex features of E, or the environment, will affect in profound ways both individuals and the stressors they experienced.

We dwell on E by way of illustrating the case for the other two assumptions. As Abner notes (quoted in Farber, 1983, p. 243): "Without an understanding of the history of labor-management conflict, the roots of burn-out are invisible and incomprehensible." From another perspective, the quality of E may overcome even very powerful stress-producing aspects of work. For example, Cherniss and Krantz (1983, pp. 198-99) describe a Catholic religious order whose members work in a residential setting for the mentally retarded, where burnout reactions are buffered by a strong sense of "ideological community." The scientists conclude:

The sisters who work in this setting violate almost every prescription that has been offered by the burnout experts. Their work is not simply a large part of their lives; it is their whole life. In fact, they literally have no life outside of the religious order and their work with retarded people. They are in contact with their "clients" seven days a week, 52 weeks a year, year after year. . . .

The prevailing view would predict that staff burnout would be rampant in this residential program, yet many of the sisters have maintained a high level of care and commitment for years. (One person we interviewed had been doing this kind of work for over 30 years.) As we talked to these people, we began to realize that burnout ultimately is not caused by over-commitment, working too long or too hard. Long hours, hard work, and the other stressors often cited as causes of burnout only lead to burnout when there is an absence of meaning in work. The burnout process thus begins not with stress but with the loss of commitment and moral purpose in work.

The phase approach further assumes that the qualities of even the "same" E will differ—not only in the perceptions of E by various Os exposed to the "same" E—but also in different issue areas, even at closely spaced times.

The basic point may be expressed in a simple contrast: $S \to O$, $S \to E$, and $O \to E$ varieties of interactions pose numbing complexities, especially given the lack of some valid and reliable molar R or Rs against which the stability of various linkages can be judged. The emphasis on burnout phases seeks to transcend this complexity by developing a valid and reliable R against which various S, O, and E interactions can be judged, *after* development of a reliable and valid R.

Let us amplify the basic contrast. Ideally, S, O, E, and R *all* require attention. Practically, however, the priority on S, O, and E not only puts the wrong foot forward first; it can also be counterproductive in that it requires very complex design, data-gathering, and interpretive decisions, if not an infinite regress. These issues can inhibit progress, while risking pessimism that progress is possible.

Right or wrong, then, the strategic choice here focuses on an R, and arguably one of the more important bottom-line *R*s—burnout. The purpose is not to finesse *S, O,* and *E,* but to provide some benchmark against which their inter-action can be estimated with some confidence. To put it another way, *S, O,* and *E* cannot be relegated to "black box" status. The phase model seeks to shift priorities, nonetheless, to see how far that will take analysis.

Eleven Tactical Opportunities/Challenges

The strategic choice seems to have been successful at least within the context of the present data sets. Their several inadequacies, of course, have been noted at various points, and need not be repeated here. The integrity of the present results badly needs testing with other designs and data sets, and tactical initiatives illus-trate some proximate challenges. They deal, in turn, with

- Distinguishing between possible types of burnout and their arenas
- Isolating "high" levels of burnout
- The possibility that naturally occurring changes in burnout phases may imply useful tactics and strategies for conscious amelioration
- Distinguishing modes of entrance to, and exit from, advanced phases of burnout
- Discovering typical pathways to and from advanced burnout
- Distinguishing "worn out" from "burned out"
- Isolating clinical and behavioral anchors of the phases
- Testing more satisfactorily for various outcomes of advanced burnout
- Describing the characteristics of groups of first-reports that covary with their apparent affinity for extreme phases of burnout
- Providing a linkage with organization culture
- Relating to ongoing lines of research

Commonly, these future research initiatives assume an initial population of perhaps 5,000 respondents, from whom two or more sets of responses could be obtained over an interval of several years. Respondents would have to be identi-fiable by the researcher, both individually and in terms of their membership in an immediate work-group of those reporting directly to a common supervisor. Ideally, a variety of "soft" and "hard" measures of performance and productiv-ity also should be available.

Burnout$_1$, Burnout$_2$, . . ., Burnout$_N$?

Analysis here focuses on the work site, and leaves open the issue of linkage with other possible burnout realms, or leakage between them. In short, there may be a "marriage burnout" as well as a "work burnout," and their linkages may be of practical as well as theoretic importance. To illustrate, variable degrees of congruence may exist between such realms, and precise description and prescription demand an ability to distinguish among the congruencies. In addition, pathways may also exist for the diffusion of burnout among these possible realms, and this implies significance for both the timing and targeting of interventions.

The issue of linkage or leakage between realms, in short, constitutes an important item on tomorrow's research agenda.

Is "High" High Enough?

In a basic sense, the future program of research rests on distinguishing high versus low scores on the three MBI subdomains–Depersonalization, Personal Accomplishment (reversed), and Emotional Exhaustion–hence, the criticality of the norms defining "high." The present norms come from a substantial population $(N > 1,500)$, to be sure, and one whose members experience stressors regularly, and with some intensity. It would be useful to test the present norms, however, and perhaps especially in occupational clusters like air-traffic controllers, who are said to experience extremely high levels of stressors.

Note one arresting point, however. The covariants of burnout phases seem to be so massive that they force themselves on our attention even when high assignments may include many scorers who are in fact moderate or even low scorers. The initial published reports about Site A, for example, defined *high* as above the median on each MBI subdomain *at that one location* (Golembiewski, Munzenrider, and Carter, 1983). That convenience set far too low a standard, apparently due to the attractive qualities of the host organization. Despite this major shortfall, however, even that convention maps patterns similar to, but less robust than, those sketched in chapters two and three. Understandably, the magnitudes of the differences between phases increase when appropriate upward adjustments are made in the scores defining high on each of the MBI subscales (Golemviewski and Munzenrider, 1984), based on Site B norms.

Can Natural Change Guide Contrived Amelioration?

Incidence data at several points show that burnout phases seem characterized by some dynamic change within a basic pattern of substantial stability. This arresting apparent fact at once justifies major research ventures and suggests their possible payoffs. The basic design would involve isolating "switchers"– those whose phase assignments change substantially between observations, perhaps six months or so apart. Certainly, a I → VIII qualifies as a switcher, as does and VIII → I. The switchers would provide dual perspective–on those trending toward VIII and those moving toward I–but it appears that this kind of design requires a large initial population. Consider the several populations reviewed in chapter six, to explain. Only about a quarter of those classified in the three most- versus least-extreme phases of burnout switch over the intervals between observations, which on occasion are a year apart.

Depth interviews with switchers could provide valuable perspective on the natural etiology and amelioration of burnout, about which we have mostly by-guess-and-by-golly hunches rather than solid information. The focal questions of such inquiry cover a broad range, which can only be suggested here. What proportion of the switchers can be classified as acute—that is, individuals who are low on burnout, who then experience some sudden and precipitating life event, and recover within a relatively short interval? Grieving over the death of a loved one constitutes a case-in-point. Improvement in such a situation would involve establishing a new balance in life, and time plus support and adaptive skills would provide the appropriate tools (for example, see Gould, 1978; Bridges, 1980). Also of great relevance would be chronic cases of advanced burnout who switch suddenly. What such switchers did, or what things were done around them, could provide useful grist for the mills seeking to grind out reasonable prescriptions for ameliorating burnout. Improvements in chronic burnout imply a need for environmental change, but data may show that to be a simplistic prescription.

Do Entrance and Exit Modes Vary?

Compelling but general reasons suggest that the direction of one's progression through the phases of burnout might be relevant, for instance, in inducing different patterns of responses by individuals. Contrast a still-worsening situation with one in which an individual reverses a situation that is still "bad" although it has bottomed-out. The vernacular certainly anticipates major differences. Illustratively, people might describe the latter condition in such terms as these: "Things are bad, but they've turned around"; and "I can see the light at the other end of the tunnel, although it's a long and dark tunnel."

The focus of inquiry on exit versus entrance could have numerous payoffs. Generally, distinguishing entrance from exit might be useful and even necessary for many theoretical and practical purposes. Specifically, for example, it might lead to distinguishing "leading" and "lagging" indicators of progressive burnout. Such knowledge would have a variety of theoretical and practical uses—in explanation, prediction, and intervention. Only longitudinal designs will provide necessary data.

Can "Typical Pathways" Be Discovered?

As noted at several points, the eight phases seem to be progressively virulent. Basically, four interacting sets of variables tend to worsen in unison, often but not always dramatically. These sets of variables include features describing the work site, symptoms of physical disease, individual performance, and measures of quantitative as well as qualitative productivity.

As has also been noted, this progressive virulence is distinguished from step-by-step movement of an individual through each of the eight phases of burnout. Empirically, this stepwise movement never seems to occur for individuals. Conceptually, such movement would be difficult or impossible to justify, as in the case of movement of an individual from Phase II to III—that is, from HiLoLo to LoHiLo.

To put it more simply, the phases seem to reflect a progressive virulence. Hence, individuals at VIII seem "worse off" in numerous particulars than those at I. But an individual will typically "skip" phases in what may be called a "personal development profile" of burnout.

Chapter six has already detailed this phenomenon, so we are merely reemphasizing the point here. One strategic research initiative could well focus on isolating "typical pathways"—or more fancifully, common flight-paths—for entering into more advanced phases of burnout, or for exiting from them. This initiative could focus on pathways or flight-paths such as those shown in Table 8.1. Rough calculations based on the persistence data reviewed in chapter six imply a rank-order of the several scenarios in cases of entrance to advanced phases of burnout. B seems the most common pathway; A seems about half as likely as B; a scenario like C seems a bit less likely than A; and a scenario like D does not appear to occur often. Given developments at Site A, this rank-ordering does not surprise. In organizations with more settled systems of appraisal, A might well be the dominant scenario.

The approach in Table 8.1 is applicable to exit from advanced burnout, as well as entrance to it. The point holds in principle, but it seems more difficult to develop scenarios appropriate for exit, which no doubt includes not only the skipping of phases but also recycling as persons "improve."

In addition to suggesting grist for future research mills, such pathways also may be used to provide a possible interpretation of certain regularities already observed, albeit with full warning that speculation dominates. Consider that Phases III, V, and VI often stand out in discussions of results—especially in connection with Type A and life events in chapter seven. There, those three phases account for the bulk of nonrandom variation, while Type A and life events seem to be associated with other phases in random ways. The pathways in Table 8.1 provide one—if only one—way of dealing with that now-and-again prominence of those three phases. That is, Case A in the table may reasonably be interpreted as chronic burnout—a "pure progression" to "full-term" burnout. Cases B and C may illustrate the broader family of acute onset which, consistently, can be associated with Type A and life stress. That is, these variables may measure vulnerability to acute episodes. Note the central role in acute episodes assigned in Table 8.1 to Phases III, V, and VI, whose central role is consistent with chapter seven's emphasis on the sensitivity of these phases to Type A and life-events differences.

Such interpretations must be tentative, given the dominance here of one-shot research designs. And the interpretation does not clearly extend to Case D in Table 8.1. This may reflect its rarity, but affirmation of that guess will require longitudinal designs with large populations.

Toward a More Differentiated Typology?

Typically, despite the divergent implications of the points above, burnout has usually been viewed as a unitary syndrome with a multiple symptomology.

TABLE 8.1
Alternative Pathways to Advanced Phases of Burnout and Associated Scenarios

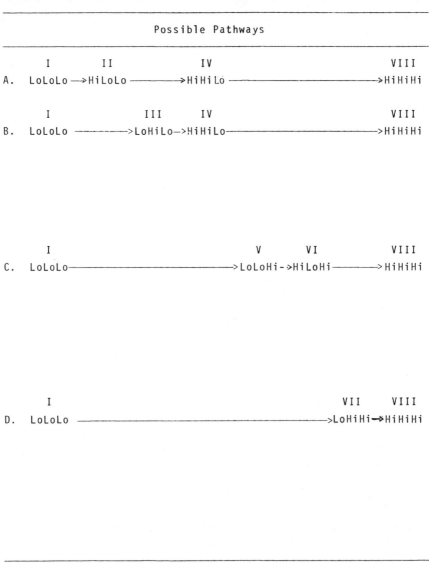

Possible Pathways

	I	II	IV	VIII
A.	LoLoLo →HiLoLo		→HiHiLo	→HiHiHi

	I	III	IV	VIII
B.	LoLoLo	→LoHiLo→	HiHiLo	→HiHiHi

	I	V	VI	VIII
C.	LoLoLo	→LoLoHi-	→HiLoHi	→HiHiHi

	I	VII	VIII
D.	LoLoLo	→LoHiHi→	HiHiHi

Proposed Scenarios

A. The profile of full-fledged burnout, a "pure
    progression."

B. Standards of performance are substantially in-
    creased in a short period; appraisals fall
    sharply; this bewilders an individual previously
    so "successful" and upwardly mobile as to have
    developed only weak systems of social support;
    and this crescendoes into herniating strain.

C. The sudden death of a spouse who has been the
    mate's "best and only buddy"; the attendant
    strain depletes emotional resources; no other
    major human supports are found and/or are con-
    sidered acceptable; the supervisor seeks "to bury
    grief in work," which further distances the in-
    dividual from human contact; and performance
    eventually suffers greatly.

D. A researcher has strong needs to be liked, and
    is successful at that but falsifies research
    data to gain broad acceptance and esteem; per-
    sonal relationships are preserved though all
    else suffers, in large part because "X couldn't
    do that"; convincing evidence of long-standing
    duplicity by X surfaces and induces his social
    supports "to cut him off" suddenly.

177

That may well be inelegant, as some existing work suggests (for example, Gillespie, 1981).

This general point can be illustrated by a brief contrast between "worn out" and "burned out" (Fischer, 1983, pp. 41–43), the distinction between which could well constitute an item on tomorrow's research agenda. The three key differentiae here seem to be sense of self-esteem, incidence, and the degree of consciousness or level of complaint. Fischer urges that we keep the two conditions separate because the "causes and the indications for their management are quite different." He articulates the three differentiae in the following way (1983, p. 42):

> We should see that the part of these victims that has become "worn out" is their sense of self-esteem. Those who are burned out, rather than worn out, cling tenaciously to a high sense of self-esteem. (In short, those who complain of burn-out are, in fact, worn out—the true victims of burn-out continue in their task in a martyrlike fashion.) It seems likely that the condition of "worn-out" is considerably more prevalent than that of burn-out and may well constitute a major sociological problem. Even though burn-out does not present such an epidemic threat to society, its victims also deserve some share of our efforts to help them.

The "burnout" cases were working "beyond reasonableness, common sense, and even concern for their own well-being and health, [and] were desperately engaged in trying to ward off something that appeared to them even more terrifying"— the loss of their "special" or "superior" status (Fischer, 1983, p. 43).

Fischer approaches behavior from the perspective of "psychoanalytic psychotherapy" (Schafer, 1976) and—although any associations with the phase model of burnout must be conjectural at this time—two points deserve note. First, straightforward designs can test for connections between the burnout phases and self-esteem, as measured by such convenient instruments as that of Rosenberg (1965a, 1965b). Initial research supports the association between self-esteem and the phases, but in a direction opposite from that taken by Fischer's intriguing hypothesis. The association only approaches significance, however ($P = .071$ in Golembiewski and Kim, 1988).

Second, some available analysis (Golembiewski and Munzenrider, 1984a) may relate to Schafer's basic distinction. Broadly, this analysis distinguishes two modes of response to all phases of burnout: active and passive, as determined by high versus low levels of job involvement, defined by norms derived by dichotomizing the Site B scores on that variable. More or less, 80 percent of those in the least advanced phases seem active and 20 percent can be rated as passive. For Phases VI–VIII, the proportions are approximately reversed. Phase by phase, individuals classified as both active and passive reflect patterns of associations familiar to readers of earlier chapters of this volume. Consistently, however, actives have a more favorable profile on all variables than do the passives, although their profiles or patterns are similar. See especially chapter nine.

It requires only a little imagination to make a hypothetical leap. Phase VI-VIII actives may correspond to Fischer's burnout, while Phase VI-VIII passives may qualify as worn out. As Fischer proposes, that would qualify the population in the study that isolated active and passive modes of response (Golembiewski and Munzenrider, 1984a) as substantially worn out, with perhaps 20 percent of that population classified as burned out.

Although conjecture can motivate testing, it does not substitute for it. See the third section of chapter nine for one use of the active/passive distinction.

Can Phases Be "Anchored"?

The regular and robust association of the burnout phases with several classes of variables merely begins the more comprehensive task of "anchoring" the phases in specific attitudes, behaviors, and values, as well as—and more importantly—in clusters or syndromes of these "anchors." Changes in phases, in turn, may well be associated with differences in these anchors, either as precursors or successors. The work site descriptors provide one such set of anchors, but attention needs to be given to a broader range of variables and especially perhaps to those that relate to basic chemical and hormonal processes.

Let us rephrase the point in terms of earlier analysis. The phases (an R) have proved useful, and this encourages of search for a far broader range of covariants that can be labeled S, O, and E—stimuli (S) like chemical or hormonal processes, differences between organisms (O), and environmental (E) features such as those tapped by worksite descriptors.

In addition, such anchoring could serve purposes far beyond that of description. In the ideal case, knowledge of such clusters will facilitate amelioration of burnout. For example, assume that the onset of specific symptoms comes to be known as a definite precursor of advanced burnout phases. Sensitivity to variations in this symptomology might serve as an early-warning system, helping us to locate and moderate stressors before their effects reinforce and build upon one another in ways that complicate remedial action.

More broadly, use of the phases might be anchored in other approaches to human behavior. For example, consider only the substantial attention that has been given to helplessness (for example, Garber and Seligman, 1980) in connection with efforts to understand and aid in the relief of the several classes of depression (Seligman, 1975). At least at first blush, the phase model of burnout can serve the same sort of purpose in two ways. One, the phases might provide an operational measure of the sense of helplessness as felt by many employees, the lack of which has been a major factor limiting research in that area. Two, the phases might also serve as an indicator of the probable onset of some of the classical depressions, and an early signal for the need for intervention.

What Constitutes Satisfactory "Outcome Measures"?

Future research must give major attention to "outcome measures," or those aspects of reality basically envisioned as being dependent variables. This research focuses on only a few of them—physical symptoms, performance differences, and productivity levels. Future research will have to expand that brief list in many ways. For example, research might well draw a blood sample before it can arrive at any decent perspective on covariation between self-reports about phases and bodily states and processes. Such a focus might well isolate leading and lagging indicators, or at least provide more guidance in distinguishing between the "dog" and the "tail."

Whatever the formidable challenges and ambiguities of such work, no doubt exists about the limitations of the present research with regard to outcome measures. The productivity data used above, for example, may well suffer from ceiling effects that set restrictive upper limits. If so, this would narrow the range of productivity scores and thus compound, confound, or even camouflage any relationships to burnout phases.

Differences in Properties of Groups of First-Reports?

Several independent studies (see the previous chapter, and Rountree, 1984) imply the affinity of immediate work-groups for extreme burnout phases. Such groups are defined as those consisting of individuals reporting directly to a single supervisor or other authority figure. Virtually all organizations have such a membership, with the "limited span of control" prescribing some low upper-limit on size—perhaps 3-10 persons reporting to a common superior at the most senior levels, and perhaps 15-30 persons at operating levels. Only a few individuals ance for the members. Patently, these HiCoh capabilities might also buffer the onset and severity of diminished personal accomplishment and heightened emotional exhaustion, the other two subdomains tapped by the present phase model in the reinforcement of any tendencies toward burnout that may inhere in personality factors, specific tasks, or environmental forces. Again, this directs attention upon features of S, O, and E that might be associated with the phase model, R. Anchoring research to a known R reduces the cross-influences of S, O, and E variables.

Major theoretical and applied potential inhere in this affinity of immediate work-groups for individuals in either the most or the least advanced phases of burnout. For example, the affinity encourages the search for different profiles of group properties, as discussed in the last section of the previous chapter. If these exist, they will surely enrich both description and prescription. To illustrate, advanced burnout may be associated with certain managerial styles and practices, or perhaps with group properties like cohesiveness, and these descriptive linkages would imply practical approaches to remedying advanced burnout. Consider cohesiveness, which measures the resultant of the forces attracting an individual to membership in an immediate work-group *minus* those forces encouraging the individual to leave it. Most HiCoh groups probably should have concentrations of members classified in the less-advanced phases of burnout—to extrapolate from the known associations of cohesiveness and productivity (Golembiewski, 1962, especially pp. 168-70). Evidence in chapters seven and nine suggests this expectation is correct.

If such a linkage with burnout phases is established, we know much about how to induce HiCoh (Golembiewski, 1962, especially pp. 149-70). Thus, how much the members like each other is an important component of cohesiveness, and conscious efforts to increase liking by selection or training might counteract the depersonalization that seems to trigger movement into advanced phases of burnout. A HiCoh group also ought to be more capable of generating and maintaining norms of high output, as well as of providing social support and assistance for the members. Patently, these HiCoh capabilities might also buffer the onset and severity of diminished personal accomplishment and heightened emotional exhaustion, the other two subdomains tapped by the present phase model of burnout.

These attractive possibilities do not exhaust the research payoffs of focusing on the immediate work-group. For example, it seems well established that HiCoh groups usually have high productivity, although a minority of them have low levels of output. In the case of both extremes, the social dynamics seem the same: HiCoh groups imply greater control over member behavior, and very high or very low productivity requires substantial control over member behavior (Golembiewski, 1962, especially pp. 168-70). But what if some HiCoh work-groups have high concentrations of advanced phases of burnout? Such a finding would require elaboration or even fundamental changes in the accepted view (Golembiewski, 1965, especially pp. 113-21), which implies an association of HiCoh with less-advanced burnout.

Providing a Linkage with Organization Culture?

Even this brief survey of properties and features of the phase model implies a strong case for the culture-relevant covariants of burnout. Consider only these implications of research on the phases of burnout:

- individual reports suggest cultural differences
- properties of immediate contexts reflect cultural differences
- direct culture descriptions relate to discrete phase distributions

The following three sections, in turn, briefly introduce these three implications. A fourth and concluding section emphasizes the several sources of analytic and applied leverage that inhere in burnout ↔ culture associations.

Individual Reports Suggest Cultural Differences

Differences in the phases suggest, but do not establish, differences in the relevant social or cultural contexts at work. Illustratively, Is and VIIIs provide these two contrasting pictures of their work sites:

Those in Phase I see a work site with:	Those in Phase VIII see a work site with:
• substantial participation	• little participation
• low job tension	• high job tension
• substantial willingness to disagree with supervisor	• general unwillingness to disagree with supervisor
• a strong tendency to enhance involvement	• a strong tendency to limit involvement
• great potential for satisfying evaluations of many facets of work	• low potential for satisfying evaluations of many facets of work

The observer can easily visualize very different contexts or cultures triggering such perceptions/reactions.

Properties of Immediate Contexts Suggest Cultural Differences

More directly, early work implies that distributions of phases are associated in predictable ways with group properties. See chapter seven, which shows that those in advanced phases see their immediate work-groups in contrasting ways:

Work-Group Property	High Concentrations of Phases I–III	High Concentrations of Phases VI–VIII
Peer Cohesiveness	Higher	Lower
Involvement	Higher	Lower
Task Orientation	Higher	Lower
Work Pressure	Lower	Higher
Supervisory Support	Higher	Lower

In powerful support of these two profiles, a successful attempt to reduce the proportion of Phases VI–VIII in an organization resulted in successful modifications in both these group properties and in others as well (Golembiewski, Hilles, and Daly, 1987). See also chapter nine.

Such variation in group properties associated with different distributions of phases suggests cultural differences, but the contrast above doubtless is too simple to be of much general use. Far more than two alternative cultures will be necessary to comprehensively describe the range found in natural-state work-groups (e.g., Bowers and Hausser, 1977). By implication, in any case, two powerful "products" associated with burnout phases—their persistence, and the affinity of immediate work-groups for those in extreme phases—in different ways suggest a significant connection between cultural variables and burnout. See chapters six and seven.

Direct Cultural Descriptors

Thus far, only a single study (Janz, Dugan, and Ross, 1986) directly seeks to associate culture with burnout and the phases. These researchers use the Corporate Culture Survey, which characterizes collectivities in terms of Shared Values, Power, and Rules. In turn, these permit calculating a Culture Index, of CI. For departments, CI correlates -.82 with the percentage of employees in Phases VI through VIII.

Leverage of Burnout ⟷ Culture Designs

The summaries above suggest that research designs involving both burnout and culture promise significant conceptual and methodological leverage. Four kinds of leverage inherent in the focus on culture ⟷ burnout designs must suffice for present purposes.

First, burnout ⟷ culture designs provide both analytic and applied opportunities, which attracts stereophonically. Change in burnout seems associated with change in the surrounding cultural context, and *vice versa*. The individual/context mating has proved serviceable in various areas of inquiry/application—delinquency, criminal recidivism, Organization Development, and so on—but the basic lesson often eludes many researchers. Chapter nine provides one test of this analytic/applied linkage.

Second, culture ⟷ burnout requires attention to several levels of analysis and amelioration—for individuals, and for several systems such as immediate work-groups of first-reports as well as the larger organization. Such linkages are crucial in the development of any comprehensive theory of organization, but tend to be neglected.

Third, the burnout ⟷ culture focus suggests the strategic significance of the immediate group of first-reports, a point that keeps reemerging in the history of behavioral analysis in various forms (e.g., Shils, 1951), but which also periodically goes into eclipse (e.g., Lakin, 1979). Right now, to apply the point, "culture" is viewed in the kind of global terms popularized by Peters and Waterman (1982), who distinguish only "tight" and "loose" cultures, and those only barely. In contrast, the present position suggests a more complicated view of culture—a kind of "building up" of a composite total culture from "local cultures." Most of the current literature suggests the "trickling down" of a monolithic or total culture, in sharp contrast.

Conceptually and methodologically, the focus on some kind of "primary group" provides numerous advantages in both research and applications, despite the apparent convenience of viewing "culture" or "organization" as monoliths. The point has been made elegantly elsewhere (Miller and Friesen, 1984, especially pp. 12–18), and the present findings at several points reinforce the usefulness of building upward from some "basic units" such as groups of first-reports. See chapter seven, especially.

Fourth, the focus on burnout ↔ culture may help with a vexing issue in behavioral analysis. The evidence increasingly suggests the appropriateness of a plural concept of change that differentiates changes in state from changes in degree within a state (e.g., Golembiewski, Billingsley, and Yeager, 1976). However, the existing formulations have a number of deficiencies. For example, change in state is now defined by complex statistical conventions that do not yield an easily interpretable "direction" for change. Some evidence suggests that variations in the distribution of phases of burnout might serve as a surrogate for estimating changes in state, as opposed to degree, which is the essence of gamma change and similar concepts (Golembiewski, 1986). Among other conveniences, these variable distributions of phases suggest a desirable direction for change— e.g., fewer VIIIs and more Is seem in general a reasonable objective of social and managerial policy. This point will be considered further at the conclusion of this chapter, immediately after we complete our list of 11 tactical opportunities/ challenges in research extensions of the phase model.

Increasing the Specificity of Other Approaches?

Finally, if only for present purposes, the phase model might well serve to increase the specificity of other approaches to work-related research. Consider here only the common usage of the Job Diagnostic Survey, or JDS, of Hackman and Oldham (1980). Those researchers propose that job features impact on "critical psychological states," as conditioned by moderators such as "context satisfactions," to generate "affective outcomes" as well as work effectiveness. The basic underlying model suggests:

```
A.   Positive                    Positive
     job factors                 outcomes
```

The findings here suggest that differences in burnout might well serve as a critical intervening variable in JDS linkages. To sample two possibilities:

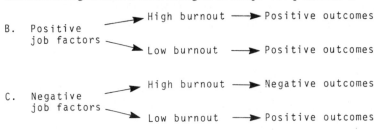

```
                          ➤ High burnout ──➤ Positive outcomes
B.   Positive
     job factors ──
                          ➤ Low burnout ──➤ Positive outcomes


                          ➤ High burnout ──➤ Negative outcomes
C.   Negative
     job factors ──
                          ➤ Low burnout ──➤ Positive outcomes
```

Case A recommends devoting resources to job improvement, but Cases B and C provide uneven support for this allocation of resources. Case B reinforces A in encouraging the allocation of resources to improving job features; and Case C would directly apply those resources to the amelioration of burnout.

These eleven possibilities are neither comprehensive nor definitive, to conclude. But they do suggest the usefulness of the phase approach in being fitted to common thoughtways, and perhaps also in transcending them in significant particulars.

Burnout Phases and Clinically Relevant Affective States

Part of the judgment concerning the conceptual usefulness of advanced burnout phases will be determined by their progressive severity, especially as judged from their "anchoring" in conditions emphasized in the clinical literatures. For example, many observers assume that advanced burnout implies depression, and is in that sense conceptually rooted in clinical symptomologies. This conclusion applies in two senses. One, the clinical literature deals with differences in states, generally if not always specifically—as in "healthy" and "less healthy" but also "unhealthy." In short, differences between types of change are implied. Two, the urgency and perhaps the character of efforts to ameliorate burnout will receive valuable guidance from tests of whether advanced phases of burnout have clinically relevant content or covariants.

Tests of this clinical "anchoring" might proceed in several ways. For example, some measures of proneness to psychiatric illness (e.g., Goldberg, 1972) might be utilized to assess the degree of covariation with the phases. Or, far more expansively, a long-term study might be begun with a large population to track variations in the phases and the mental-health histories of individuals. Directly, we cannot yet report on such attractive research designs.

The focus here is on specific affective states that seem clinically relevant, and whether or not individuals are aware of them in ways that match their phase of burnout. The purpose is exploratory, for several possibilities exist and these cannot be assessed *a priori*. Thus, individuals may be generally unaware of both resultant feeling-tones and specific contributors to them, or they may reflect various degrees of awareness. Moreover, if some wholistic awareness does exist, a central question involves the relationship between specific contributors and various levels of individual awareness. Some feeling-states may be identified with greater facility than other feeling-states, and individuals may be more in touch with some of the contributors to a particular affective state. Also, some specific feeling-states may variously "lead" or "lag" specific phases of burnout.

Such possible differentiating features can have theoretical and applied significance. Assume that self-reported affective state A proves a valid and reliable leading indicator of subsequent increases in burnout, or *vice versa*. Such a regularity would permit early diagnosis and timely remedial interventions, of course. With such a possible end in prospect, we begin a line of inquiry that is not ideal but represents some progress.

Notes on Host and Change[1]

All data come from a survey of 10 facilities in one region of a corporately managed chain of life-care retirement communities, identified in chapter three as

TABLE 8.2
Factor Analysis of MAACL Items

Subscales/Items	I	Rotated Factors[†] II	III
Genial			
Devoted	.50		
Clean	.50		
Friendly	.50		
Lucky	.49		
Sympathetic	.49		
Free	.48		
Strong	.47		
Amused	.47		
Tame	.45		
Young	.42		
Mild	.42		
Obliging	.41		
Willful	.40		
Despondent			
Frightened		.62	
Grim		.58	
Sad		.58	
Miserable		.57	
Terrified		.56	
Unhappy		.55	
Afraid		.53	
Awful		.53	
Lonely		.53	
Fearful		.53	
Terrible		.53	
Blue		.51	
Alone		.50	
Shaky		.49	
Lost		.47	
Worrying		.47	
Suffering		.47	
Rejected		.46	
Low		.45	
Upset		.45	
Nervous		.44	
Hopeless		.43	
Panicky		.42	
Furious		.41	
Agitated			
Annoyed			.61
Irritated			.60
Agitated			.59
Impatient			.58
Disgusted			.54
Critical			.53
Angry		.34	.52

TABLE 8.2 (continued)

Subscales/Items	I	II	III
Complaining			.51
Cross			.51
Discontented			.50
Displeased			.48
Disagreeable			.44
Contrary			.40
Eigenvalue	19.09	13.43	3.36
Percent of variance	14.5%	10.2%	2.5%
Percent cumulative variance	14.5%	24.7%	27.2%

†
Only loadings > .30 are reported.

Site C. Each facility has a similar formal structure, with five major departments: General Administration, Plant Maintenance, Dietary, Housekeeping and Laundry, and Resident Care.

Self-Reported Affective States

In addition to the phases, this section employs eight scales developed from the Multiple Affective Adjective Checklist, or MAACL. These scales come from two lines of analysis.

Five of the eight MAACL scales used here come directly from the long tradition of research begun by Zuckerman and Lubin. Initially, the MAACL relied on an empirical method of item selection (Zuckerman and Lubin, 1965), while factor analysis has been used recently to select items for the scales (Zuckerman, Lubin, and Rinck, 1984). The investigators conclude that the two strategies are of comparable validity, so the five major scales from both lines of work are used here. Originally, MAACL focused on "three of the clinically relevant negative affects: anxiety, depression, and hostility," using a list of 132 adjectives as stimuli for how respondents feel "today" or "now" as opposed to "generally" or "occasionally." That is, MAACL sees affect *as a state* rather than as a trait. Recently, two summary scales were added to the initial MAACL trio: Positive Affect (or Euphoria), and Dysphoria, whose general referents are indicated clearly enough for present purposes by their designations.

This analysis also deals with three additional scales derived from the MAACL. The underlying research utilizes a new response stem for MAACL—how respondent "felt in recent days" rather than "today" —and conservative research practice encourages a verification by factor analysis of the structure of responses. Analysis generates five factors with eigenvalues >1.0, and Table 8.2 provides details about the first three and easily interpretable factors, which are labelled Genial, Despondent, and Agitated.

This analysis uses all eight MAACL-derived scales because no reasonable choice could be made between the two sets. Two kinds of considerations convey a sense of the decision making that led to no-choice. On the one hand, the two sets of scales tend to be highly correlated. That is, the "new" Despondent correlates strongly with the "old" measures of Anxiety (r = .83), Depression (r = .88), and Dysphoria (r = .90). Similarly, Agitated and Hostility are correlated at a near-perfect level (r = .96). On the other hand, the three interpretable "new" factors in Table 8.2 account for less than 30 percent of the variance.

Expectations about Covariation

Table 8.3 provides some measurement details about the eight MAACL scales, and we expect that the affective states will vary regularly and robustly with the phases. For two scales—Positive Affect and Genial—scores should decrease, phase by phase. For the other six scales, scores should increase, phase by phase.

The rationales are transparent. For the six negative affective states, the decreasing emotional slack associated with the phases should induce growing emotional deficits or deficiencies. For the two positive affective states, decreases are

TABLE 8.3
Some Measurement Properties of MAACL Scales

MAACL-derived Scales	Mean	Standard Deviation	Cronbach's alpha
Anxiety	1.85	2.08	.75
Hostility	2.65	2.99	.77
Depression	1.32	1.95	.77
Dysphoria	5.82	6.06	.90
Positive Affect	10.42	6.14	.91
Genial	6.22	2.49	.63
Despondent	3.32	4.43	.90
Agitated	3.82	3.79	.87

expected because of the energy-drain of coping with advanced burnout, phase by phase.

Findings Concerning the Phases and Clinically Relevant Affects

The findings suggest a definite pattern of associations of the expected kind, but the magnitudes of the associations permit various interpretations. The table is not reproduced here, but it reflects a regularity in pattern for MAACL-derived scales by progressive phases of burnout (Deckard, 1985, p. 85). In sum, the six negative affects all increase, Phases I → VIII; and Positive Affect and Genial decrease. Moreover, all eight cases reveal a very high probability (P < .000) that nonrandom variation exists somewhere in the overall distributions of scores by phases.

The magnitudes of the patterns permit alternative interpretations, however, as Table 8.4 suggests. Thus, nearly 88 percent of all possible paired-comparisons are in the expected directions, and no statistically significant deviant cases exist. However, only 19.19 percent of all paired-comparisons achieve statistical significance, using the Least Significant Difference test, as modified for unequal subpopulations. The record of significantly different paired-comparisons varies little between: all eight MAACL scales (19.19 percent); the five traditional scales (18.57 percent); and the three scales constructed for present purposes by factor analysis (20.23 percent).

Note also that, in Table 8.4, the two positive affective states produce a substantially greater proportion of statistically significant differences, phase by phase, than the six negative affective states: 32.1 vs. 17.9 percent, respectively. This point motivates some speculation in the interpretive section to follow.

One final manipulation of the data provides us with a bit more useful information. Table 8.5 summarizes the record concerning direction and magnitude of the affective variables, considering all possible pairs of phases and the "distance" between them. In short, the greater the "distance" between phases, the greater the probability that differences in the affective variables will fall in the expected direction, and that those differences will achieve statistical significance.

Some Interpretive Possibilities

These results do not permit unequivocal interpretation, but four interpretive possibilities merit attention.

First, one may conclude that there is no irrefutably strong association between affective states and burnout phases, despite a clear tendency in that direction. This would stem in part, though not entirely, from the possibility that people are accurate enough reporters of their overall burnout state but have difficulty identifying and weighing specific contributors to the resulting states, perhaps especially with respect to negative affects. In the same connection, advanced burnout might, for different individuals, well be associated with varying degrees of specific affective states.

Explaining the results as reflecting measurement inadequacies, however, must

TABLE 8.4

Summary of Paired-Comparisons Across Eight Burnout Phases,† MAACL Scales

	I vs. II	I vs. III	I vs. IV	I vs. V	I vs. VI	I vs. VII	I vs. VIII	II vs. III	II vs. IV	II vs. V	II vs. VI	II vs. VII	II vs. VIII	III vs. IV
Anxiety							X							
Hostility			X	X		X	X	X						
Depression							X	X						
Dysphoria					X	X	X							
Positive Affect			X		X	X	X	X			X	X	X	
Genial			X		X	X	X	X			X	X		
Despondent							X							
Agitated				X	X	X	X							

	III vs. V	III vs. VI	III vs. VII	III vs. VIII	IV vs. V	IV vs. VI	IV vs. VII	IV vs. VIII	V vs. VI	V vs. VII	V vs. VIII	VI vs. VII	VI vs. VIII	VII vs. VIII
Anxiety			X	X										
Hostility		X		X										
Depression				X										
Dysphoria				X										
Positive Affect				X							X			
Genial				X										
Despondent				X										
Agitated	X	X	X	X										

[+] X denotes paired-comparison where $P < .05$.

191

TABLE 8.5
Affective Variables and "Distance" Between Pairs of Burnout Phases

	"Distance" Between Pairs of Scores						
	+1	+2	+3	+4	+5	+6	+7
In Expected Direction	73% (41/56)	83% (40/48)	95% (38/40)	100% (30/32)	100% (24/24)	100% (16/16)	100% (8/8)
In Expected Direction and Statistically Significant	0% (0/56)	6% (3/48)	13% (5/40)	19% (6/32)	58% (14/24)	44% (7/16)	100% (8/8)

be tempered. In the main, the phases have proved reliable indicators of burnout in several studies assessing concurrent validity although—as chapter three in particular demonstrates—the magnitude of the basic pattern can vary between different research sites and different panels of variables. Moreover, the MAACL has proved sensitive to variations in feeling-tone—e.g., as induced by natural experiments or drugs (e.g., Lubin and Zuckerman, 1969).

Second, one could argue that specific individual properties dilute associations, such as differences in Social Desirability, or SD (Crowne and Marlowe, 1964). SD measures the tendency to temper observations by a concern for social approval. High SD scorers should experience some difficulty in attributing to self the more negative MAACL adjectives, and hence they might generate artifactually low scores on some scales. Patently, a substantial proportion of high SD scores could reduce the magnitude of any observed associations without destroying the pattern reported above, especially if one grants the notion that SD effects are more likely to be revealed via the "obvious" MAACL instrument than via the burnout phases.

The data do not reject such an effect. Let us distinguish two clusters of MAACL-derived scales, for starters. Isolate Positive Affect, Genial, and Agitated from the remaining five scales, on the general principle that those three seem to involve the *least unattractive* self-descriptions and, hence, should pose fewer problems for high SD scorers. The differentiation does not much affect the pattern of association of affective states with the phases: 85.7 and 89.3 of all paired-comparisons are in the expected direction for the "attractive" and other set of scales, respectively. However, the robustness of the differences between the paired-comparisons differs markedly. Consistent with the SD concept, the three "attractive" MAACL scales generate 29.8 percent statistically significant differences in paired-comparisons, while the five "unattractive" scales average 12.9 percent. Similarly, as noted earlier, a substantial difference also exists in the record of statistically significant paired-comparisons for the two "positive" scales—Positive Affect and Genial. The record of this affective duo differs substantially from that of the six "negative" affective states: 32.1 and 17.9 percent, respectively.

Third, the present analysis does not distinguish active from passive modes of reacting to advanced burnout. Credibly, active VIIIs might well report that their phenomenal worlds are more attractive than passive VIIIs. Of course, this would disguise or distort associations between the phases and their affective states.

Fourth, the results do not permit making a judgment concerning whether the affective states are "leading" or "lagging" indicators. For the most part, a longitudinal research design would be far better suited in helping to make such judgments than the present, one-shot design. In short, the present data combine cases of "entrance" to more-advanced phases of burnout with cases of "exit" to less-advanced phases; consequently, no specificity about leading/lagging indicators is possible. But the possibility exists that phase X affective interaction may be distorted by the unspecified directions of individual movement through the phases.

Burnout Phases and Kinds of Change

Perhaps most significantly, the phase model relates to an issue central to all behavioral research: the effective differentiation between various types of change, without which much research must either remain uninterpretable or (worse still) will generate confusion and despair when interpretations are attempted. The current problem in this area is, in fact, so large as to defy overstatement. So, how does this analysis deal with such a grave matter? In four steps, we attempt to show how the phases of burnout may be used strategically to elucidate types of change:

- the description of three kinds of change
- unanticipated consequences of the early technology for assessing kinds of change
- the conceptual possibility of burnout phases as a surrogate for changes in state
- testing whether the phases seem to measure differences in states or only in degree

A Tripartite Model of Change

Although the position is articulated most insistently by a "small and invisible college" (Tennis, 1986), there has been *no* opposition to the radical notion that change should be viewed plurally, as a set of phenomena, rather than as a single event. Ironically, in practice, however, almost all interpretations of research are made under the assumption that "change" is "change," while conceptually, the plural concept still goes unchallenged.

Numerous models of plural change have been proposed (Golembiewski, 1986a, pp. 550-51), but the emphasis here is on one variant that uses a statistical technology to isolate types of change. This research proposes three types of change (Golembiewski, Billingsley, and Yeager, 1976; Golembiewski and Billingsley, 1980):

1. *alpha change* involves a variation in the degree of some existential state, given a reliably calibrated measuring instrument that taps a constant conceptual domain;

2. *beta change* involves a variation in the degree of some existential state, complicated by the recalibration of some portion of the intervals of the measurement continuum associated with a constant conceptual domain; and

3. *gamma change* involves a basic redefinition or reconceptualization of some domain, a restructuring of perceived reality that involves differences in state

In effect, gamma change refers to differences *between states*, while alpha refers to changes in *degree within a state*. H_2O provides a physical example. It can differ in degree—as in temperature or pressure. At several points, however, H_2O appears in different states as temperature or pressure vary in degree. The H_2O states include solid, liquid, gas, and (we suppose) plasma.

The original research focused narrowly on establishing the existence of very "large" nonalpha change, or gamma change, using Ahmavaara's procedure (1954). Basically, this technology assesses the degree of variance shared by a pair of factorial structures, which derive from pre- and post-measures of behavior with a common instrument. The measures bracket an intervention intended to impact that behavior. Nonalpha change was defined provisionally as less than 50 percent shared variance between the factor analyses of any two survey observations, considering both the pattern and magnitude of the two structures compared.

Some Unanticipated Consequences

The initial demonstration that nonalpha change seemed to exist had two major results. It reinforced in concept the need to distinguish kinds of change but, in practice, the statistical demonstration tended to traumatize both research and application. Efforts that sought to enrich both, in sum, induced pessimism or resignation about the study and practice of change. Basically, the initial technology implied a kind of analytical cul-de-sac in five different ways (Golembiewski, 1986a, p. 559):

1. Ahmavaara's procedure for determining gamma change requires a large N, which limits its flexibility.

2. Most attention to gamma change focused on aggregates of individuals, which neglects those many cases in which the individual is the unit of analysis.

3. All available technologies for determining nonalpha change require major and debatable assumptions.

4. Research fixates on testing for nonalpha change between T_1 and T_2, and neglects the tangled issue of T_1 comparisons with T_2. For alpha change, T_1 can be considered 0 and T_2 could be + or −. For gamma change, "direction" has no obvious meaning because of the fundamental change in state.

5. The covariants of the new state indicated by gamma change will be poorly mapped until the properties of alternative states are understood sufficiently to develop a taxonomy of states, *if such exist.*

OD intervenors have a definite interest in inducing nonalpha change—as in creating new cultures at the work site—but that interest was poorly served by the statistical procedures that implied the need for conceptually distinguishing types of change. Briefly, the Ahmavaara procedure permitted no assessment of whether gamma change moved in the intended "direction" and, if so, how "far." The technology could only assess whether nonalpha change occurred. Common practice usually finesses this problem. Hence, for example, OD intervenors usually assume that "change" can be reliably measured along Likert's (1967) systems of management, with System 4 indicating the direction for change appropriate to OD values.

Burnout as a Way Out of a Cul-de-Sac

The conceptualization of burnout implies at least one gamma difference or change in states, as well as multiple differences in degree. At the very least, burnout requires two states—one that is, and one that is not. Clinical descriptions certainly suggest such a difference in the states of those going into burnout, or coming out of it (e.g., Freudenberg, 1980; Maslach, 1982). Moreover, research with the phase model urges the speculation that there might be several states involved. Indeed, *perfect* empirical support for the present phase model would establish that eight *and only* eight states are required to describe the phenomenal domain labelled "burnout." Of course, the empirical data above—especially those in chapters one through five—suggest that multiple phases are appropriate, but those results are not always consistent with the usefulness of all eight phases, as now operationally defined.

These conceptual possibilities attract powerfully. Basically, *if* the phases can serve as a surrogate for estimating differences in state, that permits a way out of the analytic and applied cul-de-sac attributed above to the original test for differences in change (Golembiewski, 1986a, p. 562). That is, if the phases measure two or more differences in state, then

1. A large N will not be required.
2. The individual is the unit of analysis, and aggregations of individual scores also are possible—e.g., for work-units, given the generic problems with any such uses of individual-level data (e.g., Golembiewski, 1962, pp. 56-58).
3. The technology for measuring an individual's phase of burnout is quite direct.
4. Changes in T_1 vs. T_2 burnout have a specific direction—i.e., Phase VIII vs. I covariants powerfully reflect deficits or deficiencies: the work site has less attractive features, more physical symptoms are reported, performance appraisals decrease, and productivity falls.
5. The covariants of burnout phases are increasingly known.

This list suggests a strong case can be made, *conceptually*, for the phases of burnout as a potential surrogate for gamma change, or change in state. Indeed, it is nearly correct to note that *no* deficit or deficiency so far studied fails to map on the phases in a way that implies the validity and reliability of the several phases. And the between-phases differences are often so large as to imply changes in state.

Burnout Phases and Differences in State

The basic question thus becomes empirical: Does the phase model encompass differences that qualify as gamma? At a minimum, patently, the phase model must include at least one gamma change or difference, as contrasted with a bare difference in degree here called alpha.

The present approach to estimating gamma again uses factor analysis, which estimates the number and character of dimensions necessary to account for the variation in some collection of scores. Fundamentally, the congruencies between numerous pairs of factorial structures will constitute the present estimate of the differences in state between the structures. For example, *the* prototypic question here is whether the batches of individuals classified in phases I vs. II generate sufficiently different factorial structures in their responses to the Maslach Burnout Inventory so that the phases can be reasonably inferred to reflect gamma differences.

Technically, the congruence of factorial structures is estimated here by using Ahmavaara's technique (1954). Details aside, Ahmavaara's procedure provides us with two critical measures: an intraclass correlation coefficient; and a product-moment correlation coefficient. The intraclass correlation coefficient indicates the degree to which any two factorial structures are similar in both pattern and magnitude, while the product-moment coefficient estimates the degree of similarity in patterning only.

The square of each of these coefficients indicates the percentage of variance shared by any two factor structures, of course, and any r^2 in the .50 range or less will be taken to indicate gamma differences. This constitutes a major assumption, but probably a conservative one. Hence, when two factorial structures have 50 percent or more distinct variance, this analysis proposes they are sufficiently different to qualify as safely being alpha change, as defined here. The 50 percent cutting-point remains arbitrary, of course.

Data come from Site B, with N = 1590. For details about the analysis, see Golembiewski and Munzenrider, 1988a, 1988b, 1988c), as well as the first two chapters of this book.

No expectations are appropriate, but the present phase model would receive maximum support if tests of all pairs of phases indicate gamma differences. Gamma differences for any paired-comparison of the factorial structures on the MBI items generated by respondents assigned to one or the other of that pair, in sum, imply a change in state between those two phases.

TABLE 8.6
Analysis of Factor Structures of MBI Responses, by Phases

Paired-Comparisons of Factor Structures	Intraclass Correlations		Product-Moment Correlations	
	$r =$	$r^2 =$	$r =$	$r^2 =$
I vs. II	.44	19.4%	.53	28.1%
II vs. III	.40	16.0	.49	24.0
III vs. IV	.62	38.4	.66	48.6
IV vs. V	.49	24.0	.58	33.6
V vs. VI	.67	44.9	.73	53.3
VI vs. VII	.64	41.0	.69	47.6
VII vs. VIII	.67	44.9	.72	51.8
I vs. III	.75	56.3	.78	60.8
II vs. IV	.40	16.0	.53	28.1
III vs. V	.59	34.8	.65	42.3
IV vs. VI	.61	39.2	.73	53.3
V vs. VII	.71	50.4	.74	54.8
VI vs. VIII	.86	74.0	.87	75.7
I vs. IV	.70	49.0	.73	53.3
II vs. V	.54	29.2	.60	36.0
III vs. VI	.66	43.6	.64	47.6
IV vs. VII	.54	24.2	.60	36.0
V vs. VIII	.71	50.4	.74	54.8
I vs. V	.62	38.4	.66	43.6
II vs. VI	.54	29.2	.61	37.2
III vs. VII	.52	27.0	.61	37.2
IV vs. VIII	.70	49.0	.77	59.3
I vs. VI	.70	49.0	.74	54.8
II vs. VII	.54	29.2	.60	36.0
III vs. VIII	.71	50.4	.75	56.3
I vs. VII	.57	32.5	.63	39.7
II vs. VIII	.62	38.4	.67	44.9
I vs. VIII	.80	64.0	.82	67.2
Summary Totals =	.62	39.5%	.67	46.6%

Testing for Gamma Differences Between Phases

As Table 8.6 shows, gamma differences may be said to exist in most of the paired-comparisons of phases. To put it another way, individuals assigned to different phases in terms of their responses to the MBI items have quite different factorial structures in their heads. More specifically, on average less than 40 percent of the variance is common on the intraclass correlation coefficients, and these relate to both pattern and magnitude of the factorial structures. For the product-moment correlations, which refer to similarities in patterning only, about 47 percent of the variance is shared.

It may also be helpful to organize the data in another way. Table 8.7 is arranged in terms of the increasing "gaps" between the phases. That is, Phases I vs. II has a "gap" of 1, and so on. For all but +7, as Table 8.6 shows, differences in the "gaps" do not much influence the correlations. It is not clear why the largest "gap"—Phase I vs. VIII—also reflects the *largest common variance* between the two factorial structures, *on average*. On general principles congenial to the present line of argument, one would expect low correlations, if not the very lowest. Part of the explanation may inhere in the fact that there is only one way to generate a +7 gap—that is, Phase I vs. VIII. But for the present the answer is not known.

One might object that the results in Tables 8.6 and 8.7 imply less about gamma change than they do about the restriction of the variation in MBI scores via the focus on pairs. Three points put this criticism in perspective. First, one would expect the pattern of the factorial structures to be quite similar for all phases, although the magnitudes might well vary, because the phases are designed

TABLE 8.7

Ahmavaara Coefficients, by "Gaps" Between Phase Factor Structures

	"Gaps" Between Phases						
	+1	+2	+3	+4	+5	+6	+7
Mean r^2, intra class correlations, in %	32.6	44.7	41.4	3.58	42.7	35.0	64.0
Mean r^2, product-moment correlations, in %	40.4	52.5	46.8	44.3	49.0	42.5	67.0

to reflect the three MBI subdomains, if in different degrees. More specifically, product-moment correlations might then be higher. And so they are, but only modestly. Thus, the argument about restricting variance by focusing on the pairs has to be curbed, both by reasonable expectations and the results.

Second, another test of the restricted variation hypothesis involves estimates of congruence between 11 randomly-selected sets of *clusters* of phases: I-III vs. IV-VIII, I-VI vs. VI-VIII, and so on. The mean of the squared intraclass correlations is 64.1 percent, and that of the product-moment correlation is 69.4 percent (Golembiewski and Munzenrider, 1988a). These also reflect substantial "losses" in shared variance, although not so markedly as the comparisons of pairs of phases.

Third, one might propose that the results in Tables 8.6 and 8.7 say less about gamma than they reflect a common occurrence *when any variables are compared*, phase by phase. Three variables are utilized to test this notion in the Site B data batch: participation in decisions at work, job involvement, and job tension at work. A factor analysis is conducted for all cases (N = 1585), and it establishes a clean, three-factor structure for those variables that permits confidence that the variables do not simply measure the same domain three times. Paired-comparisons are then made of the eight separate factorial analyses conducted for those assigned to each of the phases, as they responded to the items in the three target scales. Both sets of Ahmavaara's coefficients are high when all 28 pairs of structures are compared: only six of 56 are .85 or below, and 29 are .90 or higher. The grand means for shared variance are 80.3 and 80.9 percent, respectively, for intraclass and product-moment correlations (Golembiewski and Munzenrider, 1988b).

These results do not speak to all comparisons of all variables, phase by phase, of course. But they do suggest that a simple argument about attenuation-of-variation does not seem to hold. Recall, from chapter two, that the three variables used here varied significantly in many paired-comparisons of the phases. The results also imply, consistent with the present argument, that gamma differences exist between the phases but that alpha-only differences are found between the three target variables referred to above.

This summary only suggests the central role of the phases of burnout in the study of kinds of change, but the suggestion is both attractive and consistent with earlier chapters. So, the surrogacy of the phases for changes in state can claim an attentive hearing as this beachhead gets broadened, for good or ill.

IMPLICATIONS FOR THE PHASE MODEL OF BURNOUT

These four perspectives on research and the phase model—both general and specific—imply numerous interactive possibilities for development and enrichment. The phase model "casts a long shadow," as it were. It does not suggest an analytic dead-end, but inspires us to trek down a long road.

The topics covered by the first perspective relate to the strategy underlying the phase approach. The choice was risky, going as it does against the grain of most work on stress and burnout. But the risk seems to have proved worth taking.

Second, as an inventory of eleven challenges suggests, the phase model seems well-situated in once-fertile—if now relatively dormant—areas of inquiry that seem much in need of reinvigoration. The nesting of burnout in immediate work-groups, for example, exemplifies vast areas of conventional research that can derive needed stimulation (e.g., Lakin, 1979) from the phase model, as well as contribute substantial context to it. We will not have to wait long to assess whether those eleven challenges can support useful research. Chapter nine begins some of the testing, in fact, in connection with an applied effort to reduce burn-out in a small business organization.

The third perspective on research extensions of the phase model perhaps poses more challenging problems than it now provides ready answers, but one point seems clear enough. Whatever the outcomes, the phase model requires—and perhaps even more so, deserves—testing for covariation with various clin-ically relevant affects or conditions. The results above do not discourage that search, although the interpretation of those results cannot be definite.

The fourth perspective on research extensions of the phase model seems to have much to recommend it. The focus on change is not only attractive, but it may be strategically athwart one of those lines of research that will lead behav-ioral research into a new promised land. As numerous observers have noted (e.g., Miller and Friesen, 1984), behavioral research in organizations shows major indications of being stuck. So, a conceptual boost is much needed.

All in all, then, the phase model does not imply an analytic well soon to run dry. Rather, it should be able to contribute to, and draw sustenance from, many lines of inquiry in the behavioral and social sciences.

NOTE

1. The following materials derive directly from G. Deckard, B. Rountree, and R. T. Golembiewski. (1987). Self-Reported Affective States and Burnout Phases. Mimeograph.

9. *THREE ORIENTATIONS TO INTERVENTION: EXTRAPOLATIONS FROM PHASE MODEL FINDINGS, II*

Amelioration constitutes *the* bottom line of burnout research, and this final chapter directs attention to three progressively deeper orientations to conscious intervention in social systems. The first has to do with burnout's relationship to "social support," in a way that tests the phases' claim to validity and also suggests a direct, ubiquitous approach to influencing burnout. The second orientation highlights a possibly valuable strategic feature of the burnout phases: that two modes of adaptation to each of the phases seem to exist, despite the regularities associated with the phases, especially as shown in chapters two, three, and four. The third is represented by an actual intervention in a small organization unit, an intervention that relied on social support and the modes as well as the phases in its effort at amelioration.

The chapter concludes by detailing some broader implications for the use of the phase model, and with an attempt to place that model conceptually within a two-factor theory of affect.

In the main, the chapter trends from the general to the specific—first discussing credibility of approaches to reducing burnout, then testing the realities of a specific design and its consequences, and in conclusion focusing on burnout's potential role in a more general theory of affect.

In effect, also, this chapter takes on several of the opportunities/challenges described in chapter eight. Of these, six will get the most attention:

- Differentiating possible types of burnout
- Beginning to distinguish "worn out" from "burned out"
- Linking the phases to social support, as a contribution to isolating additional clinical and behavioral anchors of the phases

- Intervening to ameliorate burnout
- Testing a "hard" measure of advanced burnout—turnover—to expand the sense of outcome measures of the phases
- Describing the characteristics of groups in relation to burnout, and hence contributing to a sense of linkages with group properties and cultures

ORIENTATION I: "SOCIAL SUPPORT" AS TARGET[1]

How to heighten the probability that interventions will do more good than harm? The notion of "social support" attracts in this regard, generally, because it implies a socio-emotional infrastructure that can cushion the personal shock that seems associated with burnout. More specifically, social support suggests low depersonalization which, it should be obvious by this time, provides front-line protection against an individual escalating to advanced phases of burnout.

The motivation to test for the linkage seems substantial. *If* social support can be related to the phases, it will serve several purposes. Such an association would imply the usefulness in ameliorating burnout of various Organization Development designs that seem effective in influencing social support (e.g., Golembiewski, 1982). Conversely, failure to find a substantial covariation with the phases would challenge the thrust of this analysis—perhaps not fatally, but seriously.

Conceptual Issues

The attractiveness of social support is patent in the concept's very definition. In Cobb's language (1976, p. 300), social support refers to a state within which "information [leads] individuals to believe that they are cared for and loved, esteemed and valued, and that they participate in a network of communication and mutual obligation."

In general, ample evidence points to the significance of social support, and also suggests that it should vary with the burnout phases, *if they measure what they purport to measure*. To augment the point, Cobb (1976) proposes a strong linkage between social support and health, a position taken by many researchers. For example, women reporting low social support experience more medical difficulties during childbirth than women reporting higher levels of support (Nuckolls, Cassel, and Caplan, 1972). Similarly, individuals with little or no social support appear to be more vulnerable to numerous stress-related outcomes (e.g., Caplan et al., 1975; House, 1981; Kasl and Wells, 1985; and LaRocco, House, and French, 1980). Of course, chapter four details the marked association of the phases with physical symptoms, and this implies another possible association between the phases and social support.

Social support remains important in research on occupational stress, in spite of numerous problems with definition and conceptualization (see, especially,

House, 1981, pp. 3-30). For example, there has been substantial debate over whether social support serves as a "buffer" that moderates organizational stressors. The positions taken run the gamut: Yes (e.g., Cobb, 1976; Pines, 1983; and Pines and Kafry, 1981), through No (Schafer, 1982). Even the "No" contingent values social support, however, with most of its adherents proposing that the main-line effects of social support are most prominent (Blau, 1981). And the perceptive House (1981, pp. 30-38) sees both buffering and main-line effects, with social support sometimes buffering the relationship between stress and health, but also impacting directly on both.

Research has busied itself with differentiating the "social support" concept, but this has resulted as much in problems as it has added to the evidence of the usefulness of the orientation. Some of these early efforts distinguish between *types* of support—for example, instrumental and expressive (Dean and Linn, 1977; Thoits, 1982). Instrumental support refers to a relationship used to achieve an end—for instance, financial assistance. On the other hand, expressive support refers to the relationship's unmediated meaning for the individual—companionship, a sense of belonging or of being loved. Other studies focus on the several *contexts or domains* in which support might be provided—in families, at work, and so on. And a few researchers emphasize the *functions* of social support—for example, listening, technical support, technical challenge, emotional support, emotional challenge, and the sharing of social reality (Pines and Aronson, 1980, and Pines, Aronson, and Kafry, 1981).

Methodological issues notwithstanding, the sense of the significance of social support has variously penetrated into practice. For instance, some organizations attempt to offset negative outcomes frequently associated with role or occupational stress by instituting and formalizing "support systems" for their employees (Caplan, 1974; Gottlieb, 1981). Support systems have been defined in the following terms (Caplan and Killilea, 1976, p. 41):

> attachments among individuals or between individuals and groups that serve to improve adaptive competence in dealing with short-term crises and life transitions as well as long-term challenges, stresses, and privations through (a) promoting emotional mastery, (b) offering guidance regarding the field of relevant forces involved in expectable problems and methods of dealing with them, and (c) providing feedback about an individual's behavior that validates his conception of his own identity and fosters improved performance based on adequate self-evaluation.

Testing for Burnout X Social Support Association

Data for testing this first orientation to ameliorating burnout come from Site B, where support is assessed by employee responses to items that relate together several domains or contexts—that is, social support from family, friends, and work-related sources. Some of the statements represent various types of positive support relationships; others focus on nonsupport, or an individual's feelings of isolation. Respondents rate each statement in terms of this response stem: how much do you agree with the following statement? Responses range from Strongly Disagree to Strongly Agree, and these anchor stems are scored as 1 and 7, respectively.

A full report appears elsewhere (Golembiewski, Munzenrider, and Stevenson, 1986, pp. 53-61), and chapter four provides preliminary details, so the treatment here can be summary in nature. The approach relies on factor analysis, which generates 5 factors among 16 items. Factor 1 describes feelings of not belonging, as well as respondents' being upset by their current predicament. Factor 2 identifies perceptions of family supportiveness, especially when help is needed. Factor 3 describes activity in non-work-related groups, such as church, social, and professional groups. Factor 4 reveals the presence or absence of significant peer-support networks in the respondent's environment. And Factor 5 relates to perceptions of being loved and being actively involved in an intimate relationship at the time of the study.

Note that most factors directly reflect the degree of social support—high factor scale scores indicate high support. Scores for Agitated-Rejection are reversed, and high scores indicate less rejection. All estimates of Cronbach's alpha attain acceptable levels for exploratory purposes. Factor 5 constitutes the least satisfactory case (.55), and the other five alphas average .67.

The correlations involving the five support scores and Total Support justify their use here, although in order to conserve space the relevant table is not reproduced. All 15 coefficients are positive, and all reflect variation that is almost certainly not due to chance. The five support factors, as expected, have moderate correlations—between .19 and .42, with a mean of .32. Total Support correlates robustly with all of the five factor scores, as expected. The mean coefficient is .67, and the range extends from .59 to .74.

Beyond such significant details, the bottom-line expectation seems quite clear: social support varies inversely and robustly with the burnout phases.

The regularity of the association of social support and the phases is clear from Table 9.1, where all overall F-values attain the .001 level. Factor 1 (Agittated Rejection) has the strongest association with the burnout phases, accounting for 15.19 percent of the explained variance, based on eta^2; and Total Support accounts for 12.45 percent. The remaining support factors account for a range of variance—from 2.59 to 5.83 percent—and average 4.03 percent.

The associations between the six social support scores and the phases are robust as well as regular, especially for Factor 1 and Total Support. Table 9.2 displays a summary of all paired-comparisons between the phases and the six factor scores. Considering all paired-comparisons, over eight out of ten are in the expected direction and nearly three in ten attain the .05 level of statistical significance. Agitated Rejection and Total Support relate most markedly and consistently with the phases. Over 85 percent of these paired-comparisons trend in the expected direction, and nearly 47 percent attain statistical significance.

TABLE 9.1
One-Way Analysis of Support Subscores and Total Support versus Phases of Burnout

Support Subscores	Phases of Burnout								F-Ratio (df = 7,1509)
	I LoLoLo	II HiLoLo	III LoHiLo	IV HiHiLo	V LoLoHi	VI HiLoHi	VII LoHiHi	VIII HiHiHi	
Agitated rejection (reversed)	23.8	22.7	22.6	21.3	22.2	20.6	21.5	18.9	39.0
Family supports	12.0	11.9	11.6	11.4	11.9	11.1	11.3	10.6	9.3
High activity	8.6	8.4	7.9	7.2	7.7	8.0	7.1	6.9	8.2
Friendships/ socially active	14.6	13.9	14.0	12.8	15.1	13.9	13.8	12.4	13.7
Intimate relationship	11.5	11.7	11.2	10.6	11.4	10.8	11.4	10.4	5.8
Total support	76.2	74.0	72.7	68.4	74.0	69.9	70.6	64.2	30.7
Number	347	105	189	120	105	173	106	368	

Note: All cases are statistically significant at or beyond P = .001.

206

TABLE 9.2
Summary of Paired-Comparisons, Support Scores × Burnout Phases, in Percent

Support Factor Scores	In Expected Direction	In Expected Direction and Statistically Significant*	In Contrary Direction	In Contrary Direction and Statistically Significant*
Agitated rejection (reversed)	89.3%	46.4%	10.7%	0.0%
Family supports	89.3	17.9	10.7	0.0
High activity	85.7	21.4	14.3	0.0
Friendships/socially active	75.0	25.0	25.0	3.6
Intimate relationship	75.0	7.1	25.0	0.0
Total support	82.1	50.0	17.9	3.6

* Refers to .05 level on Least Significant Difference test, as modified for unequal populations.

More or less, the other four factor scores provide strong directional evidence for the association of social support and burnout, but their proportions of statistically significant paired-comparisons are less impressive.

Implications for Research and Applications

These data manipulations, then, contribute in two basic senses to tentative optimism about the present approach to measuring burnout. The results add further to the evidence of the concurrent validity of the phase approach. In addition, the results also suggest a convenient—and already recognized—vehicle for intervening to ameliorate burnout by influencing social support. The last section of this chapter illustrates such an applied use, in fact.

ORIENTATION II: ACTIVE AND PASSIVE MODES

The results with social support help direct and motivate interventions to manage burnout, but only in part. The intervenor seems well-advised to keep social support at high levels, so as to avoid or buffer future stressors. But if a person is already in an advanced phase of burnout, less clarity exists about what should be done. In fact, advanced burnout suggests the danger that people may be overstimulated by designs commonly used to heighten social support (e.g., Golembiewski, 1982). Certainly, on the basis of analysis so far, advanced phases imply no great slack for coping with new stimuli. More likely, a deficit exists.

Conceptual Issues

Two related conceptual distinctions promise some possible leeway for the intervenor facing those already in advanced phases of burnout. Some observers emphasize the differences between "burned out" and (what is worse) "worn-out." In this connection, both clinical (e.g., Freudenberger, 1980) and analytical evidence suggests that active *and* passive reactions to progressive psychological burnout seem possible, and perhaps probable, and that this may be of theoretic as well as practical concern. For example, some observers note that increases in burnout beyond some threshold level often trigger a frenetic burst of activity: working longer and harder, but usually not better or smarter (e.g., Freudenberger, 1980; Cherniss, 1980). Then, a period of resignation may set in as the strains experienced by an individual further outstrip coping capabilities. In this way, "burnout" can degenerate into "worn-out." Alternatively, or in addition, the two modes may relate to acute vs. chronic onset. More or less directly, an active mode seems more characteristic of acute onset, while chronic onset might well be accompanied more often by a passivity bred of past failures to modify a recalcitrant stressor-dominated reality.

Testing for differences between the two modes challenges the theoretical specificity of the phase model. Moreover, *if* data support the existence of the two modes, dual approaches might also be appropriate in efforts to ameliorate advanced phases of burnout.

Hence, the focus here on differences in job involvement as associated with psychological burnout and some of its covariants. Job involvement (JI) serves as a surrogate variable that permits gaining some perspective on the issue of whether or not one can speak meaningfully of two modes of reaction to heightening burnout in a large population. JI is measured by self-report items (White and Ruh, 1973), with the scale having an alpha of .86 in the present population.

Data came from Site B and, as in other analyses of that site, the focus will be on two sets of variables. These measures give a sense of important work site dynamics. They condition the responses of individual employees, as well as derive from those reactions:

	Alpha
● Participation in decisions at work (White and Ruh, 1973)	.79
● Trust in supervision (Roberts and O'Reilly, 1974)	.77
● Trust in all employees (constructed for present research)	.79
● Willingness to disagree with supervisor (Patchen, 1965)	.79
● Job tension (Kahn et al., 1964)	.85

Ten additional scales are drawn from the well-known Job Diagnostic Survey of Hackman and Oldham (1980). Their terminology includes "critical psychological states" (variables 1–3 below), "affective outcomes" (variables 4–6), and "context satisfaction" (variables 7–10). The scales include:

	Alpha
● Experienced meaningfulness of work	.80
● Experienced responsibility for work	.68
● Knowledge of results	.70
● General satisfaction	.80
● Work motivation	.69
● Satisfaction with growth	.86
● Satisfaction with job security	.78
● Satisfaction with compensation	.88
● Satisfaction with coworkers	.75
● Satisfaction with supervision	.91

Here, burnout modes are considered the independent variable, and the tests below in effect seek to assess the tendency of differences in that property of individuals to covary regularly with differences in the three domains isolated by Hackman and Oldham.

TABLE 9.3
Two Levels of Job Involvement and Assorted Work Site Descriptors

	Job Involvement (dichotomized at median = 30)		T-Statistic	Probability, two-tailed
	Low (N = 799)	High (N = 768)		
A. Assorted Scales				
Participation	13.5	17.1	-18.63	0.001
Trust in supervision	12.7	15.1	- 9.82	0.001
Trust in all employees	15.3	18.7	-14.60	0.001
Willingness to disagree with supervisor	15.0	14.7	1.19	0.236
Job Tension	21.4	18.9	9.18	0.001
B. Job Diagnostic Survey				
Experienced meaningfulness of work	17.4	22.3	-22.15	0.001
Experienced responsibility for work	30.4	35.1	-16.88	0.001
Knowledge of results	20.0	21.8	- 8.45	0.001
General satisfaction	20.3	27.3	-25.48	0.001
Work motivation	30.8	35.0	-16.32	0.001
Satisfaction with:				
growth	16.4	22.5	-25.19	0.001
job security	9.0	10.7	-11.12	0.001
compensation	8.3	10.2	-11.77	0.001
coworkers	15.0	17.8	-19.73	0.001
supervision	12.9	16.3	-14.80	0.001

Testing for Burnout × Modes Association

Three tests will employ these sets of measures to assess the character and degree of effects due to modes. The first test is broadly exploratory and focuses on the association of JI with the Assorted Scales and the 10 JDS scales. A second test assesses JI interaction with the eight-phase model of psychological burnout. And a third test focuses on High vs. Low JI effects for each of the work site descriptors, separately considering each of the eight phases of burnout. This test assesses the similarity of both pattern and magnitude of active vs. passive differences.

Note that the tests are stated in interrogatory form, which befits the present state of our knowledge.

Test 1: Does Job Involvement Matter?

No reservations seem necessary concerning a first test of the relevance of active vs. passive differences in a model of psychological burnout. This initial step involves a straightforward assessment of the covariation of High vs. Low JI levels with the full panel of variables introduced above. Conservatively, the two-tailed test is relied on here to assess the magnitude of effects. For the first two sets of scales, with one exception—Job Tension—high scores imply the more desirable general state of affairs.

The results of this first test are summarized in Table 9.3. Overall, 14 of the 15 variables seem quite sensitive to JI differences, with all differences attaining or surpassing the 0.001 level of statistical significance. The direction of the differences is uniform, also. Thus LoJI implies significantly lower Participation, higher Job Tension, and lower scores on all 10 JDS scales.

With some confidence, then, the data permit the judgment that JI does matter in many central particulars. JI associations with the present variables seem quite uniform in direction, and their size and distribution are such that chance factors can be ruled out with almost absolute certainty. Except for Willingness to Disagree with Supervisor, HiJI is associated uniformly and robustly with a conventionally more attractive pattern of covariants.

Test 2: Does Job Involvement Vary by Burnout Phases?

Given the dominant associations of Job Involvement with a variety of self-reports concerning significant aspects of the work site, does the association extend to the phase model of burnout? This second test constitutes one convenient way of moving toward a clearer test for active and passive reactions to burnout.

Table 9.4 begins in an elementary way the analysis of JI variations with the phases of psychological burnout. Using the Site B population's median of 30, JI scores are distinguished as High vs. Low, and the proportions of each are calculated for the eight separate phases. The purpose is direct: to provide a picture in one large population of the distribution by phases of Hi and LoJI, which here

TABLE 9.4
High vs. Low Job Involvement, by Phases of Burnout

A. JI by Phases

		Phases of Burnout						
	I	II	III	IV	V	VI	VII	VIII
% Low JI	27.6%	34.6	39.8	58.1	42.1	52.0	76.1	76.8
% High JI	73.4%	65.4	60.2	41.9	57.9	48.0	23.9	23.2

B. Total JI Scores

									DF	F-Ratio	P =
	I	II	III	IV	V	VI	VII	VIII			
Low JI Mean =	27.1	26.2	25.3	25.4	24.0	24.9	22.7	21.6	7,777	21.173	.001
High JI Mean =	37.1	35.9	35.6	35.1	35.6	34.6	34.0	34.3	7,728	10.845	.001
Overall JI Mean =	34.7	32.9	31.8	29.7	30.9	29.8	25.4	24.7	7,1537	72.227	.001

serve respectively as surrogates for active and passive modes of reactions to various degrees of burnout.

The data show a strong central tendency for JI to vary directly with the phases of burnout, and those data also suggest the meaningfulness of acknowledging two modes of reacting to progressive burnout. For example, Phases I through VIII are quite regularly loaded by a growing proportion of LoJI. The progression is not absolutely uniform, but nearly so—93 percent of the paired-comparisons in Row A support the pattern. Row B supports and details this pattern of JI decreasing regularly, as phases of burnout progress from I through VIII, for three sets of JI scores—Low, High, and Overall. In summary, the 84 possible paired-comparisons reveal the pattern in Table 9.5. Anything over 20 percent of statistically significant paired-comparisons is normally assumed to indicate robust and regular association. In general, the present data far surpass that standard.

Test 3: Effects, by Phases, as JI Varies?

A third test is both more complex and specific. All work site descriptors will be considered individually, by phases, to test for sensitivity to High vs. Low JI. Clinical observations imply that progressive burnout may at first inspire active responses, if not agitated efforts. Often, those efforts seem counterproductive—e.g., working longer and harder but not necessarily better, as expressed in metaphors such as "wheel-spinning," "going around in circles," and so on (e.g., Cherniss, 1980; Freudenberger, 1980).

More specifically, this third test involves two basic comparisons. The first comparison uses one-way analysis of variance on each variable three times: for All respondents, for High JI, and then Low JI only (Table 9.6). The second class tests for differences between all pairs of scores, using the Least Significant Difference (LSD) test, as modified for unequal subsample sizes.

The raw data are available elsewhere for detailed inspection (Golembiewski and Munzenrider, 1984a, pp. 277-85), but only a single summary table will be relied on here to suggest the pattern and magnitude of JI affects, of active vs. passive differences. In general terms, except for Willingness to Disagree with Supervisor, not only does each work site descriptor tend to "worsen" substantially, phase by phase, but active respondents report a "better" pattern of effects, phase by phase.

In more detail, Table 9.6 establishes that JI differences affect the pattern and magnitude of associations with work site descriptors. This table reflects the results of a complex analysis. Eight tables underlie this summary, one for each of the eight progressive phases of burnout. Each component table compared HiJI vs. LoJI on the 15 significant work site descriptors, by phases, as well as by the four other measures of burnout used elsewhere in this volume—the three MBI subscale scores and Total Score. Statistically significant differences are determined by the LSD test, which assesses the magnitude of differences for all possible paired-comparisons.

TABLE 9.5
Distribution of 84 Possible Paired-Comparisons, Job Involvement, and Phases

	Paired-Comparisons of JI Scores, By Phases			
	Statistically Significant and in Expected Direction	In Expected Direction	In Contrary Direction	Statistically Significant and in Contrary Direction
Low JI	12 of 28 (42.9%)	26 (92.9%)	2 (7.1%)	0 (0%)
High JI	5 of 28 (17.9%)	25 (89.3%)	3 (10.7%)	0 (0%)
Overall JI	18 of 28 (64.3%)	26 (92.9%)	2 (7.1%)	0 (0%)

TABLE 9.6
Summary of Differences, Hi vs. Lo JI, Two-Tailed T-Statistic[†]

	15 Worksite Scales	4 Burnout Measures
A. All Cases	HiJI "better" than LoJI in 14 of 15 cases; 14 stat. signif.	LoJI "worse" than HiHI in 4 of 4 cases; 4 stat. signif.
B. Phases of Burnout		
I. Lo Lo Lo	14 of 15; 14 stat. signif.	4 of 4; 4 stat. signif.
II. Hi Lo Lo	15 of 15; 8 stat. signif.	4 of 4; 3 stat. signif.
III. Lo Hi Lo	13 of 15; 12 stat. signif.	3 of 4; 1 stat. signif.
IV. Hi Hi Lo	15 of 15; 8 stat. signif.	3 of 4; 0 stat. signif.
V. Lo Lo Hi	15 of 15; 9 stat. signif.	3 of 4; 3 stat. signif.
VI. Hi Lo Hi	13 of 15; 12 stat. signif.	3 of 4; 3 stat. signif.
VII. Lo Hi Hi	12 of 15; 8 stat. signif.	4 of 4; 0 stat. signif.
VIII. Hi Hi Hi	14 of 15; 13 stat. signif.	3 of 4; 2 stat. signif.
Totals	@ 111 of 120 comparisons, or 92.5%, show HiJI "better" than LoHI on 15 worksite scales	@ 27 of 32 comparisons, or 84.4% show HiJI "better" than LoJI on 4 burnout measures
	@ 84 of these comparisons, or 70%, are stat. signif.	@ 16 of these comparisons, or 50%, are stat. signif.

[†] T-test approximation compensates for unequal variances possibly associated with unequal sizes of Hi vs. Lo populations. The approximation is a conservative test; and two-tailed probabilities also are used to highlight robust differences only.

215

As Table 9.6 reflects, JI differences impact markedly on the panel of variables, as arrayed by phases of burnout. The terms "better" and "worse" are used as a convenience to reflect the dominant pattern of results—e.g., that for Phase I, HiJI reflects higher scores on Participation, lower scores on Job Tension, and so on, than does LoJI. Roughly, about 90 percent of the paired-comparisons favor Hi vs. LoJI, in these terms, and about 70 percent of these comparisons attain statistical significance. In short, the pattern is very consistent and robust.

Implications for Research and Applications

The present results support several findings, often strongly. These major results are conveniently grouped for present purposes under two headings: research findings, and applied implications.

Five Research Findings

The data support at least five major findings. First, Job Involvement seems a robust covariant of the present panel of work site descriptors.

Second, JI seems to vary quite regularly by phases of burnout. HiJI is associated with the least-advanced phases of burnout, in general, and LoJI with the most-advanced phases.

About 25 percent of those in Phases VI through VIII score above the median on JI. This suggests that a sizable proportion of those reporting advanced burnout retain an "active" mode of coping, even though the other three-quarters of those similarly classified may be viewed as "resigned," or at least as "less active."

Note also that only about one-quarter of LoJI are classified in Phases I through III. This implies that low burnout, in general, need not be paid for in terms of an inactive approach to work. Quite the opposite seems true, in fact.

Fourth, the pattern of HiJI vs. LoJI, as mapped on the panel of target variables, is similarly regular and robust. Thus scores on almost all target variables tend to "worsen" for all three classes of respondents—LoJI, HiJI, and All respondents—as phases of burnout progress from I through VIII. Similarly, also, the patterning is most pronounced for phases that are distant (I vs. VIII), and less dominant for paired-comparisons that are immediate neighbors (e.g., I vs. II, or VII vs. VIII). However, even in the case of phases rated +2 (e.g., II vs. IV or VI vs. VIII), for all respondents, over 25 percent of the paired-differences are statistically significant and in the expected direction; in addition, over 85 percent are in the expected direction. These data imply the usefulness of a substantial number of separate phases or stages of burnout for encompassing the variation in the work site descriptors.

Fifth, the magnitudes of HiJI vs. LoJI effects also differ significantly. The comparisons favor HiJI in over 90 percent of the cases; and over 70 percent of the differences achieve the usually accepted levels of statistical significance.

Four Applied Implications

The original intent of this research sought to determine whether active and passive reactions to advanced burnout could be said to exist, a finding which would have significant practical as well as theoretical implications. The research data above suggest a compound answer to this guiding question—yes and no. Four applied implications deriving from this compound answer are discussed below.

First, JI differences map significantly different associations on the present panel of variables *across the full range of burnout phases*. This finding has major implications but, at the present level of specificity, it does *not* support the core notion that an energetic and perhaps frenetic mode of response characterizes *advanced* phases of burnout. Rather, organization planners will find JI associated with a progressive set of effects *for all phases*. Roughly, HiJI will be associated with "better" effects than LoJI, overall, as well as phase by phase. The data definitely imply the practical utility of organizational policies and structures that encourage HiJI.

Second, the results suggest that a kind of energy-drain is associated with advanced burnout, a suggestion which neither offends common sense nor runs counter to the results presented to this point. Nearly 60 percent of all HiJI are classified in Phases I-III, and approximately the same percentage of LoJI are in Phases VI-VIII. This energy-drain suggests the usefulness of reducing burnout. The effects of burnout and JI are no doubt interactive to a degree. See also the "Implications" concluding this chapter.

Third, the present results suggest a greater margin for ameliorating burnout than had been envisioned. The present data indicate that some 25 percent of HiJI are classified in Phases VI-VIII. In substantial contrast, earlier formulations (e.g., Golembiewski, 1982, 1984b) were troubled by the apparently poor fit between advanced phases of burnout and some of the more common managerial prescriptions, such as job enrichment. Basically, the notion of advanced phases of burnout implies that the stressors experienced by an individual result in strain that threatens to overwhelm, or already has overwhelmed, an individual's coping capabilities—hence the feared inadvisability of high-stimulus designs like job enrichment for cases classified as VI through VIII, who were precisely those more likely to have work sites with properties for which job enrichment was a likely antidote—low participation, insufficient experienced responsibility for work, inadequate knowledge of results, and so on. This earlier view posed a cruel dilemma, of course.

Fortunately, the newer data suggest that there is more slack for the intervenor, and that, although the caution against high-stimulus interventions for Phases VI-VIII still applies, a sizable proportion of those in advanced stages have JI scores that imply they are still coping actively with their environment. Presumably, for example, HiJI scorers would be more likely to generate the energies required for successful job-enrichment efforts.

Fourth, considering all LoJI scores, over 27 percent are classified in Phases I–III. Such individuals may be reasonable targets for designs likely to encourage HiJI for, apparently, their work has not stressed them beyond their normal coping limits.

Obviously, the last two points require a substantial ability to target interventions to the appropriate HiJI or LoJI scorers. Far from the last word has been spoken on this crucial issue, but preliminary data suggest that nature may be helpful. Immediate work-groups, or clusters of first-reports, seem to have a definite affinity for homogeneous degrees of burnout among their members (Golembiewski, 1983b; Rountree, 1984). This suggests phenomena like "resonance" or "contagion." And, it suggests the possibility of specific targeting of interventions to intact work-units whose members are experiencing similar degrees of burnout, as the following analysis demonstrates.

ORIENTATION III: EFFECTS OF MULTIPLE OD INTERVENTIONS[3]

This section deliberately moves beyond suggestions, and reaches back to various sections of this book in order that it may move forward. For example, this section rests on the persistence of the phases sketched in chapter five, on the association of group properties and social support with burnout elaborated in chapter six and in the previous section, as well as on the distinction between actives and passives in advanced phases of burnout introduced in chapters five and eight and elaborated immediately above.

This section has one keystone quality, in short. It not only constitutes a significant test of the phase model, but it also will help assess the usefulness of ameliorating burnout via the technology-cum-values called Organization Development, or OD (e.g., Golembiewski, 1979).

This section constitutes a rare piece of work, although not a singular one. Despite the profusion of advice on how to deal with burnout, few direct interventions exist and almost none provide data sufficient to assess effects. Kilpatrick (1986) isolates 661 published studies about burnout, of which 138 (or 20 percent) offer how-to prescriptions. However, only 132 of the 661 cases rest on data-bases, and but four of these provide data from conscious interventions (Anderson, 1982; Haack, 1980; Pines and Aronson, 1983; Slutsky, 1981). This situation has changed little since Kilpatrick concluded her research.

The intervention blends prescription and research in a Human Resources corporate group, which initially numbered 31. Conventional OD designs reduce burnout, as well as improve group properties and turnover, following the phase model.

Seven major emphases characterize this action-research. Crucial associations of stress and burnout with Organization Development, or OD, will be drawn; a conceptual approach to burnout phases will be sketched; methods will be detailed; a mini-history will emphasize milestones in the HR unit's multiple transitions in response to its demanding work environment; interventions are reviewed;

results of the interventions at three points over nearly three years will be high-lighted in two sections; and implications for research and applications will be sketched.

Stress and Burnout in Planned Change

OD often rightly focuses on the "O" (for organization), but to also try to encompass individual burnout is not only attractive but seems necessary. Briefly, the world is full of "stressors," or stimuli that upset the "constancy of the [person's] internal environment" (Selye, 1974, p. 27). Stressors can herniate or energize—with effects specific not only to different individuals but to different points-in-time (Selye, 1983).

We neither can nor should avoid stressors, but we can experience too many of some of them for too long—hence burnout, which relates to the degree of strain that individuals experience, relative to their normal coping skills and attitudes. Thus, also, follow the reasons for burnout's relevance to OD, which is deeply concerned with creating favorable balances of eu-stress versus dis-stress for individuals and their employing organizations, as Warrick (1981) aptly demonstrates.

In sum, OD's interest in burnout is—or should be—*specific* and *practical*. Specifically, OD's basic orientation toward choice and change exposes individuals to potential strain. Moreover, practically, a large battery of OD designs and experience with them (e.g., Golembiewski, 1982) stand ready to guide data-based efforts to reduce burnout, and failure to tap this potential not only neglects a powerful technology but also deprives OD of a major target for applications in moving toward the vision of the responsibly free workplace (e.g., Golembiewski, 1979, vol. 1, pp. 1–132).

Conceptual Approach to Amelioration

An ongoing program of research with an eight-phase model supports burnout's depth of impact. To review, advanced phases are characterized by low levels of energy, self-esteem, and efficacy, as well as by the dreary catalog of effects documented above and also in the selected sources listed here:

- poorer profiles on self-reports relating to the work site, as in satisfaction, higher job tension, lower participation and involvement, and so on (Burke, Shearer, and Deszca, 1984; Burke and Deszca, 1985; Deckard, Rountree, and Golembiewski, 1986)
- greater physical symptoms (Burke, Shearer, and Deszca, 1984)
- lower performance appraisals
- generally lower productivity
- greater need for social support but less of it (Burke and Deszca, 1986)

The main-line linkages seem direct. Stressful work site features induce advanced phases of burnout which, in turn, are associated with such effects as a high incidence of reported physical symptoms. To suggest the flow, work site features and burnout phases each share 15–20 percent of their variance with physical symptoms in one study, but work site features explain only 2–5 percent of the variance in symptoms (see chapter three).

Advanced phases of burnout also seem to have a startling incidence and persistence. Over 40 percent of more than 12,000 respondents in 33 organizations fall into the three most-advanced phases (see chapter six). Moreover, phase assignments seem quite stable over the period of a year in about 75 percent of the cases (see chapter six).

Despite its apparent virulence, pervasiveness, and persistence, the very concept encourages cautious approaches. Although authorities often recommend high-stimulus designs for advanced burnout—interpersonal encounters, confrontations, interpersonally oriented team-building, and so on—the condition does not suggest the coping slack which such designs require. The traditional advice risks overstimulation, tersely. This seems a significant limitation on the use of OD because its theory and practice emphasize high-stimulus interventions (Golembiewski, Munzenrider, and Stevenson, 1986, pp. 191–94).

The section immediately above suggests that this conceptual impasse may be avoidable, in part, because two modes of individual response seem to exist in all phases of burnout—active, and passive or withdrawn. This distinction suggests two intervention strategies. When advanced burnout is associated with a passive mode, coping requires creating slack. Provisionally, then, intervenors might well distinguish two classes of designs (Golembiewski, Munzenrider, and Stevenson, 1986, pp. 193–94, 215–18):

High-stimulus designs	Low-stimulus designs
• interpersonal confrontations	• time off from work
• interpersonally-oriented team building	• flexible work hours
• T-groups for intact work groups	• some kinds of job rotation that require variable intensity as well as provide variety
• basic policy or structural change	• mild role negotiation
• confrontative "stress management workshops"	

Moreover, intervenors also might consider a two-stage strategy for ameliorating advanced burnout in its passive mode: to begin to reduce burnout via low-stimulus designs; and then, beyond some as-yet-undetermined level, to intervene with a broad range of high-stimulus designs to further reduce burnout and to anchor it at lower levels. For example, this first case might begin with a week's vacation, patently a low-stimulus opener.

This research uses standard high-stimulus OD designs in focusing on a head-quarters Human Resources staff group—initially numbering 31. All but two of them had active orientations to their work even though they were in advanced phases of burnout. The intervention rests on the assumption that "actives" have the emotional slack to respond to high-stimulus interventions.

Methods for Assessing Impacts

Archival data about turnover and three kinds of self-report data will assess effects of this action research. One kind of self-report permits assigning individuals to eight phases of burnout and has been described at several points. The second kind supports a characterization of the present HR population as "active"; and the final kind of self-report describes the immediate work-setting. The latter two kinds of self-reports are introduced, in turn, and then turnover gets attention. Some notes on the use of data complete this section.

Mode of Adaptation

How to estimate active vs. passive modes remains unsettled. The Job Involvement scale was used immediately above, with High vs. Low JI subgroups differing regularly and robustly on a large panel of indicators, phase by phase. Active VIIIs all but unanimously report being better off than passive VIIIs, and so on.

Here, three Work Environment Scales (WES) are used to make the active vs. passive judgment—Involvement, Autonomy, and Task Orientation (Insel and Moos, 1974). Operationally, mean *standard* scores greater than 50 on each of the three scales define "active," based on national norms for "general work-settings" (Moos, 1981, pp. 27-28). By this criterion, 29 of the 31 initial HR members qualify as "active." Specifically, the two lowest-scoring persons average 90 when their three WES scores are combined. The 29 other HR members average over 180, and over 93 percent of their 87 individual WES scores are greater than 50.

This convention requires qualification. WES scales focus not on the respondent but the respondent's *milieu*. Witness the orientation of a typical WES item: "Employees function fairly independently of supervisors." Interviews and observations confirm the assumption that perceived milieu requirements and personal responses are overwhelmingly congruent.

Work Environment Scales

Work site features are measured by the 60 WES items, which track 10 dimensions. Briefly (Moos, 1981, p. 2):

- Involvement, the extent to which employees are concerned about and committed to their jobs
- Peer Cohesion, the extent to which employees are friendly and supportive of one another

EXHIBIT 9.1
A Schedule of Non-Survey Events

	Day		
Problem sensing	1	o	HR managers surface fears
Base-line data-gathering	45-75	o	solicitation by memo of "concerns" from all employees
Begin Data Flow	115	o	Share "concerns" with all HR staff to encourage reaction and confrontation
		o	Four "interest groups" focus on special targets for improvement
Initial Action-Planning	140-170	o	Interest groups report recommendations to all HR staff
		o	HR members each report back on "5 recommendations you would most like to see implemented"
Continued Action-Planning	200	o	Begin planning to implement high-priority recommendations
Presentation to Corporate HR Oversight Committee	230	o	1984 HR turnover rates higher than expected
		o	HR Career Progression Plan proposed
Major Policy intervention	265	o	HR Career Progression Plan announced
Review, Extend, and Re-commit	295	o	10-hour meeting of all HR staff to review progress, plan future initiatives, and celebrate achievements
Major Reorganization	475	o	"Chunking" occurs: several "strategic operating areas" replace a basically-functional structure
Report on All Changes	575	o	Share all data Administrations I-IV
		o	2-hour review and planning session for adapting to the newly-decentralized Human Resources activities

- Supervisor Support, the extent to which management is supportive of employees and encourages employees to be supportive of one another
- Autonomy, the extent to which employees are encouraged to be self-sufficient and to make their own decisions
- Task Orientation, the degree of emphasis on good planning, efficiency, and getting the job done
- Work Pressure, the degree to which the processes of work and time-urgency dominate the job milieu
- Clarity, the extent to which employees know what is expected of them in their daily routine, and to which rules and policies are communicated explicitly
- Control, the extent to which management uses rules and pressures to keep employees under control
- Innovation, the degree of emphasis on variety, change, and new approaches
- Physical Comfort, the extent to which the physical surroundings contribute to a pleasant work environment

WES measurement properties are conveniently available (Moos, 1981).

Turnover Rates

The focus here is on a number of people leaving the firm divided by average HR headcount. Other measures—such as intent to leave—provide less conservative estimates of the commitment to continued employment.

Notes About Uses of Data

The four kinds of data estimate impacts of interventions, basically, and do not provide grist for planning, as is common in action research. The intervention's public focus was on "a major morale problem," and on what the HR personnel could do collaboratively to alleviate that problem. The self-report data were gathered following this survey schedule (see also Exhibit 9.1):

- Day 45:   Administration I
- Day 200: Administration II (phases only)
- Day 295: Administration III
- Day 425: Administration IV
- Day 575: Administration V

Since the major interventions occurred through Day 265, Administrations I and II may be considered as a long and short pretest, respectively. Administrations III, IV, and V constitute posttests, and are conveniently labelled short, long, and

TABLE 9.7
Respondents, by Phases of Burnout, Administrations I-V

A. All Subjects, N Varies — Respondents, in percentages, by phases

Administration	N =	I	II	III	IV	V	VI	VII	VIII
I	31	19%	0	3	3	23	23	10	19
II	34	18%	6	6	3	11	21	9	27
III	36	33%	6	11	0	11	22	6	11
IV	35	29%	6	14	0	20	11	3	17
V	37	35%	5	5	3	14	19	14	5

Grouping brackets:
- Admin I: (I-III) 22%; (IV-V) 26%; (VI-VIII) 52%
- Admin II: (I-III) 30%; (IV-V) 14%; (VI-VIII) 57%
- Admin III: (I-III) 50%; (IV-V) 11%; (VI-VIII) 39%
- Admin IV: (I-III) 49%; (IV-V) 20%; (VI-VIII) 31%
- Admin V: (I-III) 45%; (IV-V) 17%; (VI-VIII) 38%

B. Matched Subjects[†]

Administration	I	II	III	IV	V	VI	VII	VIII
I	14%	0	0	7	14	43	7	14
II	21%	7	7	0	14	21	7	21
III	36%	14	7	0	7	22	0	14
IV	21%	7	21	0	36	0	7	7
V	15%	8	0	8	23	23	23	0

Grouping brackets:
- Admin I: (I-III) 14%; (IV-V) 21%; (VI-VIII) 64%
- Admin II: (I-III) 35%; (IV-V) 14%; (VI-VIII) 49%
- Admin III: (I-III) 57%; (IV-V) 7%; (VI-VIII) 36%
- Admin IV: (I-III) 50%; (IV-V) 36%; (VI-VIII) 14%
- Admin V: (I-III) 23%; (IV-V) 31%; (VI-VIII) 46%

[†] N = 14 except for N = 13 in Administration V.

very long, respectively. Turnover data became available at approximately Day 90 for 1984, and Day 455 for 1985.

No doubt some sense of the data did percolate into the planned interventions, but only incidentally. Three general and short briefings were held for the five-person HR management team, shortly after Administrations I, III, and IV. Participants were promised a full briefing on all aggregate measurements after implementing their action plans, and this occurred at Day 575, just after Administration V.

Thumbnail History of HR Transitions

Both HR and its corporate home had grown sharply *and* raised their goals, 1981–83. To illustrate, mid-1981 saw a formal HR integration of what had been two organizationally separate activities. One dealt with operational matters like recruitment and employee relations, and the other with training and development. Close collaboration between the two was required to meet the firm's goals of major expansion while lowering turnover via better recruitment, training, and organization development. Corporate turnover in both 1979 and 1980 approximated 43 to 45 percent, while it fell in the next three years to 24, 18, and then 14 percent in 1983, even as total employment increased by more than 25 percent.

Still, in early 1984, the HR management team feared that such progress often had come at the expense of neglecting important work within HR. Staff were strained, and the VP and his directors expected "high turnover." Expectations concerning HR's contributions escalated, and so did the work load.

This concern gave birth to an OD effort whose major events are detailed in Exhibit 9.1. The exhibit does not include the five survey administrations described immediately above.

The earliest survey data confirmed the initiating concern. As rows AI and BI in Table 9.7 indicate, Administration I saw over 50 percent of the HR staff in Phases VI, VII, and VIII. The percentages are similar for all respondents, as well as for that subset of 14 who responded to each of the first four surveys. In addition, 75 percent of the total staff initially rate as Phase V or greater; and only one person among the two top levels of management scores *less than Phase V*. This not only seems high, it was the second-least desirable profile of phases observed at that time in nine organizations (Golembiewski, Munzenrider, and Stevenson, 1986, pp. 127–34). Chapter six permits the same judgment for a much larger number of cases.

The WES scores provide no particular reason for cheering in a corporation proud of its first-class status. See Table 9.8, columns (1) and (4). Recall that a standard score of 50 indicates a raw score at the mean of respondents from a large cohort in "general work-settings" (Moos, 1981, p. 27). HR Peer Cohesion is especially low, for example; and Work Pressure approximates the maximum possible score.

TABLE 9.8
Work Environment Scales, Standard Scores, on Three Administrations, N Varies

	Mean WES Scores, All Respondents[4]			Mean, WES Scores, Matched Respondents, (N=14)		
	(1)	(2)	(3)	(4)	(5)	(6)
	Administration I (N = 31)	Administration III (N = 36)	Administration IV (N = 35)	Administration I	Administration III	Administration IV
Involvement	56.3	59.2	58.8	55.5[a]	60.4[a]	59.1
TARGET Peer Cohesion	33.6[af]	46.6[a]	44.5[f]	32.6[b] [e]	39.6[b]	42.7[e]
TARGET Supervisor Support	42.4[bg]	52.0[b]	50.6[g]	43.6	48.3	49.9
Autonomy	54.1	55.6	57.8	55.6[f]	60.2	63.1[f]
Task Orientation	61.5	62.9	61.4	61.6	60.3	60.2
TARGET Work Pressure	80.9[ch]	75.6[c]	73.0[h]	82.5[g]	82.0[j]	77.99[j] [i]
TARGET Clarity	50.1	48.9	52.5	40.1[c]	41.5[c] [k]	50.8[k]
TARGET Control	55.1[d]	49.9[d]	51.4	52.1[hl]	44.3[h]	44.9[hl]
Innovation	49.6[ei]	58.9[e]	60.7[i]	54.7[di]	61.6[d]	62.6[i]
Physical Comfort	62.1	64.5[j]	59.3[j]	64.6	65.1[m]	60.8[m]

Note: Any shared plain superscript indicates P ≤ .05 by t-test, one-tailed.
Any shares superscript ' indicates P ≤ .10.

TABLE 9.9
Turnover Rates, 1984 and 1985

	1984 Corporate Rate	1984 HR Rate	1985 HR Rate
Management	7%	0%	12%
Professionals	9%	30%	22%
Technician	8%	67%	31%
Clerical	15%	66%	19%
Overall	13%	37%	20%

The 1984 HR turnover rate also proved to be high—37 percent, as Table 9.9 shows. This is almost three times the 1984 corporate average, and over 80 percent of the HR cases are voluntary. HR turnover in 1982 and 1983 approximates the corporate average.

Fitting Interventions to Transitions

The OD design sought to fit and direct transitional dynamics. Let us consider first the variable pace of intervention, and then the consistent underlying OD strategy.

Variable Pace

Expedience as well as goals for change influence the design. As Exhibit 9.1 shows, data-gathering at start-up consumed the first 100 days; active interventions spanned days 115 through 295, more or less; an anticipated reorganization urged a respite between days 295 and 575; and the design concluded with a first common HR experience under the aegis of the new structure.

The reorganization confounds the intervention, but it also provides a stiff test of the persistence of effects. Briefly, a traditional line/staff structure was quickly divisionalized (e.g., Chandler, 1962; Golembiewski, 1979, vol. 2, pp. 3-69) around separate product lines to facilitate identification with smaller and more focused efforts. Several "strategic operating areas" (SOAs) are identified and, after Day 475, nearly half of the previously centralized HR staff report directly to SOA heads. This requires for many HR staff not only a new direct supervisor, but also the development of a strong dotted-line relationship with the VP of Human Resources. In addition, both "movers" and "stayers" will maintain some common ties, for example, through periodic goal-setting meetings. The reorganization was a friendly one, with the VP of Human Resources playing a major role in its design and implementation, but its significant effects had by no means played themselves out by Day 575.

Overall Strategy

This action-research rests on a rudimentary causal network. Briefly:

Main effects are indicated by the solid lines, with broken lines indicating feedback or reinforcing linkages.

An environmental model dominates in management studies, and Organization Development (OD) represents its most focused contemporary expression. Briefly, OD provides—via values, theory, and learning designs—a coherent approach to meeting individual needs and to reducing stressors (Golembiewski, 1982), with emphasis on involving organization members in diagnosis and prescription. Conventional high-stimulus interventions based on OD theory and experience usually focus early on *interaction*—on the character and quality of relationships between people. Later attention may shift to *task*—to changes in *policies and procedures*. The combined intent is to induce an appropriate culture and process, and then to use the socio-emotional infrastructure to generate and support changes in policies, procedures, and structures.

Front-End Interventions: A Calculated Risk

The intervention strategy was conventional—high-stimulus and confrontational[5]—and may seem risky for advanced burnout. HR's distribution of phases argues against such openers, in fact, because that profile implies insufficient slack for coping with powerful stimuli. HR personnel maintained an "active" mode in all but two cases, however, and a high-stimulus design thus had a reasonable promise of reducing burnout by addressing work site issues. The high-stimulus features include: HR staff confronting superiors and peers about a range of concerns, and an energetic action-planning superimposed on already busy schedules.

In sum, the emphasis on interaction-centered designs attempts to create appropriate cultures at work. Basically, the intent is to create a low-risk and high-trust learning environment within which people can develop attitudes and skills supportive of that culture (e.g., Golembiewski, 1979, vol. 1). Since the learning group is an intact work team, social support can be brought to bear quite directly to motivate and to reinforce learning. Transfer of learning to the work site is also facilitated.

The high-stimulus and confrontational character of the initial design elements can be illustrated. For openers, all HR staff were asked to list the three best things about their department, as well as the three "concerns" they would most like to change. See Exhibit 9.2 for details, but some highlighting will be useful. In 50 percent of the responses, the "best things" involve the professionalism, skill, and education of their coworkers; and an additional 30 percent emphasize the pro-active nature of their work and its rewarding character.

These data in effect became a base from which to deal with concerns about work. Nearly half of the respondents focus on the isolation and lack of cohesion within and between HR units; and 40 percent stress the pace of work—too many projects and too many hours of work. Sharing these data in a general session (Day 115) focused on confronting the VP of Human Resources. He was widely seen as demanding and unrelenting, and HR staff had to satisfy themselves that trust was sufficiently high, and risk low enough, to warrant the expenditures of energy required to diagnose and remedy the unattractive aspects. When appropriate, this also required confronting unit heads.

After extended feedback and disclosure focusing on the HR state of affairs, four "interest groups" of volunteers were formed to gather additional information as well as to make recommendations for improvement. In effect, these recommendations (Days 140-170) deal with the "five targets" among WES scores highlighted in Table 9.8. Specifically, Peer Cohesion, Supervisor Support, and Clarity rate "too low"; and scores on Control and Work Pressure are "too high."

In sum, these front-end design features propose doing within HR what was more or less routinely done for clients. The goal involves building appropriate "processes"—a culture, values, and relationships—that will support later work on task features.

Major Downstream Response: Policy Intervention

Around Day 200, the downstream search came to highlight the lack of HR promotion opportunities. A Career Progression Plan was developed and accepted by consensus, after being blessed by a corporate committee. The Plan has several major objectives, as Exhibit 9.3 shows.

The Career Progression Plan tangibly reflects the improved HR infrastructure of processes and relationships, and also provides a clearer psychological contract with HR employees.

EXHIBIT 9.2

Summary of Responses to Two Open-Ended Items, Administration I

I. What are 3 best things about the Human Resources Department?

   1. Co-workers: 50% cite these examples: professional, skilled, talented, task oriented, dedicated.

   2. Work: 30% cite these examples: satisfying, exciting, interesting, competitive salaries, able to get things done.

   3. Opportunity for growth and advancement: 20% cite these examples: varied assignments, training, participation.

II. What are 3 things you would change about the department, if you could?

   1. Isolation/cohesion: 40% cite these examples: splits within the department: need more teamwork and cooperation between functional areas; territorialism.

   2. Stress: 40% cite these examples: too many projects, never enough time, rapid pace constantly, expected to work too many hours, no room for error.

   3. Resources: 10% cite these examples: need more clerical support, receptionists, additional personnel.

   4. Training: 10% cite these examples: need for cross-training, time to take advantage of training opportunities.

EXHIBIT 9.3
Objectives of HR Career Progression Plan

1. Clarify career progression paths and opportunities for employees.

2. Communicate these career and promotional opportunities.

3. Hire individuals whose abilities and aspirations are consistent and compatible with the level of promotional opportunity that exists for the job in which they are hired.

4. Better utilization of the talent available within human resources by increasing the amount of internal promotions in order to staff job at the professional level and above.

Overall, we want Human Resources as much as possible to be a place where each individual can achieve his or her aspirations, or get help in doing so.

Results of Action-Planning Through Day 425

What effects signal an effective intervention? Three sets of outcomes provide such evidence. In sum:

- the profile of phases of burnout tend toward less-advanced phases
- WES scores vary in three specific ways:
  - —Involvement, Autonomy, Task Orientation, Innovation, and Physical Comfort remain the same or increase
  - —Control and, especially, Work Pressure decrease
  - —Peer Cohesion, Supervisor Support, and Clarity increase
- turnover rates fall, 1985 vs. 1984

In capsule, the initial emphasis on interaction relates to two WES targets, primarily—Peer Cohesion and Supervisor Support—but increases in Involvement, Autonomy, and even Innovation might well occur. Changes in policies and procedures more directly impact the three other WES targets—Work Pressure, Control, and Clarity.

Administration III constitutes the first assessment of effects following major interventions. As for Administration IV, since no interventions are made in the 130 days prior to it, even maintenance of Administration III levels implies a potent intervention. Three emphases suffice to summarize the data through Day 425, and they all imply that intended effects occur and are maintained. In turn, changes in phases, WES scores, and turnover get summary attention.

Profile of Burnout Phases

Table 9.7 indicates that the proportion of those in Phases I-III approximately doubles for All Subjects, and nearly quadruples for Matched Subjects, comparing Administrations I and II with III. Chi-square analysis (3 × 2) shows that I vs. III changes closely approach significance for All and Matched respondents (P = .055 and .06, respectively).

Without explicit reinforcement, the shift is not only maintained for All Subjects, but is extended for Matched Subjects. Chi-square analysis indicates only random differences in III vs. IV profiles for both HR populations. In addition, the I vs. IV difference achieves statistical significance for Matched respondents, and approaches it for All (P = .088).

Changes in WES Scores

The WES scores also trend in expected ways, with All respondents providing the sharper pattern of differences.

For All Subjects, considering Administration III vs. I in Table 9.8, nine out of ten cases trend in the expected direction. Moreover, four of the eight cases on which major increases are expected achieve the .05 level of statistical significance, and an additional case approaches that level (.05 > P < .10). Moreover, for the five target variables, four trend as expected. Three achieve significance, and the fourth approaches the .05 level. Clarity trends lower, albeit randomly.

For Administration IV, all comparisons show random change only. Physical Comfort drops, although not significantly, no doubt due to ongoing construction.

For Matched Subjects, Table 9.8 shows that nine of ten cases fall in expected directions, comparing Administration I with III. Three of the eight cases for which major changes are expected in a successful intervention in fact attain the .05 level, while two additional cases closely approach it. For the five target variables, four show expected changes. One reaches the .05 level, and two additional cases approach significance. In the one deviant case, Clarity drops, although not quite achieving the .05 level.

On Administration IV, the pattern is maintained or enhanced. Clarity significantly increases; and Work Pressure falls substantially, as intended. All other changes are maintained in III vs. IV comparisons.

Turnover

Table 9.9 shows that turnover falls about 45 percent in HR, 1985 vs. 1984. No change occurs in the corporate rates, in addition, which closely approximate 13 percent in both years.

No substantial reasons encourage attributing the sharp drop in HR turnover to factors other than the interventions. If anything, 1985 was a better time than the previous year for HR personnel to seek new jobs.

Results of Action-Planning Through Day 575

Only very robust effects would survive in the face of the reorganization as well as the nine-month interval between the fifth administration of the survey and the prior planned intervention. Three emphases provide summary perspective on what seems a substantial persistence between Days 295 and 475.

Changes in Phases of Burnout

In Table 9.7, the very long posttest at Administration V shows two patterns of decay in the extreme phases of burnout. For All respondents, the decay is modest and not significant by the chi-square test. For Matched Subjects who were with HR during the full observational period, the decay is substantial after Administration IV. In both cases, however, 25 percent fewer individuals are classified in Phases VI-VIII, comparing Administration V to I. Moreover, the employees in Phases I-III increase by 104 and 65 percent for All and Matched respondents, respectively.

Opinions may differ, but the authors see a substantial persistence of changes in burnout and, despite the small numbers, this conclusion is supported by distinguishing two classes of HR employees—"movers" and "stayers." In sum, the "stayers" experience major increases in burnout over the interval between

TABLE 9.10
Summary, WES Scores, Administrations I, IV, and V

	I vs. IV		I vs. V	
	In Predicted Direction	Statistically Significant†	In Predicted Direction	Statistically Significant
I. Matched Subjects				
A. All Variables	9 of 10	6 of 8, plus one near-significant case	9 of 10	2 of 8, plus three near-significant cases
B. Target Variables	4 of 5	2 of 5, plus one near-significant case	5 of 5	2 of 5, plus two near-significant cases
II. All Subjects				
A. All Variables	8 of 10	4 of 8	10 of 10	6 of 8, plus two near-significant cases
B. Target Variables	5 of 5	3 of 5	5 of 5	4 of 5, plus one near-significant case

† Statistical significance is determined by the one-tailed t-test, $P \leq .05$.

234

Administrations VI and V, while the proportion of "movers" in advanced phases continues to decrease.[6]

That 8 of the 13 Matched cases are "stayers" suggests one possible explanation of their higher decay rate in Administration V, Table 9.7. Basically, the "movers" focus on recruiting and employee relations, which are operational and often repetitive. In contrast, not only did the "stayers" have major responsibility for planning and implementing the reorganization, but they also were enmeshed in several exhausting "due diligence" efforts required for major acquisitions. The "stayers" had high-level, generalist roles.

So "stayers" bore the brunt in the Administration IV-V interval of *the* two most significant and pressing organizational issues: reorganization and growth-by-acquisition. That period was less demanding for the "movers," despite their need to develop working relationships with both "new" superiors and the "old" VP of Human Resources. Indeed, the "movers" might seek additional budget authority from the SOA heads, who in some cases became suddenly ardent advocates of the very HR services that just a short while ago they had perceived differently. After a period of very rapid growth in staff and budget during the preceding several years, the VP of Human Resources staunchly resisted most efforts to increase HR staff.

Changes in WES Scores

Major and expected changes on the WES variables are sustained through Administration V, and even heightened, especially for All respondents. See the summary in Table 9.10. A detailed review of Administration V results appears elsewhere (Golembiewski, Hilles, and Kim, 1986), and data are omitted here to conserve space.

As shown via the phases, the HR "movers" report continued improvement on WES scores, V vs. IV and I, albeit from a lower base. Specifically, "movers" and "stayers" differ significantly at Administration IV on 5 of the 10 WES comparisons, with all 5 cases favoring the "stayers." On Administration V, only one significant difference remains—with the "movers," reasonably enough, reporting a decrease in Clarity. Essentially, the "stayers" maintain their WES scores, V vs. IV.

Trends in Turnover

The trend-line for HR turnover in the first four months of 1986 continues downward from the very high levels of 1984. In sum, the rates are: 37 percent in 1984, 20.3 percent in 1985, and 16.8 percent in 1986, annualized.

In all three years, corporate turnover closely approximates 13 percent per annum.

Implications for Research and Applications

This theory-based effort to ameliorate burnout resulted in substantial and persisting effects, and the implications for research and applications have a substantial salience. Two emphases dominate; attention first goes to a statistical demonstration of the relative significance of the phases vs. the active/passive distinction. Subsequently, our attention shifts to seven key observations about the intervention.

Do the Phases or Modes Dominate?

This analysis may seem to have failed even as it succeeded. In brief, the data can be interpreted to have established only that the modes supplant the phases in conceptual power.

Fortunately, this critical point for both research and application can be tested. And there is no need to feign suspense. The modes are useful, but the phases provide the bulk of the explanatory power. Three points provide substance to support this important (even critical) conclusion. These include an illustration, a summary of findings, and the examination of a possible deviant case.

Illustrating the Analysis

This analysis utilizes three clusters of scales to assess the power of the phases vs. modes, as seen in earlier chapters in connection with Site B. To review, the five scales describing work site features are taken from various sources:

	Alpha
● Participation in decisions at work (White and Ruh, 1973)	.79
● Trust in supervision (Roberts and O'Reilly, 1974)	.77
● Trust at all levels (ad hoc)	.79
● Willingness to disagree with supervisor (Patchen, 1965)	.79
● Job tension at work (Kahn et al., 1964)	.85

The present catalog of work site features also includes ten scales from the Job Diagnostic Survey (Hackman and Oldham, 1980).

	Alpha
● Experienced meaningfulness of work	.80
● Experienced responsibility for results	.68
● Knowledge of results	.70
● General satisfaction	.80
● Internal work motivation	.69
● Satisfaction with growth	.86
● Satisfaction with security	.78
● Satisfaction with compensation	.88
● Satisfaction with coworkers	.75
● Satisfaction with supervision	.91

And 5 final scales come from a factor-analytic study (Golembiewski, Munzen-rider, and Stevenson, 1986, pp. 62–84) of a standard list of 19 physical symptoms (Quinn and Staines, 1979). See also chapter four. This last quintet includes an overall score and four component factors:

	Alpha
● Total Symptoms Experienced	.89
● General Enervation and Agitation	.81
● Cardiovascular Complaints	.81
● Noncardiac Pains	.67
● Sleeplessness	.85

Note that all 20 alphas are acceptable for research purposes.

This analysis focuses on eight phases, distinguished by active and passive modes. Table 9.11 provides the distribution of modes X phases in Site B. There, Phase I has about three in each ten assignees who are passive, and the percentage increases quite regularly until it peaks at over 76 percent for Phase VIII incumbents. The progression is not perfect, but 93 percent of the 28 possible paired-comparisons show regular increases in the proportion of passives, phase by phase.

The analysis applies two-way ANOVA, as Table 9.12 illustrates for the variable Participation in Decisions at Work. To interpret the illustration, the means

TABLE 9.11
Actives vs. Passives, by Phases of Burnout, Site B

	Phases of Burnout								
	I	II	III	IV	V	VI	VII	VIII	Totals
Passive	97	37	75	72	45	91	83	281	781
Active	254	70	115	52	62	84	26	86	749
N =	357	107	190	124	107	175	109	367	1530
Passives per Phase, in % =	27.6%	34.6	39.4	58.1	42.1	52.0	76.1	76.6	

TABLE 9.12
Two-Way ANOVA Illustrated for Variable "Participation in Decisions at Work"

A. Variable Means by Phases and Modes

Respondents	I	II	III	IV	V	VI	VII	VIII	Totals
Passive	15.9	14.8	13.8	14.0	14.4	13.6	13.1	12.3	13.5
Active	18.6	17.0	16.2	16.2	17.5	16.5	14.6	15.4	17.1
All	17.8	16.3	15.2	14.9	16.2	15.0	13.5	13.0	15.3

B. One-way ANOVA, Phases X Participation

(df = 7, 1514)

F = 52.141

P = < .01

C. One-way ANOVA, Modes X Participation

(df = 1, 1514)

F = 373.701

P = < .01

D. Interaction, Phases X Modes

(df = 7, 1514)

F = .677

P = < .69

E. Phases, after Controlling for Modes

F = 23.918

P = < .01

F. Modes, after Controlling for Phases

F = 176.148

P = < .01

G. Betas

Phases = .31

Modes = .32

H. R^2 = .26

238

(Step A) show the expected association. Thus, actives score higher on Participation than passives in all eight phases. Moreover, as the phases progress, both passives and actives report diminishing Participation in quite regular ways. Specifically, nearly 84 percent of the paired-comparisons indicate a regular diminution, phase by phase.

Table 9.12 provides two other important data. Steps B and C show that the two Main Effects—phases and modes—each have significant covariation with Participation, and Step D indicates that the two Main Effects make distinct contributions to variance.

The analytic procedure permits greater specificity. Steps E and F in Table 9.12 confirm and detail the regularities above. They show significant effects for each Main Effect *after* the other has been controlled for.

For Participation, Step G indicates that the two Main Effects still make approximately the same contribution to an explanation of the variation in Participation, after controlling each for the other.

Finally, Step H in Table 9.12 indicates that the two effects together explain a substantial portion of Participation effects—26 percent.

Summarizing Results

It would be awkward to provide all data relevant to the analysis of the full panel of 20 variables. Following the format illustrated in the discussion of Table 9.12, however, four conclusions summarize those analyses.

First, the phases and modes almost always covary in expected and nonrandom ways with the full panel of variables. Specifically, all but one of the 40 cases show distributions that trend in the expected direction, and 38 of the 40 cases (or 95.5 percent) achieve statistical significance. The deviant cases all involve the modes: with Willingness to Disagree with Supervisor, and then with Noncardiac Complaints. This summarizes Steps A, B, and C illustrated in Table 9.12.

Second, for Step D, 14 of the 20 cases show no significant phase X mode interaction. The exceptions all involve scales from the Job Diagnostic Survey: Meaningfulness of Work, Responsibility for Results, General Satisfaction, Internal Work Motivation, Satisfaction with Growth, and Satisfaction with Co-workers. The significant interactions typically reflect differences in slopes rather than "crossovers." Hence, both the phases and the modes have distinct associations with almost all the target variables.

Third, the phases tend to dominate in explaining variance in the statistically significant cases. The mean beta coefficients for the phases approximates .31, while the corresponding figure for the modes is .19. This summarizes Steps E and F for the 38 relevant cases.

Fourth, the phases and modes together explain approximately 20 percent of the variance in the panel of variables, on average. This improves by some 25 percent on the record of the phases alone, which account for 15.8 percent of the variance in the variables in the present panel (Golembiewski, Munzenrider, and Stevenson, 1986, pp. 35, 71).

More directly, this analysis provides confirming evidence of the mutual (if differentially potent) usefulness of the phases and modes. It seems clear that the modes do not supplant the phases, but rather augment them.

A Deviant (but Suspect) Case

The previous paragraph may be too exuberant, however. Whenever possible, tests of the relative explanatory or descriptive power of the phases vs. (for example) the modes have been made. All of those comparisons, *save one*, sit comfortably with the results just summarized.

The sole major deviant case involves self-reports about performance appraisals at Site B, and their covariation with phases X modes. Several concerns about the performance appraisal data are presented in chapter five, and findings based on those data present interpretive problems. Nonetheless, a kind of truth-in-reporting requires at least brief note of this deviant case.

Using a form of analysis identical to that just reviewed, neither modes nor phases proved very useful in explaining variation in performance appraisals, *but* the modes prove more useful. Main Effects achieve statistical significance both when the phases are taken first, and when actives/passives are entered first—but just barely ($F = 2.18$ and $P = .026$). Modes achieve significance in both analyses ($P = .026$ and $P = .001$), but the phases do *not* in either case ($P = .086$ and $P = .436$). Neither test of two-way interaction achieves significance. Moreover, multiple R^2 is only .012 for modes X phases.

As noted earlier, "grade inflation" in performance appraisals precludes a robust interpretation of these results, but they are singular in opposition to the pattern of the present argument. Hence, the reason for the emphasis here on this deviant case, which may suggest some still-neglected and major weaknesses of the phase model but which—on very definite balance—does not begin to shake the evidence supporting the phase model.

Seven Summary Points

More broadly, the intervention is usefully framed in terms of seven summary highlights. First, overall, the results imply the success of orthodox, high-stimulus OD designs in improving burnout in its active mode, as well as in affecting the character of the work site. This constitutes some fresh news as well as a pleasant confirmation of old news.

The finding concerning burnout and its association with group properties is unique, and constitutes very good news for conventional OD designs, if only for "active" cases of advanced burnout. Consider burnout only. Since the trend toward less-advanced phases is more marked for Matched respondents, shifts in phases cannot be attributed mostly to personnel changes. Moreover, little favorable "natural change" probably occurred between Administration I and II vs. III and IV (Golembiewski, Munzenrider, and Stevenson, 1986, 135–39). In addition, a near-comparison group of other similarly situated professionals in the parent organization implies that HR changes in phases are not attributable to factors other than the interventions. Compare the first two administrations in Table 9.7 with this record for the near-comparisons around the time of Administration III:

I	II	III	IV	V	VI	VII	VIII
16.7%	5.6%	5.6%	13.9%	8.3%	8.3%	11.1%	30.6%

Near-comparisons provide post-only data to avoid sensitization to the MBI items, and they reflect a distribution of phases much like those among HR personnel at the time of Administrations II and III.

To complete this first point, the usefulness of conventional OD designs for advanced phases complements the strong case that has been made for maintaining low burnout via those designs (e.g., Warrick, 1981; Golembiewski, 1982). Relevantly, the success-rate literature reports no aggregate of OD applications with less than a 50 percent success rate, with most studies reporting between 60 and 80 percent (e.g., Golembiewski, Proehl, and Sink, 1982; Nicholas, 1982).

Second, the results reinforce the primacy of prior diagnosis. The results recommend distinguishing modes of adaptation to advanced burnout and, on the present showing, the combination of high burnout and active mode constitutes a reasonable target for conventional OD interventions. "Passive" cases of advanced burnout constitute a challenge for future work.

However, this research is moot on three related points of theoretic and practical significance. No one knows the overall proportion of "actives" among those in advanced phases of burnout, but it may be 25 percent or lower (Golembiewski and Munzenrider, 1984a).

In addition, the study does not tell us whether active status is a prelude to the passive mode. If so, not only would this signal the criticality of timely identification, but it also provides a conceptual explanation of what seems an anomaly—the existence of two "passive" employees in an "active" culture. If active mode derives from personality features—e.g., from high self-esteem or a low propensity to helplessness—promptness in diagnosis is less critical. This view provides an alternative explanation of the two passive cases in an "active" culture, of course.

Finally, the active/passive distinction also may relate to a basic feature of much theory on stress—the curvilinear association of stress and various outcomes like productivity. In this view, which some researchers doubt (e.g., Greer and Castro, 1986), too little stress as well as too much can induce low productivity. Those in (let us say) Phases I-III who are passive may experience a dysfunctionally low level of stressors, as for example from a laissez-faire supervisor, with low productivity being one possible outcome.

Third, experimental mortality was high, but personnel changes do not explain the changes in phases. In the main, the Matched respondents improve their phase distribution substantially more than All respondents, through Administration IV. Moreover, of those leaving, about 48 percent are in Phases VI-VIII and 28 percent are in Phases I–III, at the last-recorded observation. These are roughly the same as the weighted proportions in the Total population at the approximate times of departure—43.2 and 30.6 percent, respectively. However, about 40 percent of HR recruits fall in one of the three most-advanced phases on the first survey administration immediately after their hiring. So, recruitment and early socialization still need attention.

Fourth, there seem to be some reasonable ways of enhancing the present design. For example, a planned reinforcement experience was to follow Administration IV by three months. Uncertainty about the date of the reorganization discouraged this intervention, however, and the press of events delayed it until Administration V. Such periodic reinforcement experiences seem useful (e.g., Boss, 1983), and that design loop has long been featured in all our OD work (e.g., Golembiewski and Carrigan, 1970). Moreover, many OD action-research designs would use data on the phases and on WES scores as part of the change process. In the present case, the record of success would have reinforced effects, and perhaps heightened them.

Fifth, the research design probably generates a conservative estimate of effects. Deliberately, Administration III was held *before* a ten-hour design concluding the active interventions. Moreover, Administration IV followed that intervention by four months. Consequently, Administration III picked up only expectation effects about Day 295's major integrating experience; and fade-out had ample time to occur before Administration IV. Administration V deliberately was scheduled long after the prior planned intervention, as well as just before a two-hour general session. In addition, three already high initial WES scores—Involvement, Autonomy, and Task Orientation—permit labelling HR personnel as "active." Nonetheless, four of the six comparisons of Administration IV vs. I show increases from this high base, and one of the six attains the .05 level.

Sixth, theoretical reasons suggest that the two "passives" are not likely to respond positively to high-stimulus designs, but they do not seem to have been adversely affected. Those two persons improved their WES scores substantially, and had these sets of five phase assignments:

WES Outlier I: VII, VIII, VIII, VIII, IV

WES Outlier II: VI, VII, VI, III, VI

The Employee Assistance Program officer was alerted concerning possible difficulties, but none surfaced.

Seventh, the data through Administrative IV suggest that WES scores seem more amenable to change, and hence may be "leading" indicators. Patently, a leading/lagging distinction has both theoretical and practical value. If WES scores are "leading" indicators in a simple and direct way, their monitoring could anticipate later changes in distributions of burnout phases. Alternatively, a two-stage process is possible. Thus, when WES scores improve from a low base, they might presage improvements in burnout phases. Beyond some point, moreover, a positive WES profile might constitute a kind of "psychological floor," cushioning any impetus to regression to advanced phases of burnout and also providing a base for recovery when stressors abate.

IMPLICATIONS FOR THE PHASE MODEL OF BURNOUT

The preceding three orientations to intervention have powerful implications for the phase model of burnout. The first two identify levers for effective ameliorative action, and the third shows how social support and the modes can be used in a design to reduce burnout. As Lewin said, more or less, the successful test of a useful conceptual model will permit one to change relationships in nature in intended ways. The phase model passes that test, *this time.*

We focus upon four significant issues to summarize the aforementioned implications, *not* so much because the last word can be said about any of them, but because they each can benefit from being highlighted one more time. Again, the interrogative seems the most appropriate form:

- Is the active mode a precursor to the passive?
- Does the incidence of active vs. passive differ in organizations, especially with differences in the distributions of phases?
- Is burnout basically chronic or acute?
- Do the phases have dominant explanatory power, as contrasted with, for example, the modes and social support?

Active Mode as Precursor?

This point has grave theoretic and practical implications. If active status is a general precursor of passivity, timely diagnosis will have a high priority. Basically, it seems considerably easier to deal with Active VIIIism than Passive VIIIism, for obvious reasons. The discussion of Orientation III above supports this hunch, and implies the usefulness of ameliorating Active VIIIism through frequently applied OD learning designs. See also Golembiewski, Hilles, and Daly (1987). It is less clear how to deal safely with Passive VIII status, since it implies a person's vulnerability to overstimulation. Hence, common high-stimulus designs may be harmful for Passive VIII's, psychologically and emotionally (Golembiewski, Munzenrider, and Stevenson, 1986, pp. 242–45).

Two other possibilities exist. Active VIIIs may have disproportionately experienced acute onset, while Passive VIIIs may be persons who have been ground down by chronic features of their work environments. Alternatively, Passive VIIIism may derive from personality features, as well as contribute to them. Hopelessness or hardiness quotients might be relevant here (e.g., Maier and Seligman, 1976).

These alternative cases pose different challenges for intervention. Acute onset seems to pose the lesser challenge—with time and social support typically being sufficient to do the job (e.g., Kubler-Ross, 1981, 1982). VIIIism rooted in personality features poses a more tricky issue, and caution seems especially appropriate.

Incidence of Active Mode?

It appears that the distribution of active/passive modes may follow a general rule, as moderated by organizationally specific features. Based on the limited evidence, it appears that passivity increases more or less directly, phase by phase. At the same time, the proportions of actives vs. passives may vary substantially in

TABLE 9.13
Distributions of Phases and Actives/Passives in Two Organizations

Phases	% of Actives		% in Phases	
	Site B (N = 1530)	Site A (N = 274)	Site B	Site A
I	72.4	86.9	22.9	40.9
II	65.4	84.2	7.0	10.6
III	60.5	70.7	12.6	7.7
IV	41.9	66.7	8.1	4.8
V	57.9	80.0	7.0	13.9
VI	48.0	70.6	11.5	9.1
VII	23.9	23.5	7.1	7.3
VIII	23.4	22.7	23.9	5.8
			100.1%	100.1%

different organizations. Both points are illustrated in Table 9.13, which presents comparative data from two organizations—Sites A and B.

Roughly, Site B has twice the proportion of employees in advanced phases of burnout (VI through VIII), and also generally has a smaller proportion of actives, phase by phase. This does not surprise, of course, and supports the general ideation underlying the phases of burnout.

Burnout as Chronic or Acute?

The working answers to the two questions above reinforce the view that burnout is most economically accounted for by an *environmental model*. There, burnout is basically *chronic*, and derives from aspects of the work site—especially supervisory practices and applicable policies. The basic chronic flight-path to increasing burnout would be: I → II → IV → VIII. Advanced phases here persist indefinitely, absent basic changes for the better in the immediate work-environment. The model also accomodates *acute* onset, as from some trauma, but that seems substantially less common than the chronic variety (Golembiewski and Munzenrider, 1985, 1986, 1987). Multiple acute flight-paths exist: e.g., I → V or II → VI, as after the death of a loved one. This could escalate to VII or VIII in a difficult grieving process, absent the emotional support that can help the individual reassume a low phase of burnout within a limited period of time—no longer than six months or so.

From this perspective, relying on four major classes of variables, work site features directly impact burnout and it, in turn, affects physical symptoms. The modes of coping probably also are influenced quite directly by work site features, although broad personal differences in learning and experiences also might influence one's dominant mode of response to stressors. Hence, the modes would not impact substantially on physical symptoms, while covarying robustly with work site descriptors. Such a version of the environmental model takes this general form:

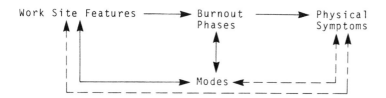

Causal linkages have been established only in one case (see chapter one), but substantial evidence supports the basic sense of the environmental model. Consider the analysis of the two modes. As the environmental model implies, the phases have similarly robust covariation with a panel of 15 work site variables and 5 measures of physical symptoms. Specifically, the mean betas are .307 and .318, respectively. For the modes, however, the betas suggest both proximate covariation with the work site features and more distal covariation with the physical symptoms. The specific means are .241 and .038, respectively.

Phases as Dominant in Explanation?

As the theoretical and applied development of the phase model proceeds, a basic question increasingly demands attention. How important are the phases in explanation and, hence, in prediction? Two modes of coping with burnout—active and passive—clearly seem to add useful specificity to phase assignments, as we have seen in chapter seven and the intervention just described. Similarly, social support also helps in understanding burnout phenomena and in ameliorating them, as this chapter documents. Many features of the design for intervention increase the degree and visibility of social support—from peers, superiors, and subordinates, as well as from executives of the parent organization keen on inducing a more humane and satisfying work site.

Patently, such developments raise the issue of what is the conceptual engine and what is the caboose. Can the phases be seen to dominate explanation? Or has research motivated by an interest in the phases succeeded in displacing them with (in the immediate analysis) social support?

Two perspectives on this question help to provide some guidance. First, the issue is not particularly earthshaking, since obviously *the combination* of explanatory elements here has an analytical potential beyond that of any one set of individual components. Second, the evidence in several places does support the conceptual primacy of the phases. For example, the analysis in the previous section of this chapter assesses the relative contributions of the phases and the modes with results that emphasize the influence of the former.

Phases $\times$ *Social Support* $\times$ *Physical Symptoms*

As the phase model evolves, it should be possible to test increasingly detailed networks of associations. This final analysis provides one example of what needs to be done by assessing the relative contributions of the phases and social support in explaining the variation in physical symptoms. All data come from Site B, and the location of the analysis at this point in the book is motivated primarily by the significant role that social support seems to play in the intervention just described.

This analysis takes a direct approach, relying on the earlier descriptions of physical symptoms (chapter four) and social support (Orientation I in this chapter). Table 9.14 provides the data array of interest here. Note that high scores on physical symptoms refer to greater experienced symptomology. In general, as expected, Total Symptoms increase as the phases progress from I through VIII. In addition, also as expected, High Support individuals generally report the lowest Total Symptoms scores.

One-way and two-way ANOVA procedures provide estimates of the variation

TABLE 9.14
Phases, Social Support, and Physical Symptoms

	Physical Symptoms, by Phases							
	I	II	III	IV	V	VI	VII	VIII
Low Support	34.7	35.9	33.7	35.7	40.1	41.3	43.5	43.4
High Support	32.9	33.2	34.2	35.6	37.7	38.9	37.2	40.9
Total Support	33.6	34.2	33.9	35.5	38.7	40.1	40.5	42.6

in the five measures of reported symptoms that can be assigned to the phases and to social support. See Table 9.15.

Total Symptoms

The analysis for Total Symptoms leaves little doubt. The phases dominate, both in the one-way ANOVAs as well as in the two-ways. The latter analysis takes two forms. Analysis first assesses the impact of burnout phases, and then of social support, after controlling for phases. In a separate run, two-way analysis then first assesses the impact of social support, and subsequently estimates the effect of burnout after controlling for social support. This analysis provides fore-and-aft perspective, as it were.

In sum, burnout accounts for the bulk of the variance in Total Symptoms. To make a ballpark estimate, the phases account for an average of over 15 percent of the variance and Total Support accounts for less than 3 percent.

Four Symptoms Factors

Analysis of the four factors generated by the 19 physical symptoms confirms the dominance of the phases in accounting for variation in the symptoms. But the details also suggest important differences between factors, which are usefully summarized here. Details about the factor analysis are introduced in chapter four, and it suffices here to remind the reader that the factors include:

I. General Enervation and Agitation
II. Cardio-Vascular Complaints
III. Noncardiac Pains
IV. Sleeplessness

TABLE 9.15
Analysis of Variance, Phases and Social Support on Physical Symptoms

	One-Way Analysis		Two Way Analysis			
	Phases	Social Support	Phases	Phases After Controlling for Burnout	Social Support	Phases After Controlling for Support
F-ratio	39.63	43.15	38.50	18.80	54.95	33.34
Probability	<.001	<.001	<.001	<.001	<.001	<.001
Degrees of freedom	7, 1472	1, 1479	7, 1437	1, 1437	1, 1438	7, 1437
% Variance	16.0	3.0	16.0	1.0	3.0	14.0

Two Way Analysis: 17.0% (Phases + Phases After Controlling for Burnout); 17.0% (Social Support + Phases After Controlling for Support)

One-way and two-way ANOVA support three basic conclusions, which are summarized here to conserve space. First, the phases explain the greater proportion of variance in physical symptoms in the case of each of the four factors. Crudely, the mean percentages of variance accounted for approximately 9 percent for the phases and 1.7 percent for social support.

Second, the variance explained varies substantially for the four factors. That variance is greatest for Factor I (20 percent), and least for Factor III (3 percent). Those with medical training will have to assess whether this statistical result is reasonable, given what we know about physical symptoms and their degrees of association with stress and burnout.

Third, social support generates some substantial F-ratios. Estimates of variance thus may be artifacts of differences in degrees of freedom. Crudely, eight opportunities exist to extract variance for burnout, while only two exist for social support.

Interpretations and Extensions

The above results do not establish causality, of course, but they do urge some rethinking of *the* conventional managerial approach to stress in organizations. Perhaps the dominant in-house prescription for managing stress has been through increasing social support, as via "support groups." This prescription often is casually offerred, although we know better. In fact, the conceptual and theoretical lacunae of this prescription have been comprehensively detailed and elegantly presented (e.g., House, 1981).

The present data and the broader program of research supporting them urge basic reevaluation of conventional thoughtways concerning stress management via enhanced social support. To begin, the phases of burnout seem to provide us with more strategic targets for interventions, in two basic senses. First, the phase model sees burnout as a basic consequence of policies, structures, and procedures at work (e.g., Golembiewski, Munzenrider, and Stevenson, 1986, pp. 240-47). This rootedness in effect implies that changes in work site features are central to the amelioration of burnout. In contrast, support groups may become fixated at the level of emotional sharing (e.g., Scully, 1983, p. 191). This sharing-only— *absent changes in the factors inducing the emotionality*—may take on the quality of gripe sessions that reinforce and can even amplify the negativism by demonstrating how broadly and persistently it is held. Indeed, employees may come to view "social support" opportunities as Band-Aids, if not as cooling-out manipulations designed to distract attention from work site conditions that negatively impact on employees. Research suggests some such effects, in fact (e.g., Shinn and Mørch, 1983).

Of course, this limitation with respect to support groups constitutes precisely their basic attraction for some managements, which are only seeking a ventilation of emotionality, since the work site features have been considered givens.

The potential strategic benefit of the phase model can also be seen as reinforced by the apparent tendency of groups of first-reports to have an affinity for those in extreme phases. Some work-units have members dominantly classified in Phases I through III; the members of other units will be classified largely in VI through VIII; and an apparently small minority of immediate work-units will be mixed. This does not surprise, on reflection, and it suggests the appropriateness of interventions that focus on individuals-in-groups.

Careful readers may conclude that this analysis does not square with chapter five, but it is important to remind them that it was *not* possible to get data on immediate work-groups at Site B. This tethers *that* analysis, but does not necessarily relate to the present argument.

Finally, much is known about maintaining individuals at the least-advanced phases of burnout, e.g., Phases I through III. The Organization Development (OD) literature details many appropriate designs (Golembiewski, 1982) whose success rates are substantial, even formidable (e.g., Golembiewski, Proehl, and Sink, 1981 and 1982; Morrison, 1978; Nicholas, 1982; Porras, 1979). The OD technology can induce a kind of coefficient of social friction that seems to make it difficult to propel individuals out of the least-advanced phases.

The intervention described above suggests ways and means of dealing with active cases of advanced burnout, of course, and that provides hope. But convincing considerations encourage a primary reliance on prevention rather than remediation.

TOWARD A GENERAL THEORY OF AFFECT

After most of the structure and details of *Phases of Burnout* had already been assembled, attention focused upon finding conceptual terms in which to better (or at least more parsimoniously) express the work reported above. In effect, in both structure and detail, we have been emphasizing two main areas: degrees of burnout, and degrees of activity in coping with burnout. A serendipitous conversation with a colleague at the University of Calgary, Wilf Zerbe, brought to our attention some work with a *circumplex model* of affect (e.g., Russell, 1979, 1980) that parallels our effort, but extends far beyond it.

So, in this brief summary statement our energies are directed toward associating the phases of burnout with a two-factor, general theory of affect. We seek at once to build on our findings but, more especially, to transcend them and generalize from them. Our effort here is limited to retrospection, but we hope to motivate as well as provide empirical tests of a theoretical position we can only begin to sketch here.

This primer on the two-factor theory and the phases has two parts. One involves some conceptual issues in the basic thought and research underlying the circumplex model. The second concerns some obvious conceptual and applied connections between the phase model and the two-factor theory.

Conceptual Primer on Two-Factor Theory

A substantial amount of research has focused on the fundamental issue of the type and number of independent factors required to account for the variation in self-reported affective states. One group of researchers concludes that as many as a dozen or more independent and monopolar factors are required—happiness, sadness, and so on (e.g., Nowlis and Nowlis, 1956). A minority but persistent and growing cadre of observers—who build on the general experience of all of us—propose that affective states are "related to each other in a highly systematic fashion" (Russell, 1980, p. 1161). As such, there is no need for a large number of independent monopolar factors—e.g., six to twelve in most cases. For example, Schlosberg (1952) proposes that a two-dimensional space suffices to map self-reported affective states, and he adds to the proposition the idea that a circular arrangement is the simplest structure for organizing the several emotions in terms of the two basic dimensions.

Russell (1979, 1980) elaborates on Schlosberg's views, both conceptually and by empirically testing the "layman's mental map of affective states" (1980, p. 1164). Conceptually, Russell focuses on two basic bipolar dimensions: passive ⟷ active; and unpleasant ⟷ pleasant. These constitute the axes of the required two-dimensional space and (by hypothesis) all affective states are defined as "vectors originating from the origin of [that simple] space." Avoiding details, several studies using multidimensional scaling procedures suggest that common affective concepts can be represented as radiating from the origin of that postulated space. Russell concludes in an abstract (1980, p. 1161) that:

> ... [eight illustrative] affective concepts fall in a circle in the following order: pleasure (0°), excitement (45°), arousal (90°), distress (135°), displeasure (180°), depression (225°), sleepiness (270°), and relaxation (315°).

See also Figure 9.1.

Four developments in this two-factor theory of affect deserve note. Russell began his analysis with three bipolar factors (Russell and Mehrabian, 1977), including dominance ⟷ submissiveness along with the two other basic dimensions. His later view is that the third dimension may capture additional variance, but only small amounts of it. Moreover, there seems to be a growing agreement that two bipolar factors are sufficient to satisfactorily express self-reported affective states (e.g., Thayer, 1978). These two required factors can be interpreted variously in different pieces of research, but opinion seems to favor degree of arousal and pleasant ⟷ unpleasant (Russell, 1980, pp. 1171–72). In addition, Russell extends earlier work proposing (e.g., Plutchick, 1962; Schaefer and Plutchick, 1966) that affective states are usefully conceived as radiating from

FIGURE 9.1
Burnout Phases in a Two-Factor Theory of Affect

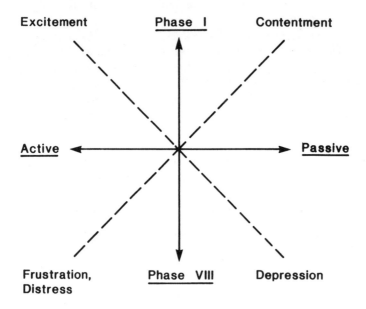

Based on Russell (1980), p. 1164.

the origin of a two-dimensional, bipolar space. Finally, Russell has developed a convenient 12-item measure of his two bipolar dimensions.

Phases and the Two-Factor Theory of Affect

This two-factor general theory of affect at once tethers and liberates the phase model of burnout. We briefly illustrate both features, in conceptual and applied terms, relying on Figure 9.1.

Quite directly, the two-factor theory summarizes the major thrust of many of the findings presented above, given the substitution in Figure 9.1 of the eight phases for the pleasant ⟷ unpleasant dimension. For example, the successful intervention just analyzed can be viewed as dealing with the two bottom quadrants. Almost all of the HR personnel were active, if in advanced phases of burnout, excepting only the two persons rated as passive. The former seem to fit in the left quadrant, of course, and the latter in the right quadrant. It requires only a little imaginative stretch to describe the dominant cluster as experiencing "frustration, distress," while the minority cluster may qualify for "depression" or a related affective state in the quadrant at the bottom, right of Figure 9.1.

Further, the effects of the interventions were such as to induce general movement toward the upper-left quadrant, where "excitement" or some close analogs seem to describe the general emotional tone.

In a related way, the two-factor theory may provide a helpful perspective on the mixed usefulness of "social support." As analysis has demonstrated, social support varies directly with the phases, but Figure 9.1 urges the need to distinguish two possible general effects and to differentiate the designs that may induce one or the other. More simply, increases in social support may lead either to "excitement" or "contentment." Those outcomes may have significantly different practical implications, of course.

Far more important, conceptually, the two-factor or circumplex model seems to liberate even as it tethers this analysis. Conceptually, the two-factor theory can be seen as integrating the burnout phases into *a general theory of affect*. To put the point another way, burnout no longer sits there uncomfortably among social science concepts, somewhat like a suspect stranger at a family outing. In the present version of the two-factor theory, burnout in fact becomes central to the analysis of affect. Consider Figure 9.1, to illustrate the point. One can conceive of many or even all affects as radiating from the (0,0) coordinates, and as reflecting various loadings of the two basic dimensions. Four of these affects are illustrated in Figure 9.1, and previous analysis has established the statistical reasonableness of viewing other affects in a "circumplex" model (e.g., Russell, 1980). Now, perhaps two dimensions will not prove sufficient (e.g., Russell and Mehrabian, 1977), but they do provide a useful conceptual place from which to start building a general model of affect.

Practically, moreover, the two-factor theory also liberates in the sense that it implies a pair of useful guides for action. The two-factor theory reinforces the active vs. passive distinction for all phases of burnout that not only seems reasonable, but also seems to require quite different kinds of designs for ameliorating burnout. Moreover, the two-factor theory suggests releasing the brakes on interventions. Directly, in its earlier formulation, all phases of advanced burnout are interpreted in terms of a critical deficit or deficiency—low *or* negative emotional slack in an individual, which in turn encourages a conservative approach to intervention. In sum, absent a distinction between modes, individuals in advanced phases might be easily overstimulated, with unattractive consequences: people in advanced phases are so preoccupied with staying emotionally afloat, as it were, that even modest waves of stimuli might overwhelm. In contrast, the two-factor model suggests more leeway for intervention. The active person in an advanced phase seems to have some emotional slack available, and that critical fact can provide a valuable margin-of-safety for interventions intended to ameliorate burnout.

NOTES

1. For a more complete technical report, consult Stevenson, Munzenrider, and Golembiewski (1984).

2. For a more comprehensive report, see Golembiewski and Munzenrider (1984a).

3. This section appears elsewhere, in substance and in substantially similar detail. See Golembiewski, Hilles, and Daly (1987).

4. All t-tests utilize pooled-variance estimates, except for Work Pressure, I vs. III, whose F-value (4.25, P < .000) requires a separate variance estimate.

5. For details of the confrontational design, consult Golembiewski (1979), Vol. 1, pp. 297–348. The intervenors consider this a basic design when a "crisis of agreement" does *not* exist.

6. To suggest the point, in Administration V the "movers" nearly double their proportion in Phases I–III—from 26 to 47 percent. In contrast, the "stayers" decrease their proportion in the same phases from 62 to 45 percent.

BIBLIOGRAPHY

Adams, J. C. (1978). Improving stress management. In W. W. Burke (ed.), *The Cutting Edge*, pp. 246-61.

Ahmavaara, Y. (1954). Transformation analysis of factorial data. *Annals of the Academy of Science Fennicae, Series B*, 881: 54-59.

Anderson, C. M. (1982). Effects of peer support groups on levels of burn-out among mental-health professionals. Unpublished doctoral dissertation. University of Washington, Seattle, WA.

Anonymous. (1987). The impact of workplace and personal stressors on manifest stress and coronary heart disease. Manuscript submitted to *Academy of Management Journal.*

Applebaum, S. H. (1981). *Stress Management*. Rockville, MD: Aspen Systems Corp.

Atlanta Constitution (1988). Heart study: Good news for driven men. January 14, pp. 1A, 10A.

Barad, C. B. (1979). Study of burn-out syndrome among social security administration field public-contact employees. Unpublished manuscript, Social Security Administration.

Belcastro, P. A., R. S. Gold, and L. C. Hays. (1983). Maslach burn-out inventory: Factor structures for samples of teachers. *Psychological Reports*, 53: 364-66.

Blau, G. (1981). An empirical investigation of job stress, social support, service length, and job strain. *Organizational Behavior and Human Performance*, 27: 279-302.

Borgatta, E. I. (1961). Mood, personality, and interaction. *Journal of General Psychology*, 64: 105-37.

255

Boss, W. (1979). It doesn't matter if you win or lose, unless you're losing. *Journal of Applied Behavioral Science*, 15: 198-220.

—— (1983). Team building and the problem of regression. *Journal of Applied Behavioral Science*, 19: 279-302.

Boudreau, R. T. (1986). Burnout in a health-care setting. Unpublished manuscript, University of Lethbridge, Lethbridge, Alberta, Canada.

Bowers, D. G. (1973). OD techniques and their results in 23 organizations. The Michigan ICL study. *Journal of Applied Behavioral Science*, 9: 21-43.

Bowers, D. G., and D. L. Hausser. (1977). Work group types and intervention effects in organizational development. *Administrative Science Quarterly*, 22: 76-94.

Bridges, W. (1980). *Transitions*. Reading, MA: Addison-Wesley.

Brown, G. W. (1974). Meaning, measurement, and stress of life events. In B. S. Dohrenwend and B. P. Dohrenwend (eds.), *Stressful Life Events*, pp. 217-43.

Burke, W. W. (ed.). (1978). *The Cutting Edge*. La Jolla, CA: University Associates.

—— (ed.). (1977). *Current Issues and Strategies in Organization Development*. New York: Human Sciences Press.

Burke, W. W. and H. Hornstein (eds.). (1972). *The Social Technology of Organization Development*. Washington, DC: NTL Learning Resources.

Burke, R. J. and G. Deszca. (1986). Correlates of psychological burnout phases among police officers. *Human Relations*, 39: 487-501.

Burke, R., J. Shearer, and G. Deszca. (1984). Burnout among men and women in police work. *Journal of Health and Human Resources Administration*, 7: 162-88.

Cahoon, A. and J. A. R. Rowney. (1984). Managerial burnout: A comparison by sex and level of responsibility. *Journal of Health and Human Resources Administration*, 7: 249-63.

Calvert, L. M. (1984). *Proceedings*. San Antonio, TX: Annual Meeting of the Southwestern Division, Academy of Management.

Caplan, G. (1974). *Support Systems and Community Mental Health*. New York: Behavioral Publications.

Caplan, G., and M. Killilea (eds.). (1976). *Support Systems and Mutual Help: Multidisciplinary Explorations*. New York: Grune and Stratton.

Caplan, R. D., S. Cobb, J. R. P. French, R. V. Harrison, and S. R. Pinneau. (1975). *Job Demands and Worker Health*. Washington, DC: U.S. Department of Health, Education, and Welfare, National Institute for Occupational Safety and Health.

Carpini, D. X. M., R. S. Siegel, and R. Snyder. (1983). Does it make any difference how you feel about your job?: An exploratory study of the relationship between job satisfaction and political orientations. *Micropolitics*, 3: 227-51.

Carroll, J. F. X., and W. L. White. (1982). Understanding burnout: Integrating individual and environmental factors within an ecological framework. In W. W. Paine (ed.), *Job Stress and Burnout*, pp. 41-60.

Chandler, A. D., Jr. (1962). *Strategy and Structure*. Cambridge, MA: The M.I.T. Press.

Chapple, E. D. and L. R. Sayles. (1961). *The Measurement of Management*. New York: Macmillan.

Cherniss, C. (1980a). *Professional Burn-out in Human Services*. Beverly Hills, CA: Sage Publications.

—— (1980b). *Staff Burnout: Job Stress in Human Services*. Beverly Hills, CA: Sage Publications.

Cherniss, C., and D. L. Krants. (1983). The ideological community as an antidote to burn-out in the human services. In B. A. Farber (ed.), *Stress and Burnout in the Human Service Professions*, pp. 198-212.

Cobb, S. (1976). Social support as a moderator of life stress. *Psychosomatic Medicine*, 38 (5): 300-14.

Cochran, R., and A. Robertson. (1973). *Social Support and Health*. New York: Academic Press.

Collins, G. R. (1977). Burn-out: The hazard of professional people-helpers. *Christianity Today*: 12-14.

Cousins, N. (1983). *The Healing Heart: Antidotes to Panic and Helplessness*. New York: W. W. Norton.

Crowne, D., and D. Marlowe. (1964). *The Approval Motive*. New York: Wiley.

Daley, M. R. (1979). Preventing worker burnout in child welfare. *Child Welfare*, 48: 443-50.

Davis, S. M., and P. R. Lawrence. (1977). *Matrix*. Reading, MA: Addison-Wesley.

Deal, T. E. and Kennedy, A. A. (1982). *Corporate Cultures*. Reading, MA: Addison-Wesley.

Dean, A. and A. Linn. (1977). The stress buffering role of social support: Problems and prospects for systematic investigation. *Journal of Nervous and Mental Disease*, 65: 403-17.

Deckard, G. J. (1985). Work, stress, mood and ecological dysfunction in health and social services settings. Unpublished doctoral dissertation. University of Missouri, Columbia, MO.

Deckard, G. J. and B. H. Rountree. (1984). Burnout in dental hygiene. *Dental Hygiene*, 58: 307-13.

Deckard, G. J., B. H. Rountree, and R. T. Golembiewski. (1988). Work stressors, burnout, and agitation: A causal path analysis. *Journal of Health and Human Resources Administration*, in press.

Deckard, G. J., B. H. Rountree, and R. T. Golembiewski. (1986). Worksite features and progressive burnout. *Journal of Health and Human Resources Administration*, 9: 38-45.

DeMeuse, K. P. and S. J. Leibowitz. (1981). An empirical analysis of team-building research. *Group and Organization Studies*, 6: 357-78.

Dohrenwend, B. S. and B. P. Dohrenwend (eds.). (1974). *Stressful Life Events: Their Nature and Effects*. New York: Wiley.

Dyer, W. G. (1977). *Team Building*. Reading, MA: Addison-Wesley.

Edelwich, J., and A. Brodsky. (1980). *Burn-out: Stages of Disillusionment in the Helping Professions*. New York: Human Sciences Press.

Egan, G. (1970). *Encounter*. Belmont, CA: Brooks/Cole.

Eisdorfer, C., D. Cohen, A. Kleinman, and P. Maxim (eds.). (1980). *Theoretical Bases for Psychopathology*. New York: Spectrum.

Elden, J. M. (1981). Political efficacy at work. *American Political Science Review*, 75: 43-58.

Etzion, D., and A. Pines. (1981). Sex and culture as factors explaining reported coping behaviors of human service professionals. Working paper No. 696181. Israel Institute of Business Research, Tel Aviv University.

Farber, B. A. (ed.). (1983). *Stress and Burn-out in the Human Service Professions*. New York: Pergamon.

Filley, A. C. (1974). *Interpersonal Conflict Resolution*. Glenview, IL: Scott, Foresman.

Fineman, S. (1985). *Social Work Stress and Intervention*. Brookfield, VT: Gower Publishing.

Fischer, H. J. (1983). A psychoanalytic view of burnout. In B. A. Farber (ed.), *Stress and Burn-out in the Human Service Professions*, pp. 40-45.

French, J. R. P., Jr., and R. D. Caplan. (1973). In A. J. Marrow (ed.), *The Failure of Success*, pp. 30-60.

French, J. R. P., Jr., R. D. Caplan, and R. V. Harrison. (1982). *The Mechanisms of Job Stress and Strain*. New York: Wiley.

Freudenberger, H. J. (1974). Staff burn-out. *Journal of Social Issues*, 30: 159-65.

―― (1977). Burn-out: The organizational menace. *Training and Development Journal*, 31: 26-27.

―― (1980). *Burn-out: The High Cost of High Achievement*. Garden City, NY: Anchor Press.

Fried, K., M. Rowland, and G. R. Ferris. (1984). The physiological measurement of work stress: A critique. *Personnel Psychology*, 37: 583-616.

Friedman, M., R. H. Rosenmann, and V. Carroll. (1958). Changes in serum cholesterol and blood clotting time of men subject to cyclic variation in occupational stress. *Circulation*, 17: 852-61.

Froggatt, K. L., and J. L. Cotton. (1984). Effects of sex and type A behavior pattern on overload- and underload-induced stress: A laboratory investigation. In J. A. Pearce and R. B. Robinson, *Proceedings*, Annual Meeting of the Academy of Management, pp. 207-11.

Garber, J., and M. E. P. Seligman (eds.). (1980). *Human Helplessness: Theory and Applications*. New York: Academic Press.

Gardell, B., and G. Johanson. *Working Life*. New York: Wiley.

Gillespie, D. F. (1981). Correlates for active and passive types of burnout. *Journal of Social Science Research*, 4 (2): 1-16.

Glass, D. C., and C. S. Carver. (1980). Helplessness and the coronary-prone personality. In J. Garber and M. E. P. Seligman (eds.), *Human Helpless-ness*, pp. 223-43.

Goldberg, D. P. (1972). *The Detection of Psychiatric Illness by Questionnaire*. London: Oxford University Press.

Golembiewski, R. T. (1962). *The Small Group*. Chicago: University of Chicago Press.

—— (1965). Small groups and large organizations. In J. G. March (ed.), *Handbook of Organizations*, pp. 87-141.

—— (1978). *Public Administration as a Developing Discipline*, vols. 1 and 2. New York: Marcel Dekker.

—— (1979). *Approaches to Planned Change*, parts 1 and 2. New York: Marcel Dekker.

—— (1982). Organization development (OD) interventions. In W. W. Paine (ed.), *Job Stress and Burn-out*, pp. 229-53.

—— (1983a). Social desirability and change in organizations. *Review of Business and Economic Research*, 18: 9-20.

—— (1983b). The distribution of burn-out among work groups. In D. D. Van Fleet (ed.), *Proceedings*, pp. 158-63.

—— (1984a). The persistence of burn-out. In L. M. Calvert (ed.), *Proceedings*, pp. 300-304.

—— (1984b). Organizational and policy implications of a phase model of burn-out. In L. R. Moise (ed.), *Organizational Policy and Development*, vol. 1, pp. 135-47.

—— (1984c) Enriching the theory and practice of team-building: Instrumentation for diagnosis and alternatives for design. In D. D. Warrick (ed.), *Current Developments in Organization Development*, pp. 98-113.

—— (1985). Performance appraisal and burn-out. In C. A. Kelley (ed.), *Proceedings*, pp. 168-72.

—— (1986a). Contours of social change. *Academy of Management Review*, 11: 550-56.

—— (1986b). Organization analysis and praxis: Prominences of progress and stuckness. In C. L. Cooper and I. Robertson (eds.), *International Review of Industrial and Organizational Psychology*. New York: Wiley, pp. 279-304.

—— (1987). Social support and burnout as covariants of physical symptoms: Where to put marginal dollars? *Organization Development Journal*, 5: 90-98.

Golembiewski, R. T., *et al.* (1986). The epidemiology of progressive burnout: A primer. *Journal of Health and Human Resources Administration*, 9: 16-37.

Golembiewski, R. T., and K. Billingsley. (1980). Measuring change in OD panel designs: A response to critics. *Academy of Management Review*, 5: 97-104.

Golembiewski, R. T., K. Billingsley, and S. Yeager. (1976). Measuring change and persistence in human affairs: Types of change generated by OD designs. *Journal of Applied Behavioral Science*, 12: 134–40.

Golembiewski, R. T., and A. Blumberg. (1977). *Sensitivity Training and the Laboratory Approach*. Itasca, IL: F. E. Peacock.

Golembiewski, R. T., and A. Blumberg. (1967). Confrontation as a training design in complex organizations: Attitudinal changes in a diversified population of managers. *Journal of Applied Behavioral Science*, 3: 524–47.

Golembiewski, R. T., G. J. Deckard, and B. H. Rountree. (1987). The stability of burnout assignments: Measurement properties of the phase model. Mimeograph.

Golembiewski, R. T., and R. Hilles. (1979). *Toward the Responsive Organization*. Salt Lake City, Utah: Brighton.

Golembiewski, R. T., R. Hilles, and R. Daly. (1987). Some effects of multiple OD interventions on burnout and worksite features. *Journal of Applied Behavioral Science*, 23: 295–314.

Golembiewski, R. T., R. Hilles, and B-S Kim. (1986). Longitudinal effects of interventions targeted at advanced burnout, active mode. Paper presented at Fourth Annual Conference on Organization Policy and Development, University of Louisville, Louisville, KY, May 23–24.

Golembiewski, R. T., and A. Kiepper. (1976). MARTA: Toward an effective open giant. *Public Administration Review*, 36: 46–60.

Golembiewski, R. T., and B-S Kim. (1988). Self-esteem, the phases of burnout, and some properties of blood chemistry. Unpublished MS.

Golembiewski, R. T., and R. F. Munzenrider. (1981). Efficacy of three versions of one burn-out measure. *Journal of Health and Human Resources Administration*, 4: 228–46.

———— (1983). Testing three phase models of burn-out. *Journal of Health and Human Resources Administration*, 5: 374–92.

———— (1984a). Active and passive reactions to psychological burn-out: Toward greater specificity in a phase model. *Journal of Health and Human Resources Administration*, 7: 264–89.

———— (1984b). Phases of psychological burn-out and organizational covariants: A replication using norms from a large population. *Journal of Health and Human Resources Administration*, 6: 290–323.

———— (1986a). Profiling acute vs. chronic burnout, II: Mappings on a panel of established covariants. *Journal of Health and Human Resources Administration*, 8: 296–315.

———— (1986b). Profiling acute vs. chronic burnout, III: Phases and life events impacting on patterns of covariants. *Journal of Health and Human Resources Administration*, 9: 173–84.

———— (1987a). Burnout as indicator of gamma change: Methodological perspectives on a crucial surrogacy. Mimeograph.

———— (1987b). Burnout as indicator of gamma change: State-like differences between phases. Mimeograph.

——(1987c). Burnout as indicator of gamma change, III: Differences of degree in worksite descriptors. Mimeograph.

——(1987d). Is burnout idiosyncratic or generic? The congruence of factorial studies of the Maslach Burnout Inventory. Prepared for delivery at the Annual Meeting, American Society for Public Administration, Boston, MA, March 30, 1987.

——(1987e). Profiling acute vs. chronic burnout, IV: Active vs. passive modes of adaptation. *Journal of Health and Human Resources Administration*, 10: 97–111.

——(1988a). Burnout as indicator of gamma change, II: State-like differences between phases. *Journal of Health and Human Resources Administration*, (in press).

——(1988b). Burnout as indicator of gamma change, III: Differences of degree in worksite descriptors. Working paper.

Golembiewski, R. T., R. F. Munzenrider, and D. Carter. (1981). Progressive phases of burn-out and their implications for OD. In *Proceedings*, Organization Development Network, Semi-Annual Meeting, September 1981, pp. 163–70.

——(1983). Phases of progressive burn-out and their worksite covariants. *Journal of Applied Behavioral Science*, 19: 464–81.

Golembiewski, R. T., R. F. Munzenrider, and J. G. Stevenson. Phases of progressive burn-out in a federal agency. *Review of Public Personnel Administration*, (in press).

——(1986). *Stress in Organizations*. New York: Praeger.

——(1985). Profiling acute vs. chronic burnout: Theoretical issues, a surrogate, and elemental distributions. *Journal of Health and Human Resources Administration*, 7: 107–25.

Golembiewski, R. T., and C. W. Proehl, Jr. (1978). A survey of the empirical literature on flexible workhours: Character and consequences of a major innovation. *Academy of Management Review*, 3: 837–53.

Golembiewski, R. T., C. W. Proehl, Jr., and D. Sink. (1981). Success of OD applications in the public sector: Toting-up the score for a decade, more or less. *Public Administration Review* 41: 679–82.

——(1982). Estimating the success of OD applications. *Training and Development Journal*, 72: 86–95.

Golembiewski, R. T., and B. H. Rountree. (1986). Phases of burn-out and properties of work environments. *Organization Development Journal*, 9: 25–30.

Golembiewski, R. T., and M. Scicchitano. (1983). Some demographics of psychological burn-out. *International Journal of Public Administration*, 5: 435–48.

Gottlieb, B. H. (ed.). (1981). *Social Networks and Social Support*. Beverly Hills, CA: Sage Publications.

Gould, R. (1978). *Transformations*. New York: Simon and Schuster.

Greer, C. R., and M. A. D. Castro. (1986). The relationship between perceived unit effectiveness and occupational stress. *Journal of Applied Behavioral Science*, 22: 159-76.

Guilford, J. (1950). *Fundamental Statistics in Psychology and Education*. New York: McGraw-Hill.

Guilford, J. P. (1954). *Psychometric Methods*. New York: McGraw Hill.

Gurr, T. (1970). *Why Men Rebel*. Princeton, NJ: Princeton University Press.

Haack, M. R. (1980). Burn-out intervention with nurses. Unpublished doctoral dissertation, University of Illinois Medical Center.

Hackman, J. R., and G. R. Oldham. (1980). *Work Redesign*. Reading, MA: Addison-Wesley.

Harris, R. T., and J. L. Porras. (1978). The consequences of large system change in practice: An empirical assessment. In J. C. Susbauer, *Proceedings '78*, pp. 298-302.

Harrison, R. (1972). Role negotiation. In W. W. Burke and H. Hornstein (eds.), *The Social Technology of Organization Development*, pp. 84-96.

Harrison, W. D. (1981). Role strain and burnout in child-protective service workers. *Social Service Review*, 54 (1): 31-44.

Harvey, J. B. (1977). Consulting during crisis of agreement. In W. W. Burke (ed.), *Current Issues and Strategies in Organization Development*, pp. 160-86.

Hendrix, W. H., N. K. Ovalle, and R. G. Troxler. (1985). Behavioral and physiological consequences of stress and its antecedent factors. *Journal of Applied Psychology*, 70: 188-201.

Holmes, T. H., and R. H. Rahe. (1967). The social adjustment rating scale. *Journal of Psychosomatic Research*, 11: 213-18.

House, J. S. (1981). *Work, Stress and Social Support*. Reading, MA: Addison-Wesley.

Howard, G. S., S. E. Maxwell, R. L. Wiener, K. S. Boynton, and W. M. Rooney. (1980). Is a behavioral measure the best estimate of behavioral parameters? Perhaps not. *Applied Psychological Measurement*, 4: 293-311.

Howard, J. H., D. A. Cunningham, and P. A. Rechnitzer. (1986). Role ambiguity, Type A behavior, and job satisfaction. *Journal of Applied Psychology*, 71: 95-101.

Insel, P. M., and R. H. Moos. (1974). *Work Environment Scale, Form R*. Palo Alto, CA: Consulting Psychologists Press.

Ivancevich, J. M., M. T. Matteson, and C. Preston. (1982). Occupational stress, type-A behavior, and physical well-being. *Academy of Management Journal*, 25: 373-91.

Ivancevich, J. M., M. T. Matteson, and E. P. Richards, III. (1985). Who's liable for stress on the job? *Harvard Business Review*, 85: 60-62, 66, 70, 72.

Iverson, G. R., and H. Norpoth. (1987). *Analysis of Variance*. Beverly Hills, CA: Sage.

Iwanicki, E. F., and R. L. Schwab. (1981). A cross-validation study of the Maslach burn-out inventory. *Educational and Psychological Measurement*, 41: 1167-74.

Janis, I. (1972). *Groupthink*. Boston: Little, Brown.

Janz, T., S. Dugan, and M. S. Ross. (1986). Organizational culture and burnout: Findings at the individual and department levels. *Journal of Health and Human Resources Administration*, 9 (1): 78-92.

Jayaratne, S., T. Tripodi, and W. A. Chess. (1983). Perceptions of emotional support. *Social Work Research and Abstracts*, 19 (2): 19-27.

Jenkins, C. D., R. H. Rosenman, and S. J. Zyzanski. (1974). Prediction of clinical coronary heart disease by a test for the coronary-prone behavioral pattern. *New England Journal of Medicine*, 290: 1271-75.

Jenkins, C. D., S. J. Zyzanski, and R. H. Rosenman. (1979). *Jenkins Activity Survey*. New York: The Psychological Corporation.

Jones, J. W. (1981). Dishonesty, burnout, and unauthorized work-break extensions. *Personality and Social Psychology*, 7: 406-409.

Jones, J. (ed.). (1981). *The Burnout Syndrome*. Park Ridge, IL: London House Press.

Jones, J., and W. Pfeiffer. (1977). *The 1977 Annual Handbook for Group Facilitators*. La Jolla, CA: University Associates.

Justice, B., R. S. Gold, and J. P. Klein. (1981). Life events and burnout. *Journal of Psychology*, 108 (2): 219-26.

Kahn, R. L. (1978). Job burnout: Prevention and remedies. *Public Welfare*, 16: 61-63.

Kahn, R. L., D. M. Wolfe, R. P. Quinn, J. D. Snoeck, and R. A. Rosenthal. (1964). *Organizational Stress*. New York: Wiley.

Karasek, R. A. (1981). Job socialization and job strain. In B. Gardell and G. Johanson, *Working Life*, pp. 75-94.

Karasek, R. A., R. S. Russell, and T. Theorell. (1982). Physiology of stress and regeneration in job-related cardiovascular illness. *Journal of Human Stress*: 29-42.

Kasl, S. V., and J. A. Wells. (1985). Social support and health in the middle years. In S. Cohen and S. L. Syme (eds.), *Social Support and Health*.

Kelley, C. A. (ed.). (1985). *Proceedings*. Annual Meeting, Southwestern Academy of Management, New Orleans, LA.

Kerlinger, F. N. (1973). *Foundations of Behavioral Research*. New York: Holt, Rinehart and Winston.

Kilpatrick, A. O. (1986). Burnout: an empirical assessment. Unpublished doctoral dissertation, University of Georgia, Athens, GA.

Klein, K. J., and T. A. D'Aunno. (1986). The psychological sense of community in the workplace. *Journal of Community Psychology*, 14: 365-77.

Kubler-Ross, E. (1981). *Living with Death and Dying*. New York: Macmillan.

—— (1982). *Working It Through*. New York: Macmillan.

Lakin, M. (ed.). (1979). What's happened to small group research? *Journal of Applied Behavioral Science*, 15: full issue.

LaRocco, J. M., J. S. House, and J. R. P. French, Jr. (1980). Social support, occupational stress, and health. *Journal of Health and Social Behavior*, 21: 202-18.

Lazaro, C., M. Shinn, and P. E. Robinson. (1984). Burn-out, job performance, and job-withdrawal behaviors. *Journal of Health and Human Resources Administration*, 7: 213-34.

Lazarus, R. S. (1980). The stress and coping paradigm. In C. Eisdorfer et al. (eds.), *Theoretical Bases for Psychopathology*, pp. 173-209.

Lazarus, R. S., and R. Launier. (1978). Stress-related transactions between person and environment. In L. A. Pervin and M. Lewis (eds.), *Perspectives in Interactional Psychology*, pp. 287-327.

Lerner, D., and H. D. Lasswell (eds.). (1951). *The Policy Sciences*. Stanford, CA: Stanford University Press.

Lieberman, M. A., I. D. Yalom, and M. B. Miles. (1973). *Encounter Groups*. New York: Basic Books.

Lief, H. I., and R. C. Fox. (1963). Training for "detached concern" in medical students. In H. I. Lief, V. F. Lief, and N. R. Lief, *The Psychological Bases of Medical Practice*, pp. 12-35.

Likert, R. (1977). Past and future perspectives on system 4. Paper presented at 1977 Annual Meeting, Academy of Management, Orlando, Florida.

—— (1967). *The Human Organization*. New York: McGraw-Hill.

Lin, N., A. Dean, and Walter M. Ensel. (1981). Social support scales: A methodological note. *Schizophrenia Bulletin*, 7 (1): 73-89.

Longenecker, C. O., D. A. Gioia, and H. P. Sims, Jr. (1987). Behind the mask: The politics of employee appraisal. *Executive*, 1: 183-94.

Lubin, B., and M. Zuckerman. (1969). Levels of emotional arousal in laboratory training. *Journal of Applied Behavioral Science*, 5: 483-90.

Lundberg, V., and B. Devine. (1975). Negative similarities. *Education and Psychological Measurement*, 27: 797-807.

Maier, S. F., and M. E. P. Seligman. (1976). Learned helplessness: Theory and evidence. *Journal of Experimental Psychology: General*, 105: 3-46.

March, J. G. (1965). *Handbook of Organizations*. Chicago: Rand McNally.

Marrow, A. J. (ed.). (1972). *The Failure of Success*. New York: AMACOM.

Maslach, C. (1982a). *Burn-out: The Cost of Caring*. Englewood Cliffs, NJ: Prentice-Hall.

—— (1982b). Understanding burn-out: Definitional issues in analyzing a complex phenomenon. In W. S. Pain (ed.), *Job Stress and Burnout: Research, Theory, and Intervention Perspectives*. Beverly Hills, CA: Sage, pp. 29-40.

—— (1976). Burn-out. *Human Behavior*, 5: 16-22.

—— (1978a) How people cope. *Public Welfare*, 16: 56-58.

—— (1978b) The client role in staff burn-out. *Journal of Social Issues*, 34: 111-24.

Maslach, C., and S. E. Jackson. (1978). Lawyer burnout. *Barrister*, 8: 52-54.

—— (1979). Burnt-out cops and their families. *Psychology Today*: 59-62.

—— (1981). The measurement of experienced burnout. *Journal of Occupational Behaviour*, 2: 99-113.

—— (1982). *Maslach Burnout Inventory*. Palo Alto, CA: Consulting Psychologists Press.

—— (1984a). Burnout in organizational settings. *Applied Social Psychology Annual*, 5: 133-53.

—— (1984b). Patterns of burnout among a national sample of public contact workers. *Journal of Health and Human Resources Administration*, 7: 189-212.

Maslach, C., and A. Pines. (1977). The burn-out syndrome in the day-care setting. *Child Quarterly*, 6: 100-13.

Mason, R. M. (1982). *Participatory and Workplace Democracy*. Carbondale, IL: Southern Illinois University Press.

Mechanic, D. (1974a). Discussion of research programs on relations between stressful life events and episodes of physical illness. In B. S. Dohrenwend and B. P. Dohrenwend (eds.), *Stressful Life Events*, pp. 87-97.

—— (1974b). Social structure and personal adaptation. In G. V. Coelho, D. A. Hamburg, and J. E. Adams (eds.), *Coping and Adaptation*. New York: Basic Books, pp. 32-44.

Meddis, R. (1972). Bipolar factors in mood adjective checklists. *British Journal of Social and Clinical Psychology*, 11: 178-84.

Meyer, A. (1919). The life chart and the obligation of specifying positive data in psychopathological diagnosis. In *Contributions to Medical and Biological Research*, vol. 2. New York: Paul B. Hoeber.

Miller, D., and P. H. Freisen. *Organizations: A Quantum View*. Englewood Cliffs, NJ: Prentice-Hall.

Mitchell, M. (1977). Consultant burnout. In J. Jones and W. Pfeiffer, *The 1977 Annual Handbook for Group Facilitators*, pp. 145-46.

Moise, L. R. (ed.). (1984). *Organizational Policy and Development*. Louisville, KY: Center for Continuing Studies, University of Louisville.

Moos, R. H., and P. M. Insel. (1982). *Manual for the Work Environment Scale*. Palo Alto, CA: Consulting Psychologists Press.

Mueller, J., K. Schuessler, and H. Costner. (1970). *Statistical Reasoning in Sociology*. Boston: Houghton Mifflin.

Mullins, A. C., and R. E. Barstow. (1979). Care for the caretakers. *American Journal of Nursing*, 9: 1425-27.

Munzenrider, R. (1986). Is burnout idiosyncratic or generic? Paper presented at Fourth Annual Conference on Organization Policy and Development, University of Louisville, Louisville, KY, May 23-24.

Munzenrider, R. F., R. T. Golembiewski, and J. G. Stevenson. (1984). Sex and other demographic differences in burnout. In L. R. Moise (ed.), *Organizational Policy and Development*, pp. 87-105.

Nicholas, J. M. (1982). The comparative impact on organization development interventions on hard criteria measures. *Academy of Management Review*, 7: 531–42.

Nowlis, V., and H. H. Nowlis. (1956). The description and analysis of mood. *Annals of the New York Academy of Sciences*, 65: 345–55.

Nuckolls, K. B., J. C. Cassel, and B. H. Caplan. (1972). Psychosocial assets, life crisis, and the prognosis of pregnancy. *American Journal of Epidemiology*, 95: 431–41.

Oskamp, S. (ed.). (1984). *Applied Social Psychology Annual*, vol. 5. Beverly Hills, CA: Sage Publications.

Paine, W. W. (ed.). (1982). *Job Stress and Burnout*. Beverly Hills, CA: Sage Publications.

Patchen, M. (1965). Some questionnaire measures of employee motivation and morale. Monograph No. 41. Ann Arbor, Mich.: Survey Research Center.

Paykel, E. S., B. A. Prusoff, and E. H. Uhlenhuth. (1971). Scale of life events. *Archives of General Psychiatry*, 25: 340–47.

Pearce, J. A., and R. B. Robinson. (1984). *Proceedings*, Annual Meeting of the Academy of Management, Boston, August 12–15.

Pearlin, L. I., and C. Schooler. (1978). The structure of coping. *Journal of Health and Social Behavior*, 19: 2–21.

Perlman, B., and E. A. Hartman. (1982). Burnout: Summary and future research. *Human Relations*, 35 (2): 283–305.

Pervin, L. A., and M. Lewis (eds.). (1978). *Perspectives in Interactional Psychology*. New York: Plenum.

Peters, T. J., and R. H. Waterman, Jr. (1982). *In Search of Excellence*. New York: Harper and Row.

Pines, A. (1983). On burn-out and the buffering effects of social support. In B. A. Farber (ed.), *Stress and Burnout in the Human Service Professions*, pp. 155–74.

Pines, A., and E. Aronson. (1983). Combatting burnout. *Children and Youth Services Review*, 5: 263–75.

—— (1980). *Burnout*. Schilla Park, IL: MTI Teleprograms.

Pines, A., E. Aronson, and D. Kafry. (1981). *Burnout: From Tedium to Personal Growth*. New York: The Free Press.

Pines, A., and D. Kafry. (1981). Coping with burnout. In J. Jones (ed.), *The Burnout Syndrome*, pp. 139–50.

Pines, A., and C. Maslach. (1980). Combatting staff burnout in a day care center: A case study. *Child Care Quarterly*, 9: 5–16.

Plutchick, R. (1962). *The Emotions*. New York: Random House.

Porras, J., and A. Wilkins. (1980). Organization development in a large system: An empirical assessment. *Journal of Applied Behavioral Science*, 16: 506–34.

Price, R. H. (1984). Work and community. Paper presented at Annual Meeting, American Psychological Association, Toronto.

Quinn, R. P., and L. J. Shepard. (1974). *The 1972-73 Quality of Employment Survey*. Ann Arbor, MI: Survey Research Center, University of Michigan.

Quinn, R.P., and G. L. Stines. (1979). *The 1977 Quality of Employment Survey*. Ann Arbor, MI: Survey Research Center, University of Michigan.

Rabkin, J. G., and E. L. Struening. (1976). Life events, stress, and illness. *Science*, 194: 1013-20.

Ragland, D. R., and R. J. Brand. (1988). Type A behavior and mortality from coronary heart disease. *The New England Journal of Medicine*, 318: 65-69.

Rahe, R. H., and E. Lind. (1968). Psychosocial factors and sudden cardiac death: A pilot study. *Journal of Psychosomatic Research*, 15: 19-24.

Raven, B. (1974). The Nixon group. *Journal of Social Issues*, 30: 304-20.

Reynolds, H. T. (1977). *Analysis of Nominal Data*. Beverly Hills, CA: Sage.

Roberts, K. H., and C. A. O'Reilly, III. (1974). Failures in upward communication in organizations: Three possible culprits. *Academy of Management Journal*, 17: 205-15.

Rosenberg, M. (1965a). *The Self-esteem Scale*. Princeton, NJ: Princeton University Press.

——— (1965b). *Society and the Adolescent Self-image*. Princeton, NJ: Princeton University Press.

Rosenman, R. H., M. Friedman, R. Strauss, M. Wurm, R. Kositchek, W. Hahn, and N. T. Werthessen. (1964). A predictive study of coronary heart disease. *Journal of American Medical Association*, 189: 15-22.

Ross, C. E., and J. Mirowsky. (1979). A comparison of life-event-weighting schemes: Change, undesirability, and effect-proportional indices. *Journal of Health and Social Behavior*, 20: 166-77.

Rountree, B. H. (1982). Psychological states in health settings. Unpublished doctoral dissertation, University of Georgia, Athens.

——— (1984). Psychological burnout in task groups. *Journal of Health and Human Resources Administration*, 7: 235-48.

Rountree, B. H., and G. J. Deckard. (1982). Quality of work life study. Mimeograph.

Rummel, R. J. (1970). *Applied Factor Analysis*. Evanston, IL: Northwestern University Press.

Russell, J. A. (1978). Evidence of convergent validity on the dimensions of affect. *Journal of Personality and Social Psychology*, 36: 1152-68.

——— (1979). Affective space is bipolar. *Journal of Personality and Social Psychology*, 37: 345-56.

——— (1980). A circumplex model of affect. *Journal of Personality and Social Psychology*, 39: 1161-78.

Russell, J. A., and A. Mehrabian. (1977). Evidence of a three-factor theory of emotions. *Journal of Research in Personality*, 11: 273-94.

Ryan, W. (1971). *Blaming the Victim*. New York: Pantheon.

Ryerson, D. M., and N. Marks. Career burnout in the human services: Strategies for intervention. Mimeograph, no date.

Sarason, I. G., J. H. Johnson, and J. M. Siegel. (1979). Development of life experiences survey. In I. G. Sarason and C. D. Speilberger (eds.), *Stress and Anxiety*, pp. 131-49.

Sarason, I. G., and C. D. Speilberger (eds.). (1979). *Stress and Anxiety*. Washington, DC: Hemisphere Publishing Corp.

Schaefer, C. (1982). Shoring up the "buffer" of social support. *Journal of Health and Social Behavior*, 23 (1): 96-101.

Schaefer, E. S., and R. Plutchik. (1966). Interrelationships of emotions, traits, and diagnostic constructs. *Psychological Reports* 18: 399-419.

Schafer, R. (1976). *A New Language for Psychoanalysis*. New Haven: Yale University Press.

Schlosberg, H. (1952). The description of facial expressions in terms of two dimensions. *Journal of Experimental Psychology*, 44: 229-37.

——— (1954). Three dimensions of emotion. *Psychological Review*, 61: 81-88.

Schwartz, M. S., and G. T. Will. (1953). Low morale and mutual withdrawal on a mental hospital ward. *Psychiatry*, 16: 337-53.

Scully, R. (1983). The work-setting support group: A means of preventing burnout. In B. A. Farber (ed.), *Stress and Burnout in the Human Service Professions*, pp. 188-97.

Seers, A., G. W. McGee, T. T. Serey, and G. G. Graen. (1983). The interaction of job stress and social support: A strong inference investigation. *Academy of Management Journal*, 26 (2): 273-84.

Seligman, M. E. P. (1975). *Helplessness: On Depression, Development and Death*. San Francisco: W. H. Freeman.

Selye, H. (1983). The stress concept. In C. L. Cooper (ed.), *Stress Research*. New York: Wiley.

——— (1956). *The Stress of Life*. New York: McGraw-Hill.

Selznick, P. (1949). *TVA and the Grass Roots*. Berkeley, CA: University of California Press.

Shils, E. A. (1951). The study of the primary group. In D. Lerner and H. D. Lasswell, *The Policy Sciences*, pp. 44-69.

Shils, E. A., and M. Janowitz. (1948). Cohesion and disintegration of the Wehrmacht in World War II. *Public Opinion Quarterly*, 12: 280-315.

Shinn, M. (1979). Longitudinal study of burnout in delinquency workers. Unpublished research proposal, New York University.

Shinn, M., and H. Mørch. (1983). A tripartite model of coping with burn-out. In V. A. Farber (ed.), *Stress and Burnout in the Human Service Professions*, pp. 227-40.

Slutsky, B. W. (1981). Two approaches to treating burn-out. Dissertation Abstracts International, 42 (5) 2086b.

Smith, B. L. R. (ed.). (1984). *The Higher Civil Service in Europe and Canada*. Washington, DC: The Brookings Institution.

Smith, F. J. (1977). Work attitudes as predictors of attendance on a specific day. *Journal of Applied Psychology*, 62: 16-19.

—— (1976). Index of organizational reactions. *JASS Catalog of Selected Documents in Psychology*, 6 (1): 54, No. 1265.

Smith, F. J., K. Roberts, and C. Hulin. (1976). Ten-year job satisfaction trends in a stable organization. *Academy of Management Journal*, 19: 462–69.

Smith, K. W., S. M. McKinlay, and B. D. Thorington. (1987). The validity of health appraisal instruments for assessing coronary heart disease risk. *American Journal of Public Health*, 77: 419–24.

Smith, P. C., L. M. Kendall, and C. L. Blood. (1969). *The Measurement of Satisfaction in Work and Retirement*. Chicago: Rand-McNally.

Special Task Force of the Secretary, U.S. Department of Health, Education, and Welfare. (1973). *Work in America*. Cambridge, MA: MIT Press.

Spicuzza, F. J., and M. W. DeVoe. (1982). Burnout in the helping professions: Mutual-aid groups as self-help. *Personnel and Guidance Journal*, 61 (2): 95–101.

Stevenson, J. G. (1986). Personal covariants of psychological burnout in field units of a federal agency. Unpublished doctoral dissertation, University of Georgia, Athens, GA.

Stevenson, J. G., R. Munzenrider, and R. T. Golembiewski. (1984). Social support and psychological burn-out. Paper presented at Second Annual Conference on Organizational Policy and Development, Louisville, KY, April 11–13.

Stouffer, S. A., et al. (1949). *The American Soldier*. Princeton, NJ: Princeton University Press.

Susbauer, J. C. (1978). *Proceedings '78*. San Francisco: Annual Meeting, Academy of Management.

Tennis, C. W. (1986). The alpha, beta, and gamma change technology: The response of an invisible college. Paper presented at Annual Meeting, Academy of Management, Chicago, IL.

Tessler, R., and D. Mechanic. (1978). Psychological distress and perceived health status. *Journal of Health and Social Behavior*, 19: 254–62.

Thayer, R. E. (1967). Measurement of activation through self-report. *Psychological Reports*, 20: 663–78.

—— (1978). Toward a psychological theory of multidimensional activation (arousal). *Motivation and Emotion*, 2: 1–34.

Theorell, T., and R. H. Rahe. (1972). Behavior and life satisfaction characteristics of Swedish subjects with myocardial infarction. *Journal of Chronic Diseases*, 25: 139–47.

Thoits, P. A. (1982). Conceptual, methodological, and theoretical problems in studying social support as a buffer against life stress. *Journal of Health and Social Behavior*, 23: 145–59.

Truch, S. (1980). *Teacher Burn-out and What-to-do About It*. Novato, CA: Academic Therapy Publications.

Turner, R. J. (1981). Social support as a contingency in psychological well-being. *Journal of Health and Social Behavior*, 22: 357–67.

Van Fleet, D. D. (ed.). (1983). *Proceedings*. Houston, TX: Annual Meeting of the Southwestern Division, Academy of Management.

Veninga, R. L., and J. P. Spradley. (1981). *The Work/Stress Connection: How to Cope with Job Burn-out*. Boston: Little, Brown.

Walton, R. (1969). *Third-Party Consultation*. Reading, MA: Addison-Wesley.

Warrick, D. D. (1981). Managing the stress of organization development. *Training and Development Journal*, 35: 36-41.

—— (ed.). (1984). *Current Developments in Organization Development*. Glenview, IL: Scott, Foresman.

Weisbord, M. (1978). The wizard of OD: Or, what have magic slippers to do with burn-out, evaluation, resistance, planned change, and action research? *The OD Practitioner*, 10: 1-14.

White, J. K., and R. A. Ruh. (1973). Effects of personal values on the relationships between participation and job attitudes. *Administrative Science Quarterly*, 18: 506-14.

Williams, A. W., J. E. Ware, and C. A. Donald. (1981). A model of mental health, life events, and social supports applicable to general populations. *Journal of Health and Social Behavior*, 22: 324-36.

Wills, T. A. (1978). Perceptions of clients by professional helpers. *Psychological Bulletin*, 85: 968-1000.

Wyler, A. R., M. Masuda, and T. H. Holmes. (1971). Magnitudes of life events and seriousness of illness. *Psychosomatic Medicine*, 33: 115-22.

Yamamoto, K. J., and O. K. Kinney. (1976). Pregnant women's ratings of different factors influencing psychological stress during pregnancy. *Psychological Reports*, 39: 203-14.

Yeager, F. A. (1987). Assessing the Civil Service's Reform Act's impact on senior manager work priorities. *Public Administration Review*, 47: 417-24.

Zuckerman, M., B. Lubin, and C. Rinck. (1984). Construction of new scales for the Multiple Affect Checklist. Unpublished manuscript.

Zuckerman, M., and B. Lubin. (1965). *Manual for the Multiple Affect Adjective Check List*. San Diego, CA: Educational and Industrial Testing Service.

INDEX

ABOUT THE AUTHORS

ROBERT T. GOLEMBIEWSKI is Research Professor at the University of Georgia, with a special interest in change within large organizations, both public and business. He received his M.A. and Ph.D. from Yale, and his A.B. from Princeton.

Golembiewski's research has been signally acknowledged, both early in his career and more recently. For example, he won the 1967 Hamilton Book of the Year Award for his *Men, Management, and Morality*; and he and his colleagues received the McGregor Memorial Award for Excellence in Applications of the Behavioral Sciences, both in 1975 and 1986, the only two-time winner of that major prize. In 1988, he received the Third Century Award as the ranking social and behavioral scientist at the University of Georgia.

He has published over 300 scholarly articles and contributions in a wide range of journals. He has also authored or edited 48 books, the last of which is *High Performance and Human Costs* (Praeger, 1988).

Golembiewski is an active consultant for both business and government. He was the prime external consultant to the Metropolitan Atlanta Rapid Transit Authority, for example, in their $2 billion program for an integrated bus-rail system. He also consults with a range of businesses, including more than 20 years with SmithKline Beckman and its various subsidiary companies such as Allergan.

ROBERT F. MUNZENRIDER is Associate Professor in the Master of Public Administration Program, and Senior Research Associate at the Center for Quality of Working Life, Pennsylvania State University at Harrisburg. He received his undergraduate and doctorate degrees at Georgia, where he has taught as a visiting professor.

Munzenrider's teaching and research interests focus on the areas of organizational behavior and development, research methodology, and computer

279

applications. He has published widely in those literatures, and is the co-author of *Stress in Organizations* (Praeger, 1986). He has consulted in both public and business arenas, as with the Federal Emergency Management Agency and Menley-James.

His research and applied interests now include a strong focus on multicultural dynamics at his Harrisburg campus. He is chairman there of the Isms Committee—which encompasses racism, sexism, tokenism, and so on. The Committee will recommend policies and procedures based on the results of a campus survey.